OUT OF PRINT
FIRST EDITION

30⁰⁰

Toward Robert Frost

Toward

ROBERT FROST

The Reader and the Poet

Judith Oster

The University of Georgia Press

Athens and London

© 1991 by the University of Georgia Press
Athens, Georgia 30602
All rights reserved
Designed by Betty Palmer McDaniel
Set in Berkeley Old Style Medium with Futura Book
The paper in this book meets the guidelines for
permanence and durability of the Committee on
Production Guidelines for Book Longevity of the
Council on Library Resources.

Printed in the United States of America

95   94   93   92   91   C   5   4   3   2   1

Library of Congress Cataloging in Publication Data

Oster, Judith.
    Toward Robert Frost: the reader and the poet / Judith Oster.
        p.   cm.
    Includes bibliographical references (p.) and index.
    ISBN 0-8203-1322-X (alk. paper)
    1. Frost, Robert, 1874–1963—Criticism and interpretation.
2. Reader-response criticism.   I. Title.
PS3511.R94Z857   1991
811'.52—dc20   90-11277
                            CIP

British Library Cataloging in Publication Data available

Then there is the literary belief . . . that believing the thing into existence.

—*Robert Frost*

To Joe—my husband
who "would declare and could himself believe"

and

To the memory of my father, Alex Link, who,
when I wouldn't believe chocolates grew on trees,
took me outside and *showed* me

Contents

Preface   *ix*

Acknowledgments   *xvii*

Abbreviations   *xxi*

CHAPTER 1
Braving Alien Entanglements   *1*

CHAPTER 2
Au Lecteur   *34*

CHAPTER 3
"Me, Myself . . . Godlike"   *74*

CHAPTER 4
Reading from Emerson to Frost   *105*

CHAPTER 5
Nature and Poetry   *137*

CHAPTER 6
Bond and Free: The Human Encounter   *175*

CHAPTER 7
Felix Culpa: Frost and Eden   *220*

CHAPTER 8
Epilogue: The Height of the Adventure   *255*

Notes   *259*

Works Cited   *311*

Index   *323*

Preface

Robert Frost was fond of saying, "My greatest inspiration when I was a student was a man whose classes I never attended" (EY 536). I can understand that. My students never sat in Frost's classes (nor did I), but Frost teaches us. I have learned to let him begin my literature classes—advanced poetry or introduction to American literature, graduate students or freshmen. I put "Design" or "Never Again Would Birds' Song Be the Same" in front of the students, and they take off. These never fail as "teachers," and they never fail to get a good discussion going, the sort of debates we love. Admittedly, the class does not exactly go on automatic pilot: I insist the students validate competing hypotheses with the words on the page; I make sure they know it is a reading lesson they are having. What happens is that even students who have no particular expertise, who said they never learned how to analyze poetry, or hated what their high school teachers did with it in digging out "hidden" meanings, leave even the first class astonished, not only at what emerged in that discussion, or at their own contributions to it, but also at the fun they had. Reader responses to that "chestnut" "Stopping by Woods" are a whole other kind of game; "Home Burial" always provokes and elicits the unexpected, the personal, and the profound. And then there are graduate students, expert, even well versed in Frost, some of them poets themselves, who engage with their fellow readers in a seminar and leave renewed, having been reminded of what it was, after all, that had brought them to graduate studies in literature. Oh yes, I had almost forgotten, one can almost hear them sigh.

Frost engages and he challenges. One reason is that, as reader response and art reception theorists tell us, he leaves openings for us to enter, where we also enter *into* the creative process—the process of making meaning. We learn that it is great fun, this game that Marjorie Cook calls "The Serious Play of Interpretation."[1] Part of the fun is that Frost does not require it—again the best kind of teacher. He stimulates, but does not require; tests us, but not to determine how much we have ingested, rather how close we are getting to poetry—his own grading criterion for the students who were in his classes. This is to see "test" as trial of the quester or the initiate. And so we open ourselves to the various possibilities of reading, close in on the strictures of form, recognize dualities and tensions, and resolve paradoxes, or at least recognize their irresolvability. With Frost, this is not only fun and intellectually challenging but emotionally engaging. And, finally, it really does teach us how to read—to value precise diction, form, prosody, to construct meaning; we learn better to tolerate the residual doubleness and tentativeness of our conclusions. We learn to trust our ability more, but language less.

And in this, of course, he has anticipated postmodernism. The irony is that he has been thought of as old-fashioned, not quite with the times of modernism, not obscure enough for the "Pound-Eliot gang," as he dubbed them. One irony is that so much of his best poetry makes wonderful vehicles for the new critical type of analysis. Another is that it is Frost who often so resolutely resists closure, just as many of his poems resist our final agreement. He encourages us to raise the most fundamental questions on interpretation; as Cook says, "Frost makes a central place in poetry for the recognition of the human need for interpretation,"[2] and I agree.

I suspect that it is this quality in Frost that has helped his stock to rise. The subtlety that Lentricchia wrote of, which eludes easy generalizations,[3] has since become better recognized, and Frost, consequently, better appreciated than he was during

Eliot's eminence as strange and commanding god. Brower, Lentricchia, and Poirier all fulfilled a great need for Frost studies— arguing that Frost was a great modern poet, that he could indeed be related to modern intellectual movements and thought, to modern poetics, philosophy, or aesthetics.[4] (Both Lentricchia and Poirier relate Frost to modern philosophy.) Brower had a superb ear and taught his readers to listen—to Frost's voices, to sound and rhythm; awareness of Frost's "defense of irony" and his toughness in the face of a tough reality out there was his greatest contribution to the argument for Frost's modernism. It no longer seems necessary to argue for Frost's place among the great modern poets—perhaps thanks to these critics, perhaps also thanks to changing perceptions of texts.

Lentricchia goes as far as to claim that the modern mind is a thing Frost's poems have helped to create (19). At the very least, I would say that Frost has helped create modern reading, with its valuing of indeterminacy and open-endedness, with the broadening of its definitions of texts. Analyzing how these values and redefinitions help us to read Frost, and in so doing to relate the poem, the reader, and the poet, is the major focus of my discussion. Poirier speaks of getting closest to the spirit of Frost's work whenever we as readers get into the action, the performance of the poem (26). This "writerly" quality is where I locate the chief excitement of Frost for a reader. Poirier considers the interpretive process to be Frost's ultimate subject (xi), but I see this process more as what Frost forces us to, engages us in, (and that, of course, is what a reader-response theorist like Iser finds most compelling and rewarding in reading).

Like Lentricchia, I find James an important key to Frost, especially the interactivity James explains and Frost requires. Where Lentricchia's interest, however, is more in James as philosopher, mine tends more toward the value for Frost of James as psychologist. James's insights also shed light on possible relations between the poet and his readers, the poet and the occasions that were his "texts." (For this reason I bring in more biographical issues than did these critics.) Both Jameses are important in my exploration of the relationships between reader and text, between Frost as writer and poet as reader. Ultimately under discussion is the reading process—a process that includes an active reader, a real and active writer, both of whom are performing both sorts of acts.

Combined, however, with Frost's indeterminacy and resistance to closure is his commitment to form and poetic conventions; but even here, he teases us, for Frost resists classification as well. He invokes traditions and conventions to set himself in tension with them: one can find in Frost's oeuvre the romantic, the classical, the pastoral (Lynen has explored Frost's version of pastoral),[5] the dramatic monologue, the masque; he delighted in that most traditional of forms, the sonnet. Yet with all of these traditions, he showed his difference, sometimes ironically (David Perkins considers him in relation to romantic irony, for example),[6] sometimes technically, sometimes, one suspects, for the sheer pleasure of resistance and difference, the defiant joy of putting his own stamp on what he still revered—the loving but rebellious son. (And if he laughs up his sleeve at any would-be pigeon-holing schoolmen with their "pastoral-comical, historical-pastoral, tragical-historical, tragical-comical-historical-pastoral," he is in excellent company!)

What Frost would be saying of criticism today one can only imagine. He would hardly have tolerated quietly either the obliteration of his authorship or his text; yet paradoxically, he shows himself to be a valuable member of Stanley Fish's interpretive community because he is so good at provoking literature from the reader. Literature in readers, after all, requires great poets to tap it greatly, to activate and inspire it. While Frost may not have been willing to be an equal partner in such a community, Fish does provide him a place, for his interpretive community includes the poets reading themselves and other poets, no doubt entering into the decision that this fourteen-line arrangement of words shall be called a sonnet. And so, even in Fish's class,

Frost would be very much alive as a fellow reader and interpreter, a role he might not have minded too much, provided we
remembered who wrote the poem in the *first* place. And provided we are the "right kind" of readers, the sort to be admitted
into Frost's community.

What Frost may not fully have appreciated in himself, though,
is that capacity of his we have been discussing—initiating readers into that select community, not just by talking about poems,
as he knew he did so superbly, but by making *us* talk about
them. True, one could say that some of his best-loved poems
are *really* caviary to the general, but then, because they are also
palatable to the "general," they are capable of teaching them to
appreciate caviar. Here, too, he is in the same excellent company
as the author of those words.

Fish considers interpretive communities to be made up of
those who share interpretive strategies not for reading (in the
conventional sense) but for writing texts, for constituting their
properties and assigning their intentions.[7] Ambiguity inheres in
the word "writing," intended as it is to apply to "reader," yet still
attached, as I believe it must be, to the act of having put those
words on the page in the first place. In the same way, the terms
in my title intend double meanings: Frost as writer *and* reader
of what he encountered; Frost in dialogue with us, the readers.
And then, back to Fish's sense of writing, Frost as helping us to
be the more poetical readers that he wanted: Frost helping us to
"write" our interpretations of his poems, which is also to share
in his making of meaning.

In the same spirit, this book is intended to work through with
my readers some of the ways our acts of reading, of encountering and constructing the poems for ourselves, parallel what
seem to have been Frost's encounters and acts of construction.
I hope to show that the phenomenology of his "reading" has its
parallels in ours, that the theories of reader response critics can
also inform us regarding the poet's acts of reading his world,
and that, while biographical and other primary material is im-

mensely useful as corroboration, the only way such a theory can truly be validated is by examining the texts of the poems themselves.

This is to see the text as inviting and entangling, as engaging the reader. This may result in resistance to being so entangled; in the case of poem or poet, to being read. I take this to be a central conflict in Frost: the need to be read, and read well, against the *fear* of being read well coupled with his possessive need to protect his creation from appropriation by others. Of course the poems reflect that conflict: the indeterminacy and ambiguity that so attract us are intimately bound up with a person whose personality and conflicting needs are reflected both in the attractions and the difficulties of the poems.

Biographies can be an important aid if one wants to understand the life better (Thompson's scholarly, complex, and controversial official three-volume biography or Pritchard's *Frost: A Literary Life Reconsidered,* a positive appreciation that manages to be honest without being either contentious or sentimental, would be my first recommendations).

But this is to be a study of Frost's poetry, more specifically the reading of his poetry. To read poetry well, Frost has told us, is to let poems illuminate one another. "Progress is not the aim, but circulation," he said. "The thing is to get among the poems where they hold each other apart in their places as the stars do" (which is also together in constellations). Brower, in support of his intention to "circulate among the poems," quotes these words of Frost and goes on to quote his "looking backward . . . to see how many poems I could find toward some one meaning . . . to learn if there had been any divinity shaping my ends and I had been building better than I knew. In other words could anything of larger design . . . be discovered" (vii–viii). Therefore this study will not be an attempt to follow either Frost's life or his poems chronologically (especially as Frost tended to save poems for later, thus obscuring accurate dating).[8] I prefer to discuss the poems as they illuminate one another in the context of the theme or artistic question under discussion. True, some issues cluster in poems of the same period, and this will be noted where it seems to be relevant. It must be remembered, though, that Frost's first book of poetry came out when he was already quite mature, obscuring the usual "early"/mature distinctions. Then too, the issues I will be raising are of the sort that do not change very much over time. Poirier, in another context, asks whether even those modernists who confront cultural crises do not do so out of mysterious personal concerns (43). Frost is driven much more openly and directly by such ongoing forces. Connections and contrasts that seem relevant, though, between poems of different periods, or common to poems of a given period, will be noted in context, especially if they will help us better to understand the reading of Frost's poetry.

It is not only beyond the scope of this book, but ultimately unjustified and impossible, to generalize from it to all poets and all reading. I suspect, however, that what we are finding about the relation between our reading of a poet and his reading of his material, between a poet and his readers, will be useful in looking at other poets and beyond that at the sometimes reciprocal, sometimes parallel, sometimes competing or threatening relations between reading and writing (the acts and the texts), between writing and being read, between reader and texts. I hope so.

Acknowledgments

Acknowledgments threaten to be a genre, which, like home movies, can evoke satire from everyone who isn't either in them or producing them. To me, though, this is one of those all too rare occasions when an obligation feels like—no, *is*—a pleasure I have long looked forward to. I confess to being an inveterate reader of acknowledgments: I know how you feel, I want to say to all those expressions of thanks that are not perfunctory but personal. The appreciation we feel on the brink of publication for the support of colleagues, friends, and family wants out, wants expression, especially if writing is what we have just been so single-mindedly engaged in.

Intellectual debts can never be truly reckoned: so much goes in by osmosis over the years, and what can specifically be traced is in footnotes. But intellectual relationships that are personal as well inspire more personal appreciation. First among mine is to Robert Ornstein, who has been and still is an example to me of a superb scholar and teacher—always *both*—who steadfastly refuses to "lose spirit in substantiation." I have benefited through the years from his insights as a reader of poetry and from his comments on my work. Likewise, Roger Salomon has not only read my work but offered thoughtful and appropriate criticism, always with tact, always with encouragement to publish my writing on Frost. P. K. Saha brought his unique insights as linguist and poet to his reading of my readings, giving generously and graciously both of his time and his ideas. William Siebenschuh has ever cheered me on; even as a busy chair in a busy season, he gave valuable, prompt, and expert editorial advice when I needed it.

To Jarold Ramsey I would like to express my great appreciation for his astute reading of my manuscript at crucial stages of vision and revision. His apt questions and suggestions—as well as encouragement—were invaluable to me.

Thanks also go to Anne Wyatt-Brown, good friend and colleague, who is always ready to read what I send her; her intelligent and incisive questions and comments when we "talked Frost" started me thinking in new ways every time. I also want to thank William Davis for helpful and stimulating conversations on Emerson. Vital to keeping up my own enthusiasm at that crucial and exhausting time of revision was the lively, intelligent conversation of my graduate students in a Frost seminar; their insights (some of which are cited in my notes) and their excitement made it an inspiring and memorable semester for me. And a big thank you to Deborah Ellis, another friend and colleague, for urging me to "send it to Georgia!"

I cannot say enough about the editors at the University of Georgia Press, whose interest in this project really kept me going. Nancy Grayson Holmes not only offered encouragement and valuable suggestions but insisted on making herself available for help and advice even through holidays and bouts of flu. Before that, it was Elizabeth Makowski who urged me on, and continued her interest even after she had left the press.

My thanks as well to Gwen Duffey for her sensitive and thorough copyediting.

Karen O'Connor-Knox gave me valuable assistance in preparing the manuscript, and in my tussles with the computer. I am very grateful for her help, but also for her efficiency and good humor when things got harried.

Grateful acknowledgment is made to the following for permission to quote unpublished material:

Estate of Robert Lee Frost, Alfred C. Edwards, executor
Janet Thompson (Mrs. Lawrance R.) for permission to quote
   from the papers of Lawrance Thompson in the Thompson-
   Frost Collection at the University of Virginia Library

Robert Frost Collection, Jones Library, Inc., Amherst, Massachusetts

Trustees of Amherst College, Amherst, Massachusetts

Dartmouth College Library, Dartmouth College, Hanover,
New Hampshire

Professor G. Armour Craig, Amherst College, Amherst, Massachusetts

Robert Frost Collection and Thompson-Frost Collection, Clif-
ton Waller Barrett Library, Manuscript Division, Special
Collections Department, University of Virginia Library,
Charlottesville, Virginia

I am also grateful to the following for permission to quote published material:

Henry Holt and Company, Inc. for permission to quote from
The Poetry of Robert Frost edited by Edward Connery
Lathem. Copyright 1916, 1923, 1928, 1930, 1934, 1939,
© 1969 by Holt, Rinehart and Winston. Copyright 1936,
1942, 1944, 1951, © 1956, 1958, 1962 by Robert Frost.
Copyright © 1964, 1967, 1970 by Lesley Frost Ballantine.
Reprinted by permission of Henry Holt and Company, Inc.

Holt, Rinehart and Winston, Inc. for permission to quote from
the following: Lawrance Thompson, *Robert Frost: The Early
Years, 1874–1915,* copyright © 1966 by Lawrance Thompson, copyright © 1966 by The Estate of Robert Frost; Lawrance Thompson, *Robert Frost: The Years of Triumph, 1915–
1938,* copyright © 1970 by Lawrance Thompson, copyright
© 1970 by The Estate of Robert Frost; Lawrance Thompson
and R. H. Winnick, *Robert Frost: The Later Years, 1938–
1963,* copyright © 1976 by Holt, Rinehart and Winston,
Inc., copyright © 1976 by The Estate of Robert Frost; Lawrance Thompson, editor, *Selected Letters of Robert Frost,*
copyright © 1964 by Lawrance Thompson and Holt, Rinehart and Winston; *The Letters of Robert Frost to Louis Untermeyer,* copyright © 1963 by Louis Untermeyer.

Jonathan Cape Ltd. for permission to quote from the poetry of Robert Frost.

Random House, Inc., Alfred A. Knopf, Inc., and Faber and Faber Ltd. for permission to quote "The Poem That Took the Place of a Mountain." Copyright 1952 by Wallace Stevens. Reprinted from *The Collected Poems of Wallace Stevens,* by permission of Alfred A. Knopf, Inc. and by permission of Faber and Faber Ltd.

South Carolina Review for permission to reprint portions of my article "The Figure a Poem Makes," which originally appeared in its Fall 1989 issue.

To my family—my husband and children, my mother—it is somehow inappropriate to say "thank you." They know what I feel, and they share this accomplishment. The cooperation and "space" I needed they gave cheerfully and with understanding. But more than that, they made me feel that what I was doing mattered a great deal to them too.

Abbreviations

CP   Robert Frost, *Collected Poems*

EY   Lawrance Thompson, *Robert Frost: The Early Years*

I   *Interviews with Robert Frost,* edited by Edward Connery Lathem and Lawrance Thompson

J   *The Journals and Miscellaneous Notebooks of Ralph Waldo Emerson,* edited by William H. Gilman et al.

LT   Lawrance Thompson, "Notes on Robert Frost"

LU   *The Letters of Robert Frost to Louis Untermeyer*

LY   Lawrance Thompson, *Robert Frost: The Later Years*

P & P   Robert Frost, *Prose and Poetry,* edited by Edward Connery Lathem

SL   *Selected Letters of Robert Frost*

SP   *Selected Prose of Robert Frost*

TJ   *The Journal of Henry David Thoreau,* edited by Bradford Torrey and Francis H. Allen

TS   *The Selected Works of Thoreau,* edited by Walter Harding

TW   Henry D. Thoreau, *Walden,* edited by J. Lyndon Shanley

V   *The Living Voice of Robert Frost,* edited by Reginald Cook

W   *The Complete Works of Ralph Waldo*
             Emerson, biographical introduction and
             notes by Edward Waldo Emerson
YT   Lawrance Thompson, *Robert Frost: The*
             Years of Triumph

Toward Robert Frost

1

Braving Alien Entanglements

One key to Frost—both the poems and the poet—is his assertion that "every poem is an epitome of the great predicament, a figure of the will braving alien entanglements" (SP 25). The "great predicament" he refers to is substantiation, what in "Kitty Hawk" he called "our instinctive venture into . . . the material." It is a predicament because we are "risking spirit in substantiation," an epitome of that predicament because in the creation of a poem, felt experience or intention "venture" into form, spirit and thought into language; chaos—the inchoate—ventures into an object that must be shaped out of its subject, by its subject, and then separated from it, only to be read by another who will mold it his way. In comparing a poem to the will braving alien entanglement,[1] Frost suggests that a poem contains within it the history of its making—the desires, struggles, conflicts, *and* results. But we know it also contains seeds of its future—the alien entanglement of its reader.

The term "braving" suggests that writing a poem involves adventure and daring.[2] The verb "brave" also includes an element of defiance, certainly of challenge; it can also suggest a show of bravado—a brave front to hide the fear one feels. A successful poem, then, is a victory, whether by virtue of its having subdued form to the need of its spirit or by virtue of its fidelity to spirit despite its engagement with form, its having become "material," a formal object.

But Frost does not speak only of the poem; a poem, he tells us, is a *figure* of the will braving alien entanglements. A poem can be the result of such an encounter or it can be a cause. It can be, itself, an alien entanglement; and it can be a figure for such "braving" in other contexts, related or unrelated to poems or to writing poetry. The implication is that any encounter of "the will" with an "alien entanglement" is a risk that nevertheless calls us out to encounter it and to show our mettle in the encounter. Further, it implies that any encounter with something or someone "alien" or "other" is potentially an entanglement; that any entanglement is with something or someone "alien." This can include an "alien," unrecognized, or unwelcome element of the self.[3] And yet not to brave such entanglement is to be forever imprisoned within the circle of the unchallenged, unchallenging self, the will untested and unmet. The verb "brave" forces the view that the alternative, not to brave, is a cowardly, unadventurous choice, protecting an almost will-less will, a spirit that never becomes manifest; a thought-feeling that never becomes the thought-felt *thing* that is a poem.[4]

Reading Frost, of course, is also a "braving [of] alien entanglements." An encounter with one of his poems can be seen as an engagement, perhaps a battlefield, perhaps a communion,[5] where reader and writer meet, risk their "wills," brave entanglement with one another. And in the potential encounter, each is risking his wholeness, his perception of self. The writer risks being misunderstood, or understood and appropriated at best. He risks being rejected or ridiculed at worst. He risks sharing ownership of his text. Sometimes Frost would say there is only one right way to read any text; at other times, he said, "The poet is entitled to anything the reader can find in his poem,"[6] and at still other times, he wanted his texts to invite in only the right readers and leave out those who were not. As he implied in "Directive," and later said of the cryptic phrase on parables in Mark, he did not want the wrong ones being saved. (Frost's looser version of Mark was that Christ implied one cannot be saved unless one knows how to read poetry.)[7] Each of these positions demands a different kind of reader, a different view of what a reader is supposed to be or do in relation to the poem. These views conflict and, in so doing, represent the conflict in the poet between the need to be entangled with "others," to be engaged with and enriched by the encounter (that is, the poet's social, additive needs), and the need to protect, to keep whole and pure and private the inner core of the self.

Surely this is a conflict every artist experiences: on the one hand, the need to share one's art and thought, one's "self,"[8] and with that the need to be recognized; on the other hand, there is the equally strong need to protect that self and that creation. Studying a poet such as Frost, therefore, can help us to understand the complex and ambivalent attitude writers can have toward their readers and the effect such conflicting feelings have on their poetic texts, on what sorts of engagement they will provoke from the reader. The exploration of these issues in one poet can have application beyond that one poet, and indeed, I believe it does. But this study presumes only the possibility of such application; for after all, it is *Frost* we are focusing on, and about a wider application there can be only unfounded conjecture. Frost himself, though, whether as example or sui generis, has provided us with fascinating questions, with teasing contradictory comments, with backhanded invitations that can always be taken as rejections both in his poems and in the incidents of his life and letters.

Whether one has been invited or one hasn't been, which of several interpretive possibilities we are to assume "right," what sort of person is addressing us, and in what tone—such are the difficulties that attract, that tempt us to enter, invited or no. Such also are the forces that work against closure and *for* openness in a text. Reader response theorists, in valuing "open,"[9] indeterminate texts, in viewing reading as interaction between reader and text, can help us to understand the ways in which a poet like Robert Frost is immensely attractive—and difficult; attractive because of those very difficulties. They help us to see the parallels between the reader of the poem and the poet reading his world, between the acts of writing the poem and reading it,[10] and may help us to understand how and why someone like Frost both needed and resisted his readers.

It is the very openness of a text, the variety of its possibilities, and its very difficulty that attract Wolfgang Iser tells us. We become entangled in it because of its indeterminacy, the gaps it presents to the reader between what is given and what must be inferred, between what is given on page 1 and what we must remake of those givens by the time we get to page 50 or 300. Our viewpoints must "wander," must be willing always to modify, construct and reconstruct, and we are always seeking consistency, whether in constructing a wholeness of the text or reconciling it with our world view and our experience; we need to make meaning where we do not readily find it, and we become entangled in the making more than in the ready-made. It is thus that we become entangled as we construct the text, and thus we construct ourselves into it as we read.[11]

We see that Iser also speaks of "entanglement," the entanglement of the reader in a text. He does not use the term "braving," but he likewise sees texts as having the power to attract and thus invite engagement, the power to engage not only the reader's feelings and interest but his creativity, his own ability to "write" in cooperation with the author. In the process, though, the reader constructs himself as he constructs a meaning of that text, includes himself in the construct and the meaning, and hence opens himself to change. He also opens his comfortable view of his world to shattering.[12] The poet, says Emerson, "smites and arouses me with his shrill tones, breaks up my whole chain of habits" (W 3:312). Reading then, no less

than writing, is "braving alien entanglements," that is, if we read
actively, as Iser would have us do. Iser's reading of the "poem
[as] . . . a figure of the will braving alien entanglement" might
very well be the poem as it is being *read*, with the reader braving
its entanglement.

Iser is speaking of the novel, not of poetry, certainly not anything as short as lyric poetry. But in poetry such as Frost's there
are gaps, there is openness, possibility left to the construction
of the reader that attracts. We are moved to search for meaning
and say: "This can't be all." And the voice that urges: "It was all"
can be right or wrong. We are moved to doubt any fixed meanings, any pronouncements by the poem or the poet. Long after
we have mined "The Wasteland," tracked down all its allusions,
and figured out how they fit into the scheme of that poem, we
are left pondering the meanings of "lovely, dark, and deep," or
"promises," or "something," or "unearthly," or "out far," or "too
lofty and original," or "letting go with the heart." These are the
gaps I mean. And their very accessibility combined with their
openness attracts and entangles, as did Frost the conversationalist, the unacademic academic,[13] the disarming, armed friend
and challenger, with his open smile and his many masks.

Frost reveled in making himself a puzzle. "Look out I don't
spoof you," he warned. He loved formulae that won't formulate,
the pleasure of ulteriority, metaphor, as the one permissible way
of saying one thing and meaning another. He left "gaps" and
collected devoted followers. He attracted. ("The gaps I mean.")
And he hurt those who became entangled, even as he himself
became vulnerable to the entanglements. He suggests bottomless depths in a poem and then laughs at the reader who looks
down deep. Yet he is never so serious as when he's joking; and,
one could infer, never so playful as when he's serious. One can
close gaps satisfyingly; one can be tripped up by them ("head
forward into the boundless" [SL 344]) and feel foolish, or hurt.
And his opening them, creating them, may all have been in the
service of protecting a core of self that cannot decide if it wants

to be penetrated or left whole, that cannot decide if wholeness is inclusive or exclusive.

Of William James, Frost used to say, "My greatest inspiration when I was a student was a man whose classes I never attended" (EY 536). (James was on leave while Frost was at Harvard.) Obviously, it was solely his writings that would have had this effect. His *Principles of Psychology* would have helped Frost to see both the sacredness of an inner, inviolable self of selves, James's concept of the pure self, and the fragmentary nature of the self: "Properly speaking a man has as many social selves as there are individuals who recognize him and carry an image of him in their mind. To wound any one of these images is to wound him" (294). James goes on to explain how such fragmenting of personality accounts for the way an officer in the military can be stern with his troops and soft with his children, how people in different relationships with a person will have different views of him, caused by the way his behavior varies with each circumstance or milieu. And James goes on to show how such difference can still result in a kind of synthesis, how these are all part of a unity, held together by that inner self. There is comfort here for the person who worries about his wholeness of self, his keeping an ego intact in the face of what he knows to be contradictory impulses and inconsistent behavior; at the same time, such a theory of fragmentation threatens one's desire for a strong, unified, invulnerable ego. One could certainly extend the concept of individual image-formers to readers of a person's poetry, and images to mean not only impressions of a person but whatever understanding one gleans of the poem, and by means of the poem. On one hand, that there can be so many ways in which a person is being "read" can inflate his ego; these various shows of interest and interpretation can be seen as additive and as investing of others in him, engaging with him, and thus enriching him, or at least attesting to his importance. On the other hand, each fresh image, each reading, is also an invasion of that self and contributes to its further fragmentation into still more, and more different, components. Frost needed to assert his being, his identity, by writing, and by telling.

We all create our selves as we tell our stories. Patricia Spacks writes that telling involves an act of mind that discovers a logic of happenings as it does not appear in experience. Putting life into words rescues it from confusion, a concept very close to Frost's definition of a poem as a momentary stay against confusion. Not just the forming but the telling are acts that rescue us and allow us to control. The act of declaring, Spacks says, implies dominance,[14] another Frostian need. In Frost's poetry and in his self-creating versions of events in his life as he told them, he was imposing order on what otherwise seemed unmanageable and chaotic. Then there is our tendency to make ourselves the stars and heroes of our own productions in the "theater of our minds."[15] One could say I tell therefore I am. But he told many versions of the same stories, put on and removed many masks,[16] and then denied them. Lawrance Thompson sees in that denial evidence of Frost's paradoxical and complicated character. We all put on a face to meet the faces that we meet in different situations, masks. And admittedly, it is somehow all one; but how to consider the complexity and contradiction of that oneness? What struck Thompson was that this complicated Robert Frost tried to deny that he *had* any masks (LT 548–49). One can see the dramatic monologues and dialogues in Frost's poetry both as adding to a complex and rich unity or as diffusing his identity,[17] fragmenting in self-defense.

This, of course, opens more invitations to construct meaning or, for some, to recover intention, or an intelligence "behind" the poem, more "gaps" that call out to be "filled" and so attract the reader. Thus does the poet let the reader know, and they meet to close them once again, to construct or perhaps reconstruct a wholeness, one vision of the poem or, for some, the poet. But to be read is to be shared and invaded, even as one is being admired or helped to wholeness. The reader takes as he adds, adds as he takes. The act of construction has also been an act of fragmentation, not only in its possibly meaning something different from some original intention, but in creating something that is now the reader's, a new construct, or at least a new version of the poem. And so even as they build and close gaps, the two must keep the wall between them as they go. The shared activity or communion results in a more complete separation. But of course, the wall was always between them—the text on the paper, the differences from one reading to another, either one person's reading from another's or Frost's saying, "The meaning of it I keep" (LY 316). Such are the walls that always separate poet from reader, readers—or readings—from one another.

Shall we, then, brave alien entanglements or keep the wall between us as we go? As we can see, the paradox is that in braving one we construct the other; in constructing, we are both sharing and shutting out. Something there is that does not love a wall, that wants it down, but something there is that needs to keep rebuilding it. That man is both of those people (a wall builder and a wall toppler), Frost said (V 8). An intriguing question might be: What if the neighbor *were* one who said "elves" for himself, who shared the speaker's mischief? Might that not be even more threatening than a taciturn neighbor, bent on erecting fences? Do good readers make good neighbors? The speaker, too, is a reader, an interpreter. He sees the neighbor carrying a stone and "reads" him as an old-stone savage armed, who moves in darkness *as it seems to him.*

We cannot escape the fact that every act of reading or writing, depending on how one looks at it, either invites or threatens alien entanglement. Threatens even as it invites, shuts out once it has let in. "I wouldn't have a poem that hadn't doors," Frost wrote in a notebook. "I wouldn't leave them open, though" (EY 397). In the refusal of Frost to explicate his own poems, there is an inherent duality: on the one hand, it is a holding back, a keeping of a meaning to oneself; on the other, it is a way of challenging the reader to do his own construction, implicitly inviting the reader to fill the gaps in meaning. Come in, says Iser's text to the reader. Come in, says Georges Poulet's reader, on the other hand, to the text, for he sees the reader allowing the text to enter him, allowing himself to be taken over, in a way to be inhabited by it. In both cases an invitation has been proffered which, if accepted, puts the reader as well as the author's "ownership" of the text at risk. Poulet's entering text does something to the reader,[18] something that causes him to lose himself, to let go of his ego for that reading time, even to be someone or something or somewhere else temporarily, and possibly somewhat changed permanently.[19] Iser's reader seems more in control as he participates in creating the text he enters, but he also is risking change as he constructs himself in some fashion into the text.[20] Either way, the reader is vulnerable to change, and either way, the author of the text takes risks in sharing his text: it becomes part of another; or its making has been shared. In both views, the relation between author and text ceases to be exclusive as soon as there is a reader, maybe even if the reader is the author himself.

But despite the fragmentation inherent in the sharing of one's text making, and hence one's ownership of the text, an author wants and needs readers to complete his act of writing or, to put it another way, to affirm the existence, as well as the worth of the self, which his writing serves both to display and to protect. Then too, the agglutinative aspect of "wandering" through minds other than his, even as other minds wander through his texts, is an important part of the contract that the writer wants and needs fulfilled. What he achieves, if he has been successful, is not his own love back but counter-love, original response, for only in evoking that, and feeling himself capable of evoking it, will he as a writer feel released from the imprisonment of self, from the mirrored labyrinth of that interior.

Frost as Reader

Frost was a reader as well, especially of the real world "texts" he experienced. He came to nature, not as a worshiper, but, among other motives, as a reader and a writer. And the creative possibilities of text construction combined with risk, the possibilities of ego enhancement as well as erosion, and the invitation to entanglement as well as the fear of it appear in the poetry as powerful contradictory, mutually reinforcing pulls.

The idea of nature as book is certainly not new; but just as perceptions of texts and how they work are not what they had been in the eighteenth century, or even the nineteenth, so Frost's way of reading nature, and constructing the readings that we in turn read in the poems, was different as well. This may be the way in which he is most modern—viewing nature as a book the "reader" helps to write. To the eighteenth-century reader of nature,[21] nature was a teacher of moral lessons, a version of some ideal that one could grasp if one were only able to read its symbols correctly. To Wordsworth nature was alive with presences, almost divine, whose "infusion" the poet awaited and welcomed. Emerson saw learning from nature mainly as a way of learning by analogy, a useful lesson and resource for the poet as well as for the intelligent seeker of answers to life's mysteries. Frost certainly benefited from such an emblematic view of nature and its place in thinking and in poetry. But the most powerful analogies with nature in Frost's poems are those the human mind imposes on what it sees, arising from a state of mind that seeks analogies for its expression or projection.[22] As Albert J. Von Frank says, the analogy between man and nature is not established by God but by man's imagination; one makes the analogy by an act of the will each time.[23] And of course we cannot forget that an important aspect of a poet's state of mind is his searching for poetic material, possible metaphors. He comes with a mind extrareceptive to what it sees, more so even than the naturalist, for the poet comes ready to see *and* to make.[24] Then, too, Frost was not content, or perhaps not able, to remain at the comfortable distance provided by analogy, nor was he willing to become a transparent eyeball, aspiring to achieve a mystic union with nature. On the contrary, aside from seeing such union as humanly impossible (he hadn't been invited), he feared it, even as he recognized its attractions, feared it because he saw more clearly the danger to life, ego, sanity, one's very humanness in giving in to such a seductive prospect. It was not only that nature could be "red in tooth and claw" but that it was dangerous where it was most inviting. There is more danger in "Stopping by Woods" than there is in "Storm Fear." That "good," that teacher, like the mythological earth mother that devours her children, must be feared as well as loved. And besides, he was too unwilling to efface his "self." He saw that the ego, for better or for worse, must be protected and respected; that how we as humans see may be, should be, uniquely human; and how each of us sees must necessarily be unique as well.

As reader response critics tell us of reading, we bring our unique combination of experience—literary, sensual, psychic, historical—to the texts that we read, and we become involved in producing "our" texts from the clues before us. What this means is that if there is any mirroring between human and nature, nature reflects what we bring to it, what we need or want or have been conditioned to see; and no two views will ever be the same even to the same reader. Nor does art mirror nature; rather nature becomes newly constructed out of a particular vision seen through a particular medium even as it is formed by it. The snow in "Stopping by Woods," "Desert Places," "Storm Fear," and "The Onset," for example, yields significantly differ- ent poems, the result of very different reactions to the natural occasion. The object of art that later emerges from an actual or imagined encounter becomes, in all its attempts and versions, what gets made of the stimulus, which may not even have been the scene described in the poem and which may be written ten years later in response to something quite different.

The Frostian observer whose voice we "hear" in the poems can remain in control of his "reading" to the extent that he re- mains in control of his vision: he can shift his perspectives in order to "see" in varied or desired ways; he can control what he sees by making something of his own out of that vision. Indeed

Frost made poems out of such visions and made poems about the process of doing so. To use the imagination in this way, and to use language to do so, is not only to privilege imagination but to give the "maker" or "seer" at least the illusion of control over nature; to do so in language is to attempt control by means of language.[25] When Frost spoke of everything in nature being the hem of the goddess's garment, synecdoche, every small thing touching a larger one, he was also making claims for metaphor in poetry and the ways it has of helping us to express reality and to manage it.[26]

But this is still to maintain the synecdochic, the analogic distance and the control such distancing implies. When one feels a seductive pull to the woods, to the beauty of nature, or simply the invitation it offers to withdraw and escape from more human, more "civilized" promises, when one allows too strong an identification with nature, the identity rather than the analogy, one can fear loss of humanity as well as loss of self. It is then one feels the danger of alien entanglement, and in Frost this is expressed more powerfully than Wordsworth or Emerson ever expressed it. The woods become a "text" or represent a text at once far more protective and concealing—certainly more dangerous—than any Iser envisioned. Yet the danger of feeling shattered or lost, and the attendant response to construct out of the encounter and construct the self in the constructing, *are* elements of reading that we find in Frost's reading of nature, a term that, we must remember, was not "just pretty scenery . . . but the whole goddam machinery" (CP 558) including human nature (CP 469) to Frost.

We shall be discussing in greater detail the various relationships between speaker and nature in Frost's poetry, from the more manageable analogy to the more frightening identity. In this respect, too, we can see parallels between reading nature and reading texts in print—the values and the dangers of identification in reading both kinds of text. Personal identification as an important factor in reading is discussed by Inge Crosman

Wimmers, who considers interpretation "to include both text interpretation and self-interpretation,"[27] with self-understanding
as a way of giving a text its significance and veracity. Pertinent
to discussion of the stances taken by Frost's speakers, pertinent also to Frost's dramatic quality, is her discussion of role-
playing—identification, projection, association building, sympathy, and antipathy—which make of reading "a complex and
tense confrontation" (156), with empathy as "the central concept operative in all understanding" and reading as a process
of role-playing that leads to understanding (157). Once interrelationship between text and reader is activated, it sets in
motion analogies between aesthetic experience and the reader's
life (129). We can certainly relate this to the ways in which Frost
saw the potential in nature both for analogy and identification,
aesthetically as reader and productively as writer.[28] Wimmers
takes care, though, to remind us that there is a connection between empathy and narcissism and warns of the necessity of
critical perspective to temper identification.[29] Here we can point
to Frost's humor and his irony as saving.

Frost recognizes (more so than Emerson or Wordsworth give
evidence of doing) that identification with nature means it is not
only nature out there but its manifestations within that create
our identity with it, our ability to construct art with it; in so
doing, we construct ourselves into it and, in the process, further construct ourselves. To be this kind of reader is to read as
Poulet describes: to admit the text into our inner being, to give
ourselves over to it, and allow it to inhabit us for the time of the
reading. Obviously, with a text as powerful as nature, this can
be glorious and it can be threatening. Abandonment cannot be
total—we do not dare allow it to be; yet the reward of daring is
to dare, entanglements must be braved if we are to experience,
or read, or write.

To an artist or to any person, the greater the seductive power
of nature in any of its manifestations, the greater the fear of
being swallowed by it, losing that self and that control, artistic

or human. In addition, the artist/reader of the natural world, in his struggle to *form,* is always wrestling with Proteus, in danger, even, of becoming Proteus, so absorbed is he in shaping, in inhabiting, and being inhabited by alien shapes. The result he fears is that he no longer has a recognizable form of his own, and this, too, is what Frost was not willing to allow. I suspect that his powerful need to assert and impose his own ego, his views, his personality, his readings, his ownership of his text, were responses to the very real fear of that very real danger—loss of self, fragmentation to the point of losing sight of or control of or touch with the "pure self." But, if out of the struggle will come something shaped, then the artist must enter into it; besides, without the struggle there is no exigency to shape. Thus we return to what Frost has said over and over again is the great predicament: substantiation—spirit into form.

This shaping of a new object out of an encounter with that which is unformed could, in fact, be the best defense against the feared loss of self; to create a new object is to assert an ego-retaining power in the face of what threatens to blur perceiving subject and perceived, entangling object. If, as James said, the mind working on the data it perceives is like a sculptor working on stone (287), then even perception is a shaping experience.

In all of this, there is a double-edged relationship between the seeing/feeling/conscious subject and the object that it apprehends, whether the object be poem to the reader or natural phenomenon to the poet, and here James can be helpful to us, as he surely was to Frost. On the one hand, James gives us that image of the mind as sculptor, participating in the constitution of the world; on the other, he insists on maintaining a distinction between a state of mind as a subjective fact and the objective thing it knows (172). "We must avoid confusing what the consciousness is for what it is a consciousness of," warns James (196). Yet knowledge is constituted by a new construction that occurs altogether in the mind. The thing remains the same whether known or not. When once there (in the mind), the knowledge may remain there, whatever remains of the thing (219), but knowledge has been constructed in the mind, out of knower *and* known.[30]

We might go on to raise the question of where interpretation fits in. Rather than the relation between knower and known, is it knower to potentially knowable, the thing to *be* known, and therefore having no existence outside the act or process of knowing? In recognizing the influence of James on Frost, and also on the phenomenologists[31] whose thought underlies reception theory, we find that a reader response theorist such as Iser provides a logical as well as a useful approach to the reading of Frost and to the understanding of Frost's "reading." As James might say, what we "know" of the poem is a construct in our minds, but knower and known remain separate, united only in the act and the form of the knowledge that has been "sculpted," and that is unique to that knower. "In a sense the statue stood there from eternity. But there were a thousand different ones beside it, and the sculptor alone is to thank for having extricated this one from the rest" (288).[32] Certainly James would apply this literally to the artist—plastic or verbal—as well as metaphorically to the general knower.

Frost, with his terrible need to keep his ego intact, his fear of losing himself, never seems to wish, like Keats, to "be" the sparrow pecking at the gravel; he does not speak enviously of an imagination that can enclose a gigantic and powerful force in the claustrophobic confines of a serpent. If we can take Keats at face value, we can assume the protean aspect of poetry making[33] would surely not have seemed the fearful threat to Keats that it must have to Frost.

Frost's way was different: rather than trying to be that sparrow pecking at the gravel, he let the sparrow be just a sparrow. His alternative was not that of the pathetic fallacy, for he had been too well versed in country things, but he did project his psychic needs and fears onto natural phenomena and onto his dramatis personae, from his willful boys to his insane women, from his lonely men to his torn or loving couples. Typically, he could have it both ways: expressing dramatically conflicts he could not or would not have explicated or analyzed or expressed; but this, too, is an act of fragmentation, of invitation and rejection. To identify any one created voice with "the" voice of a dramatist is foolish and naive, but to form a sense of personality from their totality, or their cacophony, or their argument, their very variety, may not be. Through the very distinctiveness of those various personalities, those wonderfully "living" voices and their speech tones, the stories still remain Frost's to tell. Frost's love of the immediacy of gossip was surely related to his desire as a poet to capture tones of voice; his love of listening and telling stories like gossip, a way of asserting his own identity and his need to enter into dialogue.[34] When our stories are appreciated, when our listeners lean forward and say, "And then?" "You don't say!" "Imagine that!" we have entertained and we have made contact, but we have also impressed them with a version of ourselves, one we hope they will admire and lean closer to and also carry away with them; then they will retell it their way and establish in their own right a value and a desirable identity with *their* listeners. In telling—narrative or dramatic, especially through dramatic voices—then, there is further evidence of what we have already seen as the paradoxical combination of self-creation, self-assertion, self-protection, self-diffusion, and ultimately fragmentation.

Where exactly the voices in the dramatic lyrics, monologues, or dialogues correspond to Frost or those he knew is perhaps better left to those more interested in reconstructing a life, to those who allow themselves to be drawn nearer, into the gossip circle, and, of course, Frost, who loved gossip, would never mind were he not its subject.[35] What is relevant to this study, however, is the relationship of the real man, his self-creation or his creation by others, to the poetry and how we read it; to how the speaker in a Frost poem sees what he sees, what he makes of it, and how that might be analogous to the process by which Frost saw and wrote. We might also want to notice when the "voice" we hear is that of a spectator and when a participant, when it is *presenting* a spectator and thus places scene or event at a further remove, allowing the poet still more distance, more opportunity for irony. We might want to ask how the way Frost read the text of nature or human drama, for example, is a way of reading and writing that illuminates the poetry or the poetic method for us, the readers of his poetry. In other words, how did Frost "read"? Want to be read? Where do the readers of his poems come in, or is that irrelevant? More important than asking how this or that person or event influenced Frost or stimulated a particular poem is to ask how this relationship, this event, this reaction was characteristic of Frost's method of inviting or rejecting, of asserting or questioning.

Frost as Text

Perhaps it is because, despite our awareness of masks and roles, we feel so strong a presence in the poems, hear so individual a voice, that we keep trying to find the man behind the masks. What we find validates not our readings but our conviction that man and poems present analogous difficulties, challenges, and fascination. That there are so many different views of Frost, even on the part of a single friend or biographer, let alone between conflicting biographers, parallels the difficulties his poetry presents to his readers. So does his tendency to present so many different versions of himself, to solicit "readers" and tellers of his life and personality only to reject them. Similarly, Frost's poetry is often most elusive when it seems most accessible. Both in what the biographies tell us and what the differences between them tell us—even more telling, what we learn from the stories *of* those biographies—we are given better to understand the extent to which Frost's possessiveness of self *and* text was in conflict with the need to share them, to be read right by the right readers of both. Always there was the fear of any threat to the intactness of his ego coupled with the need both to tell and to entangle, and hence to risk being entangled. The story of the Thompson biography, for example, is a study in its own right, but because it also seems such a telling dramatization of these issues, it merits some discussion, for Frost the man must be seen as yet another text that has been variously read, that reflects both the reader and the read—the biography making subject and the terribly complex protean object. Each "life," of course, is another example of the agglutinative, synthetic process of putting Frost together, but in being *A Portrait of the Artist*, each is different from the other and, of course, from aspects of the man. As we have seen with the poems, so with the life: to construct out of it, to share in the making of this identity that is the man, to interpret him is also to take, to fragment, to share in his "possession," his "ownership" of the text that is Frost. Stanley Burnshaw quotes Frost as having said to him: "I want you to save me from Larry [Thompson]." [36] Burnshaw reads this as a plea, I assume, to set his name aright, his fear that a wounded name will be left behind, as he may well have feared. But I see yet another possibility, another fear, one that Frost may not have been fully or consciously aware of: that of having shared his life-text too much with another, a fear that his life was to be another person's construction, and while he wanted to be biographed and known, his contradictory need was to be left inviolate as an entity that only he possessed. He used to say he liked being made of, meaning made a fuss of, made the center of attention. He needed that, hungered for it. Yet the other side of that idiom is that he becomes made something of, becomes, for example, the hero of Larry's "novel," the construct of Larry's interpretation. He had invited and then, I suspect, deeply feared the collaborative construction that was to be a biography.

Unfortunately Thompson did not live to write the book he had wanted to write next—*Robert Frost and Lawrance Thomp-*

son: The Story of a Biography. It has the stuff of a splendid novel, perhaps a tragic one. It is the story of friendship gone sour, of mutual trust turning to mutual mistrust, of hurt, suspected betrayal, and just plain surfeit. Thompson realized Frost felt he knew too much, realized that he needed to make of this life a good book that had some kind of unity, with a character at its center that held together as a character, not simply a collection of facts in chronological order. He was drawing from life, maybe, but he was creating a book with Robert Frost at the center as its main character. Thompson, the teacher of literature, the critic, the academic interested in novels, was profoundly conscious that, with no intent to falsify or distort,[37] he was, in some ways, novelizing as well. He had told Stearns Morse[38] that he viewed Frost "from the point of view of one who had for years lectured on the novel." Indeed, Thompson writes of his structural concerns, his need for a unifying theme, and he also writes of his determination to remain at least as faithful to his subject as one can to that kind of subject.

> What comes first is CONFLICT OF MOTIVE AND FEELING. This
> is a stripping to the essential (as [D. H. Lawrence] sees it)
> which I could keep in mind, profitably. It would mean sort-
> ing out the primary from the secondary. It might tell you
> how and where to start—with tensions. Start with retro-
> spection: the kinds of questions he asked at the end of his
> life, in terms of cause and effect.[39]

> My but there is the making of a fine novel, in matching two
> lives like hers [Elinor's] and his, and in watching the inevi-
> table tragedy develop from it. . . . In the biography I want
> some of that briefly sketched for the discerning. I see it as
> a chain of cause and effect; a chain that is predicated in the
> minor tragedy of their very strange and dark courtship.
> (LT 150)

It would be hard to find an example of a man whose appar-

ent inconsistencies can be explained as part of a larger consistency. And to me, that is the major goal of my biography.
(LT 305)

Furthermore, he discussed these issues with Frost, even as late
as 1953, when the relationship was already very strained.

On the subject of twisting facts, for example: "Frost pointed
out that we were caught between two desires: the desire for
truth (ie, the specific details as to exactly what happened in
combat zones) and the desire for a neat story" (316). Frost also
said the importance in a good biography is for the biographer
to have some ideas of his own; he told Thompson not to make
it too detailed and exhaustive and exhausting, but sprightly.
Everything depended on those ideas. Not that those ideas managed to encompass or capture the subject, but merely that those
ideas gave the biography some shape: a beginning, middle, and
end (532)—the stuff of narrative, of story, and this, a concern
shared by Frost regarding the telling of his story.

Frost was relieved by these discussions, and so was Thompson, for Frost did not want just a standard biography either, and
here we see again those contradictory needs and impulses in
Frost. He wanted the truth told, but he feared it. He wanted to
be the hero made into that book, but he hated the person who
was doing it to him. Perhaps at bottom was Frost's competitive
spirit: whose life was it anyway, whose story to tell? For Frost
was constantly presenting himself, telling himself.[40] It was not
just that a biographer might reveal facts or character traits that
were potentially damaging; it was that the biographer was also
creating a Robert Frost in competition with Robert Frost. The
doing of this task, the act of making, may have been as threatening in its rivaling Frost's act of self-making and self-presenting
as anything that might have been revealed.

The fawning biographers or presenters of Frost—Robert Newdick, for example, or Elizabeth Sergeant, or Hyde Cox—were
not feared by Frost, only tolerated; they irritated him, and he

did not seem to respect them. He would dangle bait to potential biographers, then tire of them, and withhold from them. Newdick was checking everything with Frost to make sure he would approve what he was saying and how he was saying it. Even Newdick, though, was forced to see that Frost was not always perfect, that, consequently, there were comments or incidents he would want to gloss over or omit.[41] Thompson, on the other hand, was one whom Frost had appointed and to whom he was making everything available, one in whom he confided and seemed to need as a friend, especially during that difficult time in his life following the death of Elinor (1939). He also discussed with him the method of the biography. He seemed to respect Thompson, not always as a fellow grown man, for he exploited him and used him, too; but as a biographer he took him seriously enough that he may have felt, later in their relationship, the need to be "saved" from him.

What difference does it make that we know Thompson, in limiting the surgery on his brain tumor, risked his life in order to keep his brain fit to complete this lifework? Surely the motivation had to be something more powerful than scoring points against a man who had given him plenty to resent; surely it had to have been motivated by an inability to let something go unfinished that he felt such a personal and artistic investment in. One senses the tragic dimension of the hold and the pain when one sees, in a notebook, begun upside down and backwards:

SMALL PLANS GRATEFULLY HEARD OF
Cambridge, Aug 12, 1939

Only fair that this should start upside down, for my world has been turned topsy-turvy. I promise myself to try hard. Aside from that I have little faith in being able to walk on the ceiling. Perhaps the illusion will pass; perhaps the ground is nearer my feet than the ceiling. I hope so. . . . "It's like being invited down to Stratford by the bard."
Simply this: without my even hinting that I thought I

could do it, I sat facing Frost and discussing Newdick—and slowly heard him say he would like to have me undertake the writing of his biography.

Or this: (2/24/40) "Lucky he doesn't know how much I love him." Or this: "But my first reaction is one that will not leave me—my downright inability to do the task *worthily*" (LT 1).

And then, written in 1963: "[Thompson says he is writing] from the heart, so I'll put it in here just as I wrote it: First of all, here I am, pretending that I'm anxious to go up and see Frost when the truth of the matter is that I'm still so puckered at the way he has treated me that I really don't care whether I ever see him again, alive or dead. . . . The irony . . . of our going through the motions, to see if we can arrange what neither one of us wants to have arranged" (LT 866). How very sad this is, this love-hate drama. "The way he has treated me" seems the giveaway.

But always there is evident the concern, at least the professed concern, with being careful and fair. Thompson wrote how he discussed the issue with Frost because he was "worrying a good deal about the difficulty of writing biography, and had decided that all biography was some kind of distortion or fiction. I wished I could ask him what he, Frost, would emphasize as being most important, as a way of corroborating or checking what I was doing. But I had decided that it wasn't cricket to do that." The discussion, it seems, "broke the ice. . . . Frost shifted gears to a better mood," resulting in a feeling of closeness, a good ending for the summer (LT 530).

And this, as an example both of his interest in psychology and of his concerted effort to rise above his resentments: "It's easy enough to get mad at the old bastard, but when you get down deep enough to understand that he was victimized by a whole set of drives which he couldn't control, then the value of explaining the complication is the value of treating them sympathetically and of giving him credit for having intermittently triumphed over his troubles as well as he did." He goes on to say, it is easy enough to drag out all Frost's faults. In spite of flawed human qualities, Frost was at times very lovable, helped people. "Must keep reminding myself of this. Put it in the introduction. Take bearings from that before returning to the problem of writing the introduction" (LT 1514).

But, in its simplicity, perhaps the following, from Thompson's handwritten notes, sums up both the recognition of any "teller's" limitation combined with an almost impossible ambition: "Every once in a while I have a gleam of insight which gives me hope that I can get into Frost" (Sunday, 16 February 1958).

What difference does any of this make, other than to give us a perspective on a perspective, and a complex, changing one, at that? And to remind us that it is *one* perspective,[42] not only among several biographies and personal accounts, but among the "texts" of Frost that any reader is constructing at any given time.

The biographies, of course, are still other texts that we read, each in its own right or in relation to one another—or to the poems, or to our biases and expectations. Because Frost forces us to confront the act of reading itself as we wrestle with how to read him (the poetry, the man, in toto), it might repay us to relate a teasing question of biographical method to these extended acts of reading. While Thompson was working on his biography, in October of 1965 to be exact, and after he had submitted *The Early Years* to the publisher, he came across Karen Horney's theory of neurosis and found it to be the very description of Frost. There are phrases Thompson quotes and underlines seven times in his copious notes on Horney. Donald Sheehy, in an excellent and fair-minded article, analyzes the influence of Horney's psychology on Thompson's Frost—on his conception of the man, on his shaping of his biographical text, and on his "feeling free to be judgmental without believing himself to be hostile."[43] Sheehy finds the reference to volume one as "now still being revised" proof that Thompson was revising it in light of his reading of Horney (although it would require close analysis of Thompson's actual revisions to make a strong statement on the extent of the influence). Horney makes much of the search for glory and its importance to the neurotic personality. Not only has Frost himself spoken of the importance of glory[44] (without having read Horney), but Thompson, in his introduction to the letters, published a year *before* his reading of Horney, alludes to Frost's "unquenchable thirst for honor and glory" (SL ix). We must also be alert to the fact that where such analysis of what seems undeniable influence stops short is the impossibly complex question of susceptibility, predisposition, inner necessity, call it what you will, of that precise influence and the magnitude it may be assuming. Thompson himself raises the most tough-minded, introspective questions about what there is in him that has prodded him to this project and to proceeding as tenaciously as he did (LT 1544). At an early stage in his conceptualizing man and scheme for the book, Thompson showed a psychological bent in approaching his subject: "I'm interested in the motives behind Frost's *fears*. My task is to watch the separate FEARS, and study the beautiful variety of SEPARATE growths which spring from them in Frost's life and art. Don't forget to sort them out, *as* being separate. And get back of those fears, eventually, to some deeper source."[45]

To move out to the territory between reader and biography: alerted by Burnshaw to the Horney-Thompson connection, I read Horney's book and could not help seeing the connections that Thompson had made, but of course I had read Thompson and could not ever completely un-read him. This, too, raises problems and questions that are not easy to answer: how do we reckon with the psychological parallels that are indeed there, the psychological conflicts one can (not must, but certainly can) see in the poems, even more overtly in the letters? The value of bringing biography to poems obviously carries the attendant dangers of reductiveness and distortion, but what of the equally possible distortion that poems bring to biography or to the man on the platform, that the man on the platform brings to our reading of the poems—a distortion whose "correction" seemed no small part of Thompson's agenda once he got over his own distant reverence. The process, wherever one takes it up, reminds me of Norman Holland's feedback loops, which presume not only that we bring something to a text or experience but that every experience and every text modifies what we bring to the next one. How humbling it is to see how difficult it is to see. Witness this example of poems, poet, biographer, readers, and rereaders of both: more specifically, my reading of Sheehy reading Thompson reading Horney to reread Frost, whom he had already "read" in person and before that—*and* after that—in the poetry; my reading Horney through the lens of Thompson reading Frost; and all the preceding quite purposely avoiding the question of why I, or Thompson, or Sheehy—or you, for that matter—have chosen this subject, this person, these poems, to interest us. Even if we put aside these last questions, and I resolutely try to, we must continually remind ourselves how necessary it is to attempt to disentangle the skeins of text, poet, reader, and life even while we recognize how impossible it is to do so.

Likewise, in discussing Frost's need both to share and to keep, we must remember that vital to this conflict, parties to it, of course, are we, the readers. How we see ourselves and our roles will determine the extent to which we feel threatened or at risk, or even whether or not we see ourselves as parties to the contest that Frost seemed to need to set up. We may take Frost, the reading of poetry, his or anyone's, or our roles as readers in any way we choose. But to understand Frost better, I believe, is to understand that Frost might have seen us much as he saw other poets, biographers, friends, and members of the family: potentially allies *and* enemies, potentially fulfilling as well as potentially threatening, potentially synthesizing and potentially fragmenting, and, as with all of these relationships, potentially rivals for possession of the man and the text. Always in contest, it seems, Frost was surely in contest with other poets, perhaps in contest with nature, and, I submit, in contest with his readers. As the right readers he claimed to be seeking, or the wrong ones he tried to hide meaning from, as the critics he ridiculed and disparaged and feared, or as friendly players in the high game of poetry (playing in the noblest sense that Frost meant when he invoked that word), or as any combination of these, serious readers engaging with the texts would have seemed to Frost to become players in that contest.

To us, as readers, it may seem no contest at all: we may see the engagement as personal enrichment, as a game of solitaire, as a puzzle to be solved, as an aesthetic experience, as a clue to a life, as a linguistic exercise—one could go on and on. But to understand how Frost's poetry works, and how that way of working has its analogue in his personality, is to see the poem as, among other things, a kind of contest: sometimes the battle-field, where reader and poet meet, sometimes a record of a battle with nature, or with his own nature, or a battle with language, the fight to form. The paradox is that for the poet to win it is to lose it; to be penetrated as a poet, to have the poem battled with and to have been the magnet drawing the reader, to have created a poem that entangles a reader and engages him, whether in cooperation or in contest is to have won. It is important to see, as Frost may not have, that whatever the nature and the terms of this engagement, any conflict it presumes has its beginnings in Frost himself, who, as reader of nature, wanted to be invited but wouldn't go in, whose poetic doors invited in and then closed out.

This, of course, raises the perennial question of how life and poetry are related, but here our task will not be a simple-minded tracing of influences, or "real" occasions, but rather how the living personality and the poetry are analogous, how the questions of needing to invite and needing to reject, of opening doors and closing them, of wanting to be met and entangled with and wanting to hide and be left alone, are everywhere apparent in the poetry, as well as in the reports and letters of living people who loved, hated, but above all were attracted to the man.

For he was a man who attracted and then feared the closeness of those he attracted.[46] Thompson, interviewing Raymond Holden after Frost's death, comments: "Here . . . you have the familiar configuration: someone who starts by admiring Frost just this side of idolatry, and who winds up—disappointed" (LT 1439). An excellent case in point is the contradiction on views of Frost as a teacher. To some, he was the inspiring master and the master teacher; to others, he was just plain lazy and disorganized. To all, he was a conversationalist they would sit up all night to hear—one who was willing to sit up all night to talk to them. One could point to those younger aspiring writers whom he nurtured and encouraged. In one of his many marvelous pronouncements on education, he said that the advantage of a course was that students would then "have a claim on [him]" which would lead to their seeking him out outside the classroom (I 70). And yet John Ciardi, in one of his many astute observations on Frost, said that Frost was a magnificent and inspirational presence among students but was not capable of being a teacher of the sort that generates a truly sympathetic interest in his students because he would not allow himself to be invaded by students.[47] *Invaded*—it is what we are discussing; the word fits in with the threatening aspect of closeness and with the combative nature of the writer/reader contract, or contract as we are discussing it relative to Frost. Ciardi's analysis of Frost as teacher reminds one of James's comparison between the sympathetic and the narrow, unsympathetic personality, contrasting the expansive, inclusive outlines of the one with the entrenched, secure region of the other, concluding that "the outline of their self [the sympathetic] often gets uncertain enough, but for this the spread of its content more than atones" for they feel themselves "integral parts of the whole of this brave world" (313). In this trade-off is the rub, for Frost would have wanted and needed those sympathetic relationships but feared

the blurring of outlines. It must be said that Frost did not necessarily repel the sorts of "invasion" we are discussing. At times
he resented it; at times he had to protect his poetry from such
distraction, his time and concentration from fragmentation. But
he also needed it. Indeed, he attracted, and *was* attracted; and
in very similar ways, his poems attract, inviting, yet doing so in
a way that suggests an inviolable core.

The Dancer and the Dance

Most important for this work is the way these insights fit
into the notion of Frost's (for want of a better term) intertextuality: the difficulty of separating life from work, reader from
text, reader of the life from writer of the life from reader of the
writer of the life's Life. In all of this, the line between poem and
poet keeps blurring, at times seeming distinct, at times indistinguishable. Can we tell the dancer from the dance?[48] A related
question is: Is the dance a solo or a pas de deux with the reader?
For if the dance is a performance, we must decide whose performance it has been—and who the audience is, if indeed there is
one, or has to be one.

The marks on the page, the author, the reader, the many possible meanings, evocations, interpretations, effects, their possible contexts—theories abound to relate and separate these elements, to privilege or cancel some at the expense of others. One
way to separate these elements, but still see them in relationship,
might be to visualize a series of concentric circles. At the center
might be the "subject" of the poem—the natural occasion, the
object or experience that is being given form, being dramatized,
or shown by the poet. It may be the apparent occasion as that
appears to the reader, but let us assume it to be the stimulus
in fact or experience that triggered the vision that triggered the
poem. The innermost ring would be the perceiving poet. The
next one might be the poem, with its speaker "reading" a natural
event or occasion, the phenomenon or relationship discussed in

the poem. Another is the reader of the poem. One might want to add a further ring, a reader of the reader's reading, much as a teacher will be a reader of his student's reading or one critic of a colleague's interpretation. One may or may not want to insert a ring between poet and reader, the intermediary "ring" of biographer reading the poet, whose reading of any of the inner rings we may wish to take into account.

From each of the circles, though, one could look in either direction, toward the center or outward. To move inward from any ring is to "open" oneself both to entanglement from within or invasion from without. The perceiving poet is drawn in toward, in Frost's case let us say, nature, fact; he is also opening out to the possibility of forming into a poem. That poem, once formed, draws the reader both to see the center through it and to become entangled in it, in what lies within poem, poet, or natural occasion; at the same time, the reader becomes vulnerable to "attack" or invasion from the readers of his readings, and so on out. Every act of reading has its analogue in another act of reading or being read. Thus reading Frost is entering a series of concentric circles into which one feels an invitational pull, with each "entrance" into a circle making an opening for an act of construction, which in turn renders the construct, and constructor, vulnerable to being entered, to further construction, which, as we have seen already, also presumes fragmentation, diminishment, or re-construction by someone else into something else. We have seen this whether it is the poet constructing out of nature, the reader out of the poet, other readers out of one's reading. At the same time, Frost's sleights of word undermine us as we move in either direction. The reader, in interpreting a text, in becoming engaged with it, has invaded that text, and very possibly the author's privacy. To read a Frost poem is also to reconstruct Frost reading his material, as well as Frost writing out of it. And it is to be reached out to by an entangling poet, and drawn in toward the center, as he had been. Of course, to reduce anything so complex to geometric diagrams is grossly to oversimplify, especially as any one scheme seems to preclude possibilities that are not in that neat diagram, and further, as these circles exist on a plane, having no third dimension, let alone infinite dimensions. Of course, to suggest a temporal sequence falsifies as well: the complex act of reading is never simply linear. We could be seeing the poem itself as the read or written object at the center.

In the actual reading process, in the communion uniting fact, artifact, writer, reader in one synthesis of the successful reading, we might more easily visualize a spinning gyroscope made up of inviolate circles, yet connected by the axes of a unified reading or natural fact. Each "circle" could be identified, could be seen in various relations to another and to the whole. But once the gyroscope spins, it is all one, and we cannot tell the dancer from the dance until we stop once more to analyze. And then we may be dead wrong.

Frost was fond of saying we look at A the better to understand B, the better to understand C, the better to understand D, the better to understand A, coming full circle. Reuben Brower quotes Frost in seeing the poems as forming among them, between them, in connection with one another "a constellation of intention."[49] As with the poems among one another, so it is with what we may find outside the poems but still within the totality of "reading" Frost. Unless we are card-carrying New Critics, we need not confine our constructions to single poems. One can construct a larger text: the oeuvre that is Frost, and this could be the collected poems, or could include the man, his letters and talks, the reports of him and constructions of him by others.

Certainly, any work that even pretends to be about any part of such an oeuvre must be conversant with the other parts and show awareness that, whether or not we will ever understand the relationships of the parts, the intertextuality of those various and fascinating texts, we must be aware that some relationship is surely there. To be a scholar is to court Frost's scorn for "conscientious thoroughness along projected lines of logic" on the part of that "schoolboy" who "can tell you what he knows in the order in which he learned it." Playfully, he puts him in contrast to the poets, who "stick to nothing deliberately, but let what will stick to them like burrs where they walk in the fields" (SP 20). But burrs can hurt as well, and fields can tempt us away from school, even to the possibility of getting lost. How to be both the careful scholar, and that bit of poet the poet requires to "construct" his poems in reading them? (It is surely no coincidence that some of Frost's best readers have been poets: Ciardi, Dickey, Jarrell, nor that Frost was such an excellent, and careful, reader of other poets as evidenced from his comments, for example, on Keats, Milton, and Shakespeare.) The existence of this work already assumes an accepted invitation: "You come, too," Frost tells us at the beginning of every poetry collection. We come, too, and, in doing so, enter into Frost's game, playing in all of Frost's senses of that important word. As readers we brave the alien entanglements he offers us, and, unfortunately, we, too, become caught in the predicament of forming as we read, and as we write, of risking poetic spirit in schoolboy substantiation.

In poetry, however, the great venture of the spiritual into the material can be seen another way: it is the poet who takes the material and makes of it something "spiritual," that is, something that one imagination has created to speak to, to stimulate, another imagination. It is a sort of invitation to the spirit. Let us not forget that in the line "The fact is the sweetest dream that labor knows," Frost is not simply celebrating fact but calling even fact a dream. Fact and dream, spirit and material, are formed into a poem. Frost spoke of a poem as a napkin going into a napkin ring, with the ring as the poem and the napkin spreading out again for other people.[50] One could focus, though, on the radiation of possibilities that the *forming* has made possible. The test of a poem, Frost said, was whether it got through to the reader—and in this sense it was per-formance—through form.[51]

If James is right that "the breaches between [different men's thoughts] are the most absolute breaches in nature" (226), then the intimate act of reading the poem, with its multiple and complex possibilities of meaning and feeling, may be the closest one person can ever come to another's meaning. Reading the poems gets closer to a poet, as person or as poet, than any version of the facts of his life can.[52]

Which returns us to the conflict for Frost between seeking ideal readers and fearing them, between wanting to be "read" and fearing it ("The Fear of Man"). For being read can be seen as a way out of the isolation and alienation implied in James's statement. This notion of James's, combined with his view of the privacy of "the self of selves," encourages us to view all acts of mind as issuing from the unique affective life of a person.[53] If, as Frank Lentricchia tells us, "verbalization can be amplification of the hidden interior," and if Frost indeed "creates a self in publicly accessible linguistic shapes" (125), then writing a poem that is to be read is reaching out of that purely private self in an attempt to be shared and joined; it is a way out of the great personal or existential loneliness. But at the same time, it is an opening of that private self and a risking of its inviolability, no small venture for Frost.

Still, I do not see the major conflict as just between revealing and concealing but between being left inviolate and alienated, or being read and constructed, hence shared with another potential possessor, who, in the act of reading becomes a violator of the poet's core Self. (Frost, like Paul of "Paul's Wife," was a "terrible possessor.") Frost spoke of "endless . . . things in pairs ordained to everlasting opposition" (YT 413), of "a man's heart [as] a bursting unity of opposites" (EY 427), and we shall be noting many such dualistic pairs. This duality that is held in unity by the poet who does and does not want to be shared, read, "invaded" by the external "objects" in nature or human relationships, who "invades" these "objects" as they become subjects of his poetry only to have them help "invading" readers into the poems, and with it all, the positive need to be read and read closely—this duality is surely a fundamental duality of Frost as a *poet*. To read him closely is to invade the poem and the poet, to be a vital party to that conflict; ultimately it is the reader who is the alien entanglement that Frost, as a poet, most needed and feared.

This study will attempt to read Frost actively—to dare to try qualifying as the "right," albeit sometimes threatening, reader. Reading Frost will be an act of reading the poetry; it will also be seeing Frost as reader. Then too, if we are to be sympathetic readers as James saw the quality of sympathy, we as readers must risk the certainties of our outlines in the attempt to avoid narrowness—the attempt to enter Frost's "brave world." This will be an attempt to brave the alien entanglement that is Frost and that Frost braved, an attempt to meet him on the ground that is his poetry.

2

Au Lecteur

Frost is willing to grant us some interpretive "sway," as he puts it; on the question of "who has a right to do what with [his] poetry," he concedes: "The right kind of people can take it their way. There's a good deal of sway in it. And of course that's the fun of it" (V 77). Our license to have fun with the poems, as Frost would have it, then, is to be the right kind of person; perhaps we can modify that to presuppose the right kind of reader, which may or may not be the same thing. But Robert Frost trains his readers, provides not only textual cues within poems but whole poems that seem instructions in how to read. He also sets us problems that parallel his own: for example, he did not want to be "just" a "nature" poet (I 34), and we feel the conflicting pulls in his poetry between love of the fact, the material, the concrete for its own sake, and the *use* of that immediate fact as a means of saying something else. This dilemma runs parallel to the question of how to read Frost. He seems to ask: How shall we see the material world, actual experience? How shall we use it? And the reader, in trying to understand Frost, can follow him in his many roles, identify and approximate his various stances, follow his dramatized, possibly unrelated, personae to the crater of the ant, to the brooks or the woods, and ask herself: How is Frost seeing nature, reading and using the factual world?

Other questions follow: How is the way the speaker presents a scene a function of what that speaker seems to need, what he brings to it, or wants to take away from it? And parallel to that: How is what we see in that poem affected by what we bring of ourselves, our training, our expectations, our "repertoire"?[1] If we do not ask ourselves such questions, we run the risk of being "hypocrite lecteurs," assuming that what we see on the page is totally "other" and apart from ourselves, that as reader-spectators we can see another's "monstres," or dissect his visions or texts with impunity and without involvement, without being participants as well. Perhaps it is as willing or unwilling participants that we are most the poet's "semblables."[2] And perhaps that "frère" involvement is what Frost at once most needed and most resisted. Even as he invites us and rejects us, he instructs us and tests us. After all, the "right readers" *can* take it their way. He has said so.

Frost as teacher of reading[3] shows us invitations, but he also warns us. It may help to let Frost demonstrate how he has his protagonists read the texts of nature and, in reading, become participants, not merely spectators in relation to what is seen. He shows us that reading is, first of all, seeing and that seeing is not only selective, not only possibly deceptive, but always see-ing *from*—from a particular place or stance, a particular vantage point, as illustrated in the poem of that name:

If tired of trees I seek again mankind,
   Well I know where to hie me—in the dawn,
   To a slope where the cattle keep the lawn.
There amid lolling juniper reclined,
Myself unseen, I see in white defined
   Far off the homes of men, and farther still,
   The graves of men on an opposing hill,
Living or dead, whichever are to mind.
And if by noon I have too much of these,
   I have but to turn on my arm, and lo,
   The sun-burned hillside sets my face aglow,

My breathing shakes the bluet like a breeze,
  I smell the earth, I smell the bruised plant,
  I look into the crater of the ant. (CP 24)[4]

The poem begins with a move from viewing trees to viewing mankind. The speaker will shift his angle of vision and his
place of vision. He has had to look up to see trees; now he
climbs up to a slope, one where cattle "keep" the lawn, and
from there he is able to look not upward but outward, looking,
but himself unseen. This desire to look without becoming involved is entirely consistent with the view he takes of mankind.
He sees no people; he sees homes, and, further off, graves. To
him they seem interchangeable as he is lolling like the junipers,
concerned only with his own surfeit and boredom. Even his
sentences are loose and rambling, weighted with participials, an
artificial phrase like "hie me" and an indefinite relative clause
added as an afterthought on line 8.

As the sonnet "turns" at the sestet, so does he, literally, on his
arm.[5] He turns back again from mankind to nature, but this time
he looks down, and he looks close. The hill no longer seems to
belong to the cattle; it is no longer the place from which to view
the distance. We are not conscious of anything as large as a hill,
for our attention, directed by the speaker, is now focused on a
spot of that hill, on just the amount of hill that close vision and
smell can take in, and we look not only at that spot of grass but
at another hill, a hill upon the hill, the crater of the ant. The
speaker looks not from the hill, or merely at it, but also *into* it.
Vision now is moving inward as it moves closer, and the objects
of vision have gone in size from trees to ants. With this change,
of course, his own stature changes relative to what he sees and
to his angle of vision: he goes from Brobdingnag to Lilliput. He
seems ant to the trees, God to the ants.

He is close enough to the earth to feel the glow of the sun-
burned hillside, to smell the earth; his own arm has probably
bruised the plant, and his breathing shakes the bluet "like a

breeze." Godlike yes, but we see that the feeling here is not just power over this handkerchief spot of nature but oneness with it. His inhaling and exhaling—his very breathing—is totally bound up with what he sees. Consistent with such immediacy is the change in style from the cumbersome, rambling structure of the octet to the tight sentence structure of the end of the poem—five simple declarative clauses in the space of four lines. Following the metrical jolt of the "turn" in line 10, the sonnet not only moves in simple sentences but in metrical regularity to its close.

We seem to have begun with nature, trees, and ended with nature, ants; we have gone from large and imposing to minute and vulnerable; we have moved from distance up or out to proximity down and in. The speaker, by comparison, has gone from insignificant, passive, and indifferent to powerful, active, and involved. Thus there have been two swings within the poem: nature to mankind and back to nature. Yet at the end we see not only the grass and the bluet but the crater of the ant—home, incidentally, of another highly structured society. The word "again" in line 1 indicates that the vision began with "mankind"; thus we have not simply two changes but what amounts to a pattern of back and forth—mankind, trees, mankind, nature, and possibly even the society of the ant. The joke of the swing back and forth between mankind and nature, between see-er and seen, is the impossibility of fully escaping either, so bound together are they, so does one reflect the other. Ants, too, form societies; the pronoun "these" is linked conspicuously by rhyme to "trees"; yet its reference is "the houses of men . . . the graves of men." We see that man is in nature and nature is in man, and we also see the impossibility of separating completely the "reader" of that text of nature from the "text" itself.

Yet the poem is not only concerned with what the man sees as he alternates in his attention between mankind and nature but, rather, with modes of seeing. The person has the ability to adjust his vision; he takes an interest in a variety of views for a variety of reasons. He needs, at times, to look at nature after looking at gravestones and then to look back at mankind. His interest is in the "further range" as well as the close, the minute and particular as well as the immense and distant. The word "vantage" implies advantage or superiority. The superiority of this man's view does not lie simply in the panoramic vision that height affords. It is the superiority of one who is able to shift his vision, to adjust it as his needs and curiosities dictate, and thus to exercise some control over what and how much he sees. His superiority lies both in the number and variety of things he sees and in the various ways he sees other objects and himself relative to them.[6] Another advantage is his capacity to arrange what he sees by means of varied and shifting perspectives.

This vantage point could be the artist facing his material, which, in the final analysis, is humanity, nature, himself, or the reader confronting a text that does so. Even though, within the poem, we have no evidence of a wholly new creation, or even any alteration of the perceived objects, we do have evidence that when seeing combines involvement with detachment, close vision with distance, when it also shifts perspectives, it structures the seen in various ways and makes *seeing* a creative act. This is a necessary prelude to the shaping of raw material which the writer will do, but it is also the sort of seeing the active reader engages in to construct meaning from what is on a page.

Even more active reading is required when we are given pieces but no unified vision, fragments that must be made coherent and meaningful. "The Wasteland," of course, is the prototypal poem of fragments shored up against ruins but, less obviously, so is "Range-Finding." In its fragmented vision, its dependence on the reader to piece the narrative together and to place it in its larger context of war, it is surely one of Frost's most modern poems. There is no human figure actually in the poem, no "I," no "he." We are shown the drama of the battle's effect "before it stained a single human breast." The only human presence is that of the narrator, narrating an incident whose nonhuman participants play their parts between the shooting of the bullet, which precedes the poem, and the finding of its target, which is likewise outside the poem. They are *between* spatially if not temporally, for by the time the spider withdraws at the end of the poem, we can assume that the bullet has indeed stained that human breast. Insect vision, however, is limited to visible space and cannot be aware of what lies outside its view either in time or space. Only the speaker and the reader project the bullet beyond the poem and recognize that the speed of a bullet exceeds the speed of the spider's movements, that the effect of the bullet precedes the spider's "finding nothing." Inside the poem we have only the action of the bullet and the reaction on the part of the creatures of nature.

> The battle rent a cobweb diamond-strung
> And cut a flower beside a ground bird's nest
> Before it stained a single human breast.
> The stricken flower bent double and so hung.
> And still the bird revisited her young.
> A butterfly its fall had dispossessed
> A moment sought in air his flower of rest,
> Then lightly stooped to it and fluttering clung.
> On the bare upland pasture there had spread
> O'ernight 'twixt mullein stalks a wheel of thread
> And straining cables wet with silver dew.
> A sudden passing bullet shook it dry.
> The indwelling spider ran to greet the fly,
> But finding nothing, sullenly withdrew. (CP 159)

Even in the nonhuman world, the battle cuts, rends, and dispossesses. A flower is stricken and bent double, a butterfly clings flutteringly to its place of rest, but the effects of the battle are fragmented, as each creature sees and feels only what affects its own peace and routine. We see several ranges of vision in the poem, each sharply limited. The bird is as indifferent to the flower as the spider is to the human breast; she "still revisited her young." Although the butterfly had only to adjust the height of its place of rest, it has been frightened. Still, its only concern was with its rest, not with the flower. "Nothing" to the spider meant "no fly," and ironically this meant a spider frustrated in its desire to wage its own war. Its diamond-strung web might now be less effective in providing the battleground it needs against the fly, but even of that the spider is unaware. We see, then, a range of damage on the path of the bullet and multiple ranges of vision perceiving it. The only complete view is that of the human being who writes or narrates or reads the poem. Yet the title, "Range-Finding" (the use of the participial "finding" in the title), undercuts even this superior knowledge.

The soldier who fires the rifle is "range-finding." He looks into his sight and approximates distance and wind direction in order to determine the most accurate trajectory for his bullet. His vision of the target may preclude his vision of the flower and the cobweb. Complete success, accurate range-finding, re-sults in destruction of human life, a comment on ways in which human awareness and intentions are more deadly than nature's indifference. In seeing multiple views and possibilities, we who read the poem, and surely the poet-narrator, are also "range-finding." We too are determining our distance from the target—indeed even the nature of the target (both within the poem and *of* the poem). We too are trying to focus our vision on the space traversed by the projectile, and we are finding that, as our per-ception of our target shifts, we must adjust our range-finders to determine its distance from us.[7]

In so doing we are showing our vision to be unsure and in-complete. In view of all the points of view, the kinds of vision, the diverse ranges, we are forced to ask how we are to see the fragments in this poem. The major source of fragmentation has been the disjoining of cause from effect by virtue of limited vision. The creatures of nature have no conception of cause; they are only capable of responding to effect, that portion of effect which upsets them at the moment. The flower is a victim although it has not been a target, but what lies between purpose and result—what lies beyond it—these are considerations the creatures are incapable of and the soldier cannot allow himself if he is to pull the trigger.

Even if we ignore the moral questions raised by what we know to be intentional destruction, we cannot ignore the relationship between the rifleman and nature. We are shown a spider who is too limited to see what war is, yet who seeks its own victim. By implication, surely, we are shown the possible limitation on the part of the range-finder-soldier who seeks his own victim with no conception of what happens to the flower, the butterfly, and the bird. But there is no soldier mentioned in the poem, and while his presence is implied, we cannot know how he felt about his shot or his target; we certainly cannot know the extent of his awareness. Yet perhaps this is irrelevant, for in his role as predator, he fits into a predatory nature; for the moment that he must be an unthinking instrument of destruction, he is part of the "jungle." He shares the qualities of the spider laying the snare for the fly.[8]

Thus we find a distinction between the soldier who is identified with nature and the poet-narrator who remains apart from it. It seems that the only true awareness of the whole drama takes place in the poet and the reader, and even that is called into question as we shift our range and our focus, as we cast about for the correct distance, or the best way to join parts into wholes. It is in our constant attempt to do so, in our ability to see more, and with a moral vision, that we have the "vantage point" here. It is when we need to do this that we feel most apart from a nature that has no will and most fully engaged in what we are reading. Any bitterness we detect in the poem lies in our recognizing that the narrator-observer, who understands what has happened and who needs to share his horror, will never find in nature the solace, the understanding, the response that he needs. Without this poet-narrator we have nothing more than a scene—a "no-man's land"[9] quite literally lacking even the Frostian speaker we are accustomed to hearing.

To expect more from nature is to sentimentalize it, and one

can easily ridicule and reject such an attitude. It leads to an anthropomorphic view of nature and its poetic extension, the pathetic fallacy. Not so easy to ridicule, though, is the need to feel that birds can weep for a burned-out house. Here, because loss and destruction naturally evoke a need for sympathy, it is more painful to realize man's separateness from nature. For our own protection, we must recognize "The Need of Being Versed in Country Things":

The house had gone to bring again
To the midnight sky a sunset glow.
Now the chimney was all of the house that stood,
Like a pistil after the petals go.

The barn opposed across the way,
That would have joined the house in flame
Had it been the will of the wind, was left
To bear forsaken the place's name.

No more it opened with all one end
For teams that came by the stony road
To drum on the floor with scurrying hoofs
And brush the mow with the summer load.

The birds that came to it through the air
At broken windows flew out and in,
Their murmur more like the sigh we sigh
From too much dwelling on what has been.

Yet for them the lilac renewed its leaf,
And the aged elm, though touched with fire;
And the dry pump flung up an awkward arm;
And the fence post carried a strand of wire.

For them there was really nothing sad.
But though they rejoiced in the nest they kept,
One had to be versed in country things
Not to believe the phoebes wept. (CP 300)

The force of this poem lies in the opposition between the illusion of parallels between nature and humans and the reality that there is no connection. The midnight sunset is no natural phenomenon although it may have the same visual effect: it is a house burning. The chimney, which "was all of the house that stood," is compared to "a pistil after the petals go." The dry pump flings "up an awkward arm," and the fence post *carries* wire. Thus that which is destroyed and inanimate is expressed as if it were living and acting, and acting, in fact, on behalf of the birds who are finding these remnants congenial and useful to their needs. The other side of this illusion is that the birds seem to be weeping and sighing but are, in fact, part of the life that continues. Nesting in these remnants, they find lilac and elm, though touched with fire, renewing their leaves "for them." They neither weep nor know what weeping is, nor do they understand the meaning of a house destroyed by fire, nor distinguish between live lilac and dead pumps, which were all equally *there* "for them."

Frost tells us, though, that only the seasoned country man would know enough to realize this. The city sentimentalist might think phoebes weep for what has been just because they make a weeping sound. "One had to be versed in country things/ Not to believe the phoebes wept." (That "not" is further emphasized by the change in meter of that last line; it is the only one in the poem which requires stress on the first syllable of the line.) The title, however, goes beyond this straightforward knowledge. It is not just that we are being given a lesson in country things, a warning against anthropomorphizing a nature that neither understands, nor cares, nor *is* anthropomorphic. It is that we *need* to know this before we can proceed to appreciate nature or come to terms with it in any way. We need to be well versed as human beings in relation to nature, or even as writers in danger of becoming sentimental and committing the pathetic fallacy; we need, as readers, constantly to remind ourselves that we must be aware of the extent to which we have difficulty sepa-

rating what we need and expect of a text—natural or printed—
from what is actually there. We must understand when we are
meeting that which we encounter on its own terms, when we
want it on our terms, and the difficulty of ever being fully able
to know exactly which is which.

The question of how to read, or how much to read into, a
text does not simply arise from the reading of a Frost poem. It
is a question about which he wrote poems, such as "A Missive
Missile" and "Maple." The latter is a long poem that is not one of
his best; it is not widely known or anthologized, but it seems to
deal with the issue of nature as metaphor, indeed with the larger
question of the function of metaphor—the burden it imposes,
the traps it sets, the rewards it provides.

To summarize the poem briefly: "Maple" is a girl's name, but
teachers and friends usually insist on calling her "Mabel." Her
father confirms, when she is still a young child, that "Maple"
was indeed correct: her mother had given her that name before
she died in childbirth, and the father assumes it bid her "Be
a good girl—be like a maple tree./How like a maple tree's for
us to guess" (CP 222). He had promised to tell her more about
the different trees and more about her mother later, when she
was older. She never forgot this discussion, as he assumed she
would; the seeds he sowed merely slept and came to life when
she grew older and pondered her name once more.

> Its strangeness lay
> In having too much meaning . . .
> Her problem was to find out what it asked
> In dress or manner of the girl who bore it. (223)

She grew up, searching for herself and educating herself in
the process. Her secretarial education brought her to the city,
where, raising her eyes while taking dictation one day, she reminded her boss of a maple tree. Since he had thought her name
to be "Mabel,"

they were both stirred that he should have divined
without the name her personal mystery.
It made it seem as if there must be something
she must have missed herself. So they were married,
and took the fancy home with them to live by. (225)

They went to her girlhood home on a pilgrimage to see if
there were some special tree, but they found none. They hesi-
tated to press her father for the answers; her husband feared
invading his privacy—some personal memory that should remain between him and his dead wife. They gave up the search,
clinging "to what one had seen in the other / By inspiration. It
proved there was something." They "kept their thoughts away
from when the maples stood uniform in buckets," relating her,
rather, to autumn maples. Once they came upon a maple whose
scarlet leaves were shed at her feet, "but its age kept them from
considering this one" (226). They gave up the search. Frost
concludes:

Thus had a name with meaning, given in death,
Made a girl's marriage, and ruled in her life.
No matter that the meaning was not clear.

.   .   .   .

Better a meaningless name, I should say,
As leaving more to nature and happy chance.
Name children some names and see what you do. (CP 227)

In this conclusion we find that Frost is taking back with one
hand what he had given with the other, disparaging names with
too much meaning at the end of a poem that ends in failure
to see enough meaning. He ends on a note of criticism—that a
name with meaning is too much of a burden for a girl to carry,
that it directs, it causes, it does not simply name or label. Yet
the name had brought her together with a man in a good marriage. To live by a fancy is not all bad; to search for meaning
creates a more meaningful life, whether one finds the correct

meaning or not. Thus it was in the *search* for meaning, not in
the finding of it, that her life became enriched; it was in her husband's intuitive perception of meaning that love came to them
both. To analyze the ways in which they felt they had failed in
their search is to enter into the whole question of how to read
a metaphor: the danger of overreading, and the opposite pitfall
of being too literal, or even too narrowly analogical. To be good
like a maple, or scarlet like a maple, or beautiful like a maple is
not to *be* a maple. Finding a point of similarity with a maple is
far narrower than finding the essence of "mapleness."

Her husband recognized her "mapleness," and she in turn
responded to that recognition, yet neither one could define it
or understand it. Instead of really looking at maples, they kept
looking for clues, for the particular maple, the particular message. Maple and her husband had rejected one because it would
not have been there when her mother named her.

> Could it have been another maple like it?
> They hovered for a moment near discovery,
> Figurative enough to see the symbol,
> But lacking faith in anything to mean
> The same at different times to different people. (CP 227)

This is surely the voice of the poet, intruding to criticize
inability to be figurative enough, to allow metaphor some flexi-
bility, some openendedness. The misunderstanding begins with
the father's interpretation of the mother's intent:

> Well, you were named after a maple tree.
> .   .   .   .
> She put her finger in your cheek so hard
> It must have made your dimple there, and said,
> "Maple." I said it too: "Yes, for her name." (CP 222)

We see that the father begins the assumption that the name
was "after *a*" tree. It probably was not with *a* tree in mind, nor
was the intent to "name *after.*" He creates the simile "be like

a maple" and assumes it to mean "good." The mother seemed to say, "She is like a maple," or perhaps, "Be a maple," and we too may ask "how?" The problem did not lie in the difference between simile and metaphor, the presence or absence of "like" or "as," for in their deep structure they could be the same, with an analogical connection present in both. Rather the real difference is between specifying a single property or feature (as in the as + [adjective/adverb] + as or the adjective + like structures) and leaving open the possibility of any number of analogous features. The father goes on to say "*How* like a maple tree's for us to guess" (emphasis mine), but it is this range of possibility they fail to explore. They are too afraid to "guess." I agree with Max Black's argument that neither the comparison view nor the substitution view of metaphor has the rich potential of the interaction view: that the principal subject (in this case, the girl) interacts with the subsidiary subject (maple) along with its system of associated commonplaces and the newly created implications.[10] Frost may have relied on the substitution view in his definition of metaphor as "saying one thing in terms of another," but in the poetry he exploits interaction. In "Maple," for example, the subsidiary subject—maple—had an effect on the principal subject—Maple-the-girl; Frost surely expects his "right" readers to open themselves to the fullest range of shared meaning and newly created implications. In "Maple" we see that the problem, rather, lay in insisting that the metaphor be tied too firmly to one attribute, or to one tree.

There are various attributes of a maple which we can think of and which the couple see. The problem is only that they fail, for one reason or another, to apply them to her. The mother named the baby at her death, but it was also in her season of bearing. Birth and death came together at that moment in her life; yet the young couple could only focus on the image of the maple in fall—season of death, yet also season of its greatest beauty. In keeping their thoughts away from the sap season, they missed the "steam," the rising sap, the scorching by fire, the bearing.

They missed the inner sweetness, looking, as "she [had always] looked for herself . . . more or less outwardly." That the maple's inner sweetness occurs at a time of minimum beauty, and that the greatest outward beauty occurs at the time of death, is a paradox which escapes them entirely.

> Even in fall, though:
> Once they came upon a maple in the glade,
> Standing alone with smooth arms lifted up,
> And every leaf of foliage she'd worn
> Laid scarlet and pale pink about her feet. (CP 226–27)

One reason they failed to relate her to this tree was "a filial diffidence [that] partly kept them from thinking it could be a thing so bridal"—too beautifully undressed—again missing the fact that this, like the spring maple of rising sap, sweetness, and bearing may have been exactly what her mother would have wished her to be and to have. That and the beauty and the up-turning, up-reaching that had attracted Maple's husband to her, and the roots that spread out far, not just in deep.

Since all these are attributes of a maple, any maple, any time, Frost seems to be demonstrating that to be too literal, or to remain at the level of one-to-one analogy, is to limit the range of one's understanding. At the same time, however, being too analytical, trying too hard to find the "secret," can be the stumbling block to finding the secret. Simply coming upon those maples—any maples—and relating to whatever it is that is magnificent at that time, that is what Maple was too self-conscious to be able to do.[11] Her husband's one great contribution was his inspired and intuitive recognition of the "inner mystery" of her being. She, after all, could not "read" herself, but he found what she missed, and their marriage became a combination of his perception and her mystery—the ideal relationship between reader and poem.

Thus metaphors, as we see in this poem, are dynamic and creative, and they do not only illustrate, they can influence what happens,[12] or at least change the way we see when "the principal

subject is 'seen through' the metaphorical expression." Maple became more like a maple because she thought she was supposed
to be like a maple. Names, words, *can* enter into the creative
process and be formative. They can mean different things to different people and yet mean all of this at once. Still, they can
be *mis*read. Parallel to this is the way we can misread nature.
Maple could not literally be a maple, nor was she related to any
one maple or quality of a maple. The solution would have been
to find the "system of shared commonplace" evoked by maples
and girls[13] and apply those that were appropriate. The problem
was her inability to distinguish the literal from the figurative,
the identity from the analogy. Her problem, too, was the limitation of her imagination (we remember it was "fancy" they
took home with them) and of her ability to reconcile herself
to mystery—the mystery of her own being, the mystery of her
husband's intuitive apprehension of her essence, what Karsten
Harries considers the transcendent possibility of metaphor to
express the not-present.[14] What makes this poem important for
our purposes is its pivotal position in the relationship between
reading nature and reading poetry—or any metaphor, reading
any natural phenomenon or experience as metaphor. While it is
an invitation to see nature as metaphor, it is a warning to do so
with delicacy, tact, and care.

In "Time Out" Frost most explicitly compares nature to a
book that we can "read," but rather than tell us what he reads,
he tells us how to do it. While he "reads" with his fingers the lesson of nature's cycles, the major realization of the poem is that
the slant, the slope, and the corresponding attitude they gave
him in his climb up the mountain created the analogy between
mountain and book; or more accurately climbing a mountain
and reading a book. It was the slope that both gave his head
which made the two activities analogous, and it took a pause
in the activity to make him realize it. The lesson of life learned
from flowers is subordinated to the lesson he learns about how
we learn. Whether with nature as book, or literal book, to read

well we pause as we read; we bring to it an attitude, and we *reflect*. We do not rest in simple analogy—that is merely to re-flect as a mirror reflects. (And this kind of reflection *can* be done with a hard and level stare and *can* be prey to causes and sects.) The thoughtful observer-reader-artist also reflects in the sense of thinking deeply; and the result, of course, will be re-arrangement, reassessment, images with more than one possible reference. Not content to rest in pure analogy with nature, we must add to what we see our further reflections on what we see; we add our selves, our questions, and our imaginations to the facts before us, and if we are not entirely lacking in imagination, like Maple, we form new connections with what we see, and we extend our range of understanding beyond the fact or the simple analogy. If we are poets, we transform what we see and think into the new wholes and new creations that are poems. If we are "poetic" readers, we perform analogous reading acts. In this respect, it may be useful to see Frost's "Time Out" in connection with "The Poem That Took the Place of a Moun-tain," where Wallace Stevens, in reversing the book/mountain analogy, suggests this possibility even more strongly:

There it was, word for word,
The poem that took the place of a mountain.

He breathed its oxygen,
Even when the book lay turned in the dust of his table.

It reminded him how he had needed
A place to go in his own direction,

How he had recomposed the pines,
Shifted the rocks and picked his way among clouds,

For the outlook that would be right,
Where he would be complete in an unexpected completion:

The exact rock where his inexactnesses
Would discover, at last, the view toward which they
    had edged,

Where he could lie and, gazing down at the sea,
Recognize his unique and solitary home.[15]

By the time we finish this poem, we are not certain whether
the poem from which he looks out is the poem he read in the
book or a poem he wrote, or whether one simply reminded him
of the other. Again, it is the *outlook* that is important in determining what is actually seen, and it is by means of that view
that the speaker arrives at self-understanding and "completion."
Stevens, however, makes more specific the active nature of the
looking out: in order to achieve the "outlook that would be
right" he had to *recompose* what he saw.

It is this that Frost seems to do as well, not only with respect
to composition, but with respect to his way of seeing the world
around him. He objects to mere "sunset raving" (SP 36) and felt,
according to Lawrance Thompson, that "great art abjures a sense
of the beautiful—the purely emotional and sensational, in order
to be more concerned with fact as emblem of the spiritual and
the mystical" (YT 568; SL 596). Seeing nature as emblematic is
certainly not new with Frost. As we have noted before and will
discuss subsequently in greater detail, Emerson was a powerful influence in this respect. Swedenborg, whose ideas Frost's
mother preached to him, had written: "One would swear the
physical world was purely symbolic of the spiritual world." (EY
70). Frost is not a Swedenborgian. As he put it: "I was brought
up a Swedenborgian. I am not a Swedenborgian now. But there's
a good deal of it that's left with me. I am a mystic. I believe in
symbols. I believe in change and in changing symbols. Yet that
doesn't take me away from the kindly contact of human beings.
No, it brings me closer to them." (I 49)[16]

His world of symbols, then, is not necessarily concerned with
the spiritual world. The "impulse from a vernal wood" is not,
for Frost, some immanence communicating spiritual mysteries;
rather, it is an insight that forces him to reflect as he reflects;
and, of course, his way of relating the natural world to human

experience gives the poems their psychological and philosophical immediacy and their emotional depth. Still, Frost has said that in what we observe there is "always, always a larger significance. A little thing touches a larger thing." [17] He used to call himself a synecdochist: "I believe in what the Greeks called synecdoche: the philosophy of the part for the whole; skirting the hem of the goddess. All that an artist needs is samples." [18]

But where does that put the artistic creation fashioned from the "samples"? Does it remain part of that "larger thing" or separate from it? If we assume the hem of the goddess to be the hem of a garment that clothes what must never be seen, that inviolable, knowing secret that sits in the center, the closest the poet can get is still only to what covers her, or perhaps clothes her just so she *can* be viewed and touched, or at least "skirted." Touching it, though, could mean touching *on* it—perhaps sometimes successfully. More crucial, perhaps, to Frost, would be the possibility that one who so succeeds would be a *part* of (rather than apart from) what he has touched (on). A comforting view, this, artistic creation as a kind of at-onement.

Thompson focuses more explicitly on the spiritual meanings Frost may have attached to the term synecdoche. He reminds us that Frost called synecdoche a "philosophy" (not a figure) of the part for the whole [19] and that, in connection with synecdoche, Frost had said, "My motto is: something has to be left to God." But it is important to distinguish spiritual views from poetic ones, even though one view may well inform or lead to the other. Frost speaks of the poetry belief and the God belief together (SP 45), but they are not necessarily the same. To understand how Swedenborg or Emerson claimed to see the things of the world is not to assume that Frost saw those things the same way; all we have is samples to show us that he used them poetically in similar ways. His synecdochic worldview may have been one that saw the poetic, not necessarily the divine or spiritual, potential in a doctrine of correspondence. Synecdoche is a figure, not a religion. Its poetic and/or religious potential, whether by belief or by active creation or both, may indeed have given the poet comfort. Holland interprets Frost's synecdochic view as the only way he has of dealing with realities too vast to manage: the small, the emblematic, the poem, the incident, as world in little, as manageable.[20] His theory helps us to see how the poem-in-the-making might have allowed Frost to feel not only more "in touch" with the universe but more in control of at least a *part* of it.

Both Thompson's philosophical/spiritual reading of Frost's "synecdochism" and Holland's psychological one are important and illuminating, but more to the point here is the way it gave Frost poetry, or rather gave him some of what he needed to create poetry, gave him a way of seeing, not only actual scenes or dramas in nature but potential ones. It is difficult, for example, to believe that Frost really came upon that deadly drama in white that the speaker of "Design" claims to have come upon. That tableau, the fact that the speaker just happened upon it, and, of course, the very randomness of such a perfect design of darkness provide a "sample" that we surely feel was imagined.[21] We might conjecture regarding what went into that bit of imagining: Thompson tells us he was mulling over the question of design; who knows but that concept may have suggested a literal design in nature, the web. The drama that became even the early version seems an invoked rather than an experienced sample, a *possible* sample, both of design in randomness and randomness in the service of design, and all of it a "sample."

To become better readers of Frost's ways of "reading" and imagining requires us to ask how such a worldview—what he called synecdoche—worked for him as a poet and what it asks of the reader or does to help us. Is the pebble a *part* of the Whole Truth or is it only a pebble—perhaps not even that, but an illusion of a pebble? In its whiteness, is it a *sign* of the purity of truth, or does its absence of color suggest that "blanker whiteness," absence of meaning, its elusiveness the elusiveness of truth? How *do* terms like metaphor, symbol, or synecdoche, not to mention natural fact, help him—help us? This question is especially pressing in light of the fact that we do not actually find a great number of obvious figures in the poems.[22] It seems to me that seeing the universe as synecdochic provides a way for Frost to find a middle ground between two worlds: a world of natural fact that he will not deny or devalue as being what it is—real, the things we love for what they are, a nature that he will not regard as a mere copy for him to "use" while he imagines and longs for an ideal universe,[23] and a Wordsworthian nature—active and alive with presences that he is too pragmatic to accept as real. Samuel Levin posits a theory of metaphor that asks us to take a metaphor literally, as the literal expression of a "metaphoric world," a world we cannot necessarily conceive (that is, have a concept of) but conceive *of* (have a conception of), a *possible* world, where one could imagine that a sea laughed or that trees wept. He claims, as of course he had to, that such a theory must necessarily be limited to the reading of a poet, like Wordsworth, whose romantic conception of the universe included such possibility, whose worldview included an active nature, whose poetic aspiration was to invoke from nature and his own imaginative receptivity such moments of heightened awareness and feeling, moments in which flowers could be happy and seas laugh.[24]

But Frost is too rooted in realism. When in his poems winds hiss or bark, when leaves invite, or trees intend, he is more likely to be showing how human emotional states are being projected onto nature. (We shall explore this more fully in chapter 5.) Surely it is this assumption that saves Frost from the pathetic fallacy, this ironic double vision of the naive, needing man on the scene as a consciousness separate from the poet who *is* versed in country things which allows us to see Frost's animated trees, judgmental animals, and social or philosophical birds as modern creations. Just in case we do not get the joke, poems like "Come In" or "The Need of Being Versed in Country Things" assert our separateness as well as the poet's from such a nature. They warn us against being fooled by the pathetic fallacy and against sentimentalizing an unfeeling, uncaring, indifferent nature. Yet in both poems, underneath the bravado of one, the country wisdom of the other, lies a sort of wistful longing for what one can no longer believe; and when one cannot believe in fairies, or that birds or trees weep, one takes the next step in remove from those fictions, finding them similar, analogous, representative of the real world or some aspect of it. Synecdoche, then, can be, as George Bagby points out, a way of seeing reality,[25] what we could call a worldview, and Levin might say that if one's worldview is synecdochic, then what the artist "sees" is true of that world.

The point is that, once the poet sees the universe as emblematic, he will find designs for his art, emblems for his ideas, and ways to create a nature that will allow them to fuse. As Dewey wrote: "The painter did not approach the scene with an empty mind, but with a background of experiences long ago funded into capacities and likes, or with a commotion due to more recent experiences. He comes with a mind waiting, patient, willing to be impressed and yet not without bias and tendency in vision."[26] Seeing the world as figure draws from the poet the poetry that comes from the associations he makes along a system of shared commonplaces,[27] as objects in nature become now principal subjects, now subsidiary subjects. As we will discuss in more detail and from different perspectives in a subsequent chapter, Frost was not content to rest in analogy. As P. K. Saha says, analogy is a caterpillar crawling on a leaf; metaphor is a monarch in flight.[28] Those objects Frost was enlarging had to be able to encompass any part of the universe—material, spiritual, human, psychological—had to be open to vast possibilities. Or, as metaphor, the smaller thing had to be able to express multiple meanings or to represent multiple possible realities, whether of human relationships, psychological trauma, or speculation on the divine.

Indeed, Frost has elevated metaphor to be "the whole of

poetry" (LT 25), saying that a poem is a new metaphor inside or it is nothing, that it is everything out of its place, a triumph of association.[29] How then to account for poems like "Stopping by Woods," "Out, Out—," "Mending Wall," or "The Pasture"? For these poems seem so factual—scenes, small dramas, whose voices and situations can stand alone and unassociated. We might want to know if we can, must, ought to, or better not take them only literally. In Frost we never fully lose the "realness" of the literal term, or subsidiary subject, when it becomes figure. That "cord" tying the actual to "higher" possibilities can break[30] without harming the poem because that earth, those facts, are rich enough with experience and beauty to survive independent of the cord and whatever it may lead us or attach us to. One can relate this to Samuel Coale's statement: "An emblem is like a natural object; in the poetry it represents that natural object and is significant without "symbolic" definition".[31] We cannot help noticing, however, that the word "significant" has still crept into his definition. There is a difference between "clogging" a poem with symbolism (LU 376) and allowing its implicit possibility. We cannot deny that many of the poems allow, even enjoin, us to find "something more," whether by means of a giveaway sub-sidiary term, a context such as our seeing "The Pasture" placed at the front of all Frost's collections, or just some "sense" we have and must therefore also mistrust that there is "something more" here. That "something more" can be classed as symbolic, the missing "Y" in Nowottney's view or as class four metaphor in Perrine's scheme, where nothing on either side is said explicitly, but, implicitly, associated thoughts will fill our heads.[32]

Any story we value has intimations of something more, Frost claims, and on those grounds alone, he gives us leave to make his tiny valuable "stories" something more and potentially dif-ferent "somethings" from one reading to another. "The aesthetic moral is: to go any poem one better, not one worse . . . just get another poetic something going—one step more poetic any-where" (V 82). A poem, he says (metaphor, he says elsewhere), is like a current carrying the eel grass with it, combing it like hair, and thus combs it in different directions without uprooting it from its initial clarity, its fixed meaning (LT 415kkk). Perhaps to the poet the fixity is in his "meaning" or intention, the combing, the metaphoric currents he activates that make it radiate, that can push and pull it in different directions, giving it possibilities for different "looks"; as readers, however, we may feel that where we cannot recover that fixed "meaning" we are bound to recognize the fixity of the words on the page which create a "fact" or "scene" but still allow it to be combed by the associations that those words evoke. The poetry that sways on its anchor has both deftness and definiteness (V 77).

The lyrics seem to me to be easier to take metaphorically than the longer dramas. How can one reconcile the intense realism of "Home Burial" with Frost's claim that a poem is nothing if it is not a new metaphor inside. It might be helpful to see it, as David Lodge (following Jakobson) sees realistic fiction, closer to the metonymic than the metaphoric mode,[33] given that the metaphors within it radiate ever greater possibilities for its meaning to be realized. The realistic drama on the whole might represent a larger reality, or be contiguous with it, rather than analogous to, or symbolic of, something selected from another category. Lodge points out that at higher levels of generality a literary text is total metaphor, the text being vehicle and the world tenor. "The metonymic text . . . seems to offer itself to our regard not as a metaphor but as a synecdoche, not as a model of reality, but as a representative *bit* of reality" (109). And so we have come full circle, for Frost has suggested as much in his relating "intimations of something more" to synecdoche although he creates new difficulties in his terribly grand inclusiveness: "All figures are really all one figure. It's a live, live thing for the mind to rise to" (LT 25). "Metaphor, parable, allegory, synecdoche—all the same thing! . . . all the figures are one figure" (V 42). The difficulty of such inclusiveness of figure is of a piece with the difficulty of a synecdochic worldview so all inclusive as to be no help at all. If everything is part of the same whole, we are caught in a tautology—everything is everything. Or, more to the point, anything can be made to be representative of something that is a part of all creation and therefore a sample, a representation, a piece or a touching of it.

As readers, as students of his poetry or of the craft, we may want to make some finer discriminations, to understand more precisely how a given poem, line, metaphor, synecdoche, or metonymy is working. More fruitful, perhaps, might be to examine, in these realistic dramas, which elements are metonymic in their representative qualities and which are metaphoric. In some cases, one might be able to read both ways. The reader of "Mending Wall" is not likely to think the neighbor is really an old-stone savage armed; we can say he resembles one in that he carries a large stone and/or in that he represents an old and unexamined tradition. We can say that he represents, in the speaker's time and world, a very real type of person or mentality, or—viewed synecdochically—part of larger humanity, or need or characteristic in the nature of human beings, or animal territoriality. But there is something here we can take literally. The speaker says he sees him this way. We, then, are free to assume that the speaker is using simile, not really seeing him this way, but only comparing him with stone-age savages or using that image to represent real world characteristics. But we might also allow that the speaker is having a sudden involuntary vision that he shares with us. For an instant this is truly what he sees, and thus the realistic quality of the drama is maintained. We cannot feel the same confidence in Frost that Levin feels in Wordsworth, that the poet is experiencing such a world; rather he gives the reader his more detached, ironic portrayal of such a speaker, his visions or similes, and such a neighbor for us to construct in any way we can.

And this brings us to another way we might interpret Frost's synecdochism: The stories we value, let us remember, are those that "have intimations of something more [special] than itself.

It almost always comes under the head of synecdoche, a part, a hem of the garment: touch the hem of the garment for the whole garment. And that's what it's about all the time" (V 42). The part for the whole, the synecdochic act he refers to here, is the act of *reading*. The way we take the poem, the poem as synecdoche in a larger meaning, the act of reading that poem as synecdoche in the larger act of reading poems, and beyond that, in finding meanings or, better yet, meaning—this too is synecdochic. It is the view in which he expects the right reader to join him. "Success in taking figures of speech is as intoxicating as making figures of speech," he has said (SP 96).[34] The implication once more is that the reader must act poetically in his reading, that right reading is a poetic act, a synecdochic one.[35]

We remember, though, the lesson of "Maple," the warning that to go symbol hunting may lead us away from meaning or force us into too narrow a view. We remember, too, that Frost loved the facts for their own sake as well as for the sake of the "larger thing." In some of his greatest poems, we are not only left a great deal to ourselves in deciding what the poem "means," if decide that we must; we are also left to decide whether, in fact, we are in the presence of metaphor at all, whether we are not simply in the presence of "fact," a drama, or some collection of material reality we are simply to "see" as passive spectators, stories we are simply to "hear" as willing listeners.

How, in "Birches," do we divide the experience of the poem from the meaning of the poem? Where exactly does occasion become "something more"? The greatness of this poem lies precisely in blurring these distinctions, while at the same time remaining concrete, specific, and in the realm of immediate feeling and experience. The dividing lines between identification with the experience and figure enlarging it, between contemplative detachment and emotional nearness, are simply not there. (Long before "So was I once a swinger of birches," we have felt the closeness of the speaker to the situation and to the boy.) Yet while the lines dividing them are not there, the art uniting them is. The poem is, from beginning to end, concrete and accessible; yet the mood of the poem, the tone, the language, lead us to the conviction that there is more here, much more, than a discussion of birches and the technique of swinging them. But *what* we do not quite know, for the referents are left open—to use Frost's expression, the poem "opens doors";[36] and we feel that we understand where those doors might lead because we are led in our own contemplations to the same feelings. At the same time, we are never forced by the poem to see any one of them as the "meaning," nor are we forced to choose between them.

In the same spirit of openness, Truth is presented as a digression breaking in. The direct progression of thought would be: "I like to think some boy's been swinging them. . . . I should prefer to have some boy bend them / As he went in and out to fetch the cows." But that is what he would like to imagine; it is not what he actually sees—birches permanently bent. It is not the truth. Truth yields ice storms; imagination yields boys. Then the word "matter-of-fact" pulls us up short and sends us back to what he is calling "matter-of-fact."

> Often you must have seen them
> Loaded with ice a sunny winter morning
> After a rain. They click upon themselves
> As the breeze rises, and turn many-colored
> As the stir cracks and crazes their enamel.
> Soon the sun's warmth makes them shed crystal shells
> Shattering and avalanching on the snow-crust—
> Such heaps of broken glass to sweep away
> You'd think the inner dome of heaven had fallen. (CP 152)

Actually, truth as the speaker tells it is not matter-of-fact at all; it is highly associative and figurative.[37] The nonverbal fact of the ice storms and the bending they cause is unadorned. It is in the telling it, then, in the thinking about the fact, that Truth is conveyed by means of imagery and imagination. The inner dome of heaven falling, girls on hands and knees drying their hair, this is what we are told, and we may ask what, then, is truth?

It may be that which can only be expressed by means of metaphor—"parables . . . and indirections"—of associations that lead us from a blinding singleness of vision to a multicolored, multifaceted perception of reality, possibly less precise but richer with the associations that inform it and the imagination that raises it above mere fact. That bending under the weight of storms, never to be straight again, combined with the echo of Shelley's "dome of many colored glass," life, which "stains the white radiance of eternity, / Until Death tramples it to fragments," belongs somehow with the image of those girls on hands and knees drying their hair. Together these images and associations tell the truth as Truth cannot tell itself. Even if one has never heard of "Adonais," there is that concrete, magnificent view (and apt sound) of the birches clicking and crazing as they turn many-colored in the sun before shedding heaps of broken glass. This scene would remain only beautiful, were it not that

> They are dragged to the withered bracken by the load
> And they seem not to break, though once they are bowed
> So low for long, they never right themselves. (152)

Frost's joke about matter-of-factness, like all his jokes, turns on serious self-defense;[38] it only thinly masks the realization that there is nothing matter-of-fact about this truth.

The relationship between fact and imagination as Frost posits it here illustrates once more that dilemma we feel between the pull of facts and of nature for their own sakes, and the contrary pull toward the imaginary, the purely emotional or philosophical. In "Birches" the subject is literally the swing between earth and that which is higher—*toward* heaven. In saying toward heaven, however, the poem suggests that the swing is also between the reality of earth and the call of the spirit, and again we see Frost's typical "between-ness," the pull of contraries that keeps him in balance. The dominant metaphor of the poem is, in fact, not birches [39] but swinging birches. The triumph of that boy's swinging is in his learning how to keep his poise:

> . . . climbing carefully
> With the same pains you use to fill a cup
> Up to the brim, and even above the brim.
> Then he flung outward, feet first, with a swish,
> Kicking his way down through the air to the ground.
>   (CP 153)

Climbing high, kicking outward, the need to escape, those girls, those heaps of broken glass, and later the desire "to get away from earth a while," all suggest that in life which requires poise, the art of keeping one's balance. The "many-colored glass" stanza in "Adonais" resolves itself in an exhortation to "Die." It follows the question "Why fear death?" This and Frost's "I'd like to get away from earth awhile" suggest the temptation toward death which we find elsewhere in Frost, balanced, however, by the fear of death, which looms even larger in Frost's thought. This section, in its weariness, its depression with "life [that] is too much like a pathless wood," has been compared with the opening canto of *The Inferno*,[40] with its sunless woods, its mid-life depression, its straying from the path. Dante's pathless wood also leads to an upward climb. His speaker, too, will reaffirm life, but he begins in fear, and he will need to pass through hell.

> It's when I'm weary of considerations,
> And life is too much like a pathless wood
> Where your face burns and tickles with the cobwebs
> Broken across it, and one eye is weeping
> From a twig's having lashed across it open.
> I'd like to get away from earth awhile
> And then come back to it and begin over.
> May no fate willfully misunderstand me
> And half grant what I wish and snatch me away
> Not to return. Earth's the right place for love:
> I don't know where it's likely to go better. (CP 153)

Certainly we can wonder for a moment what love has to do with what he has been saying. Love of the earth and the facts, love of the earth and its birches for one thing. Love as it relates to those bending girls for another. Love—indeed all emotion— as it relates to the poem's concern with climbing, experiencing, swinging, and kicking, yet learning control, learning poise and balance, exercising its refusal to remain earthbound, balanced by its return always to earth.

The passionate little girl in "Wild Grapes" is pulled up by a birch—a birch that controls her. Unlike the boy of "Birches," she could not control the birch. She grasped the top, which had been proffered to her; she did not climb from the bottom, testing her launch out as she went. Having been caught up by the birch, she could only hold on until she dropped, or she could let go and jump. She was not yet big enough, nor skilled enough, to handle birches; she did not go about it right, and so it "had" her. In fact she never did learn how to let go with the heart. "Birches," by contrast, swings more evenly between abandon and control, whether the subject is death, love, or birches. We see that one can lose one's life—or at least one's balance—by lack of restraint in the need to escape, or the need to imagine, or the need to love. Lack of restraint in emotion and imagination can destroy art as well.[41]

A poem such as this one can have the authentic ring of felt experience at the same time that the experience is metaphor, as it becomes a poem about love, art, life, and death. In this poem the questions that have previously been raised as artistic questions cease to be questions; they simply function together as elements of art without showing their limits, their outlines, or their mechanism. The questions that a poem like "Maple" raises rather crudely are here resolved with no questions asked.[42] How much may be legitimately "read in" to such a poem? How much should we read in? Everything, or nothing. The poem remains Frost's even as it becomes the reader's.

"Mowing" takes still farther the issue of difficulty in distinguishing where fact leaves off and metaphor begins. As if a poem like "Birches" shows too much, is too laden with meaning, too much metaphor (even though we cannot find the seams connecting it to fact), Frost seems at times to want to retreat from metaphor, to deny it altogether with a sort of antimetaphor poem that makes no claim to mean anything other than the experience it presents—mowing and leaving the mown grass to "make" itself into hay. In "Mowing" fact and poetic act are so inextricably fused that we do not draw lines of analogy. The fact *is*, seemingly with no intervening imagination or act of mind. The transformation of grass to hay *is* the poem, and the whispering of the scythe is what we hear.

> There was never a sound beside the wood but one,
> And that was my long scythe whispering to the ground.
> What was it it whispered? I knew not well myself;
> Perhaps it was something about the heat of the sun,
> Something, perhaps, about the lack of sound—
> And that was why it whispered and did not speak.
> It was no dream of the gift of idle hours,
> Or easy gold at the hand of fay or elf:
> Anything more than the truth would have seemed too weak
> To the earnest love that laid the swale in rows,
> Not without feeble-pointed spikes of flowers
> (Pale orchises), and scared a bright green snake.
> The fact is the sweetest dream that labor knows.
> My long scythe whispered and left the hay to make. (CP 25)

Of this poem, Frost wrote to Thomas B. Mosher: "In 'Mowing,' for instance, I come so near what I long to get that I almost despair of coming nearer" (SL 83). It seems to me that what he "longs to get" and feels he did get in this poem is the fusion between fact and poetic act by means of sound. It seems no coincidence that at this point in his career he writes and speaks so much on the subject of the "sound of sense."[43] The relationship between mower, scythe, ground, and grass becomes hay in the making and poem in the making at the same time. This is truth and art at once in its barest, most factual skeleton. We are convinced the scythe whispered because we hear it whisper. Like the mower, we cannot be sure what it whispered, but we are convinced *that* it whispered.

Since Frost was so concerned at this time with "sound posturing," and since he felt this poem came closest to what he "longed to get," it seems worthwhile to examine how sound functions in this poem. Simplicity of expression, unadorned fact, these are not the only understatements of the poem; this is whispering against a backdrop of silence, and therefore the reticence in choice of words and total lack of figure is paralleled by reticence in using the voice. Perhaps the "lack of sound . . . was why it whispered and did not speak." Voicing loudly would have been too great a contrast with the silence, too obtrusive. Besides, voicing is too articulate; it is too definitely speech, which is too undeniably expressive of a particular idea, and scythes are not capable of speech or idea. They are capable of the sound of whispering, and therefore this sound of the scythe remains credible. In this poem it is also audible. Consonant with refusal to voice out loud is the scarcity of explosive (obstruant) voiced consonants. The only one that really stands out is the /g/ in "gift" and "gold," and that is precisely what he is denying. The whispering of the poem is executed by means of all the "s" sounds (25 /s /—10 /z /) and all the "w's" (21). In the first three lines alone, there are 9 /w/ or /hw/ sounds and 8 /s/ or /z/ sounds, there are 17 "w" "s"—or whispering—sounds, which continue for the length of the poem. In addition to duplicating the sound of the scythe, the poem duplicates the rhythm of the scythe by means of repetition of words, phrases, and rhymes: "whisper" appears four times; line 2 is almost repeated in line 6 and again in line 14:

(2) and that was my long scythe whispering
(6) and that was why it whispered
(14) my long scythe whispered

The rhyme of "my," "why," "my" and the assonance with "scythe" are all part of the repetition that parallels the rhythmic swing of the scythe. Nowhere does Frost use the word "sigh" along with his whispers, but the sound /sai/ appears three times and suggests not only repetition (the /ai/ sound appears nine times) but still another nonverbal, emotive expression that we "hear" between scythe and grass.

There seems something loving and private between this scythe and this field—and it excludes the mower. He swings the scythe that initiates the sound and ultimately causes the hay "to make." Without his doing the mowing there will be no whispering and no hay, but having done this much to cause hay, he is still limited with regard to final result. That he asks, "What was it it whispered? I knew not well myself," shows that he feels himself removed from scythe and grass even while he mows. He hears the whispering, but he does not quite hear the message; he can only conjecture, and as he does, he combines his own idea and meanings with the sounds he hears. That he hears is more important than what he hears (an interesting comment on the whole question of "messages" from nature; confidence that nature can be read is not the same as confidence in reading it correctly). We are told of "the earnest love that laid the swale in rows." It is a love that deserves unadorned truth, it is a love that labors, and it is a love that scares a bright green snake. The destructive aspects of mowing are acknowledged in this line, as they are in the previous one. In fact, the dactylic opening of it jars the serenity of the poem, but the emphasis in this poem, unlike the "Mower" poems, unlike "The Exposed Nest," and "The Tuft of Flowers," is on the creative aspect of the destruction. There can be no hay without cut grass. The "mowing" proceeds by means of the intimate relationship between scythe and field on to the making of hay. If the figure (for poetry) is the same as for love, then the figure for love is the same as for poetry,[44] and both are inevitably tied to the labor and to the rending that accompany creation, be it mowing, loving, or writing. The "it"—that which the scythe whispered—"was no dream of the gift of idle hours," no mooning or daydreaming or resorting to romantic fancy; it was the product of labor and of reality.

One of the realities in this poem is that very limitation which the mower feels. At the end of the poem, the scythe "left the hay to make." At the beginning, the mower knew not well himself what the scythe was whispering. Here surely is another "figure" for a poem riding on its own melting (SP 20), a creation not being made but "making." There is evidently only so much the mower can do; the rest is out of his control. The created work assumes at some point a life of its own; as in "The Woodpile," the work at some point participates in its own creation. "The greatest pleasure in writing poetry," said Frost, "is in having been carried off. It is as if you stood astride of the subject that lay on the ground, and they cut the cord, and the subject gets up under you and you ride it. You adjust yourself to the motion of the thing itself. That is the poem" (P&P 375).

Perhaps because the poet is "maker," and because love and labor and truth are associated with each other and with art, the making of a poem has entered into the discussion along with the making of hay. Both seem to belong together in the poem, and yet nowhere is an analogy drawn between them. We could draw them in our reading; yet we do not want to "weaken" the poem with "anything more than the truth." "What you do to the facts falsifies them. What facts do to you despite your resistance, transforms them to poetry" (I 21), Frost said, and one feels that in this poem the facts of mowing have become transformed into the facts of art as well. Yet this poem that asserts "The fact is the sweetest dream that labor knows" rests on fact.[45] Even as Frost resists the "easy gold" of fantasy (underscoring his rejection of romanticism by means of allowing an archaic "literary" word like "fey" to obtrude itself), he resists as well the use of any figures of speech. Every word in this poem narrates, shows, points to what is actually there, what actually occurs.

Except one—the implied comparison in saying the scythe

whispered. This could be a personification of the scythe, for only people whisper; it could be an implied simile: the scythe made a sound like whispering. But no, we are told in no uncertain terms, "My long scythe whispered." We are told it with three consecutive stresses that do not simply state, but assert, and imply, "You had better believe it!" And we do believe it, precisely because, as we have seen, the poet has managed to *make* it whisper to our ears as well.

There are three strong assertions in the poem. The first is line 9, significantly the conventional turning point of the sonnet: "Anything more than the truth would have seemed too weak." This line too is made to stand out by means of its reversed stress pattern, beginning with a stressed syllable. What follows is no longer conjecture about what the scythe was whispering but the mower's statements about truth, fact, and labor. (While the contrast in tone is so pronounced between octet and sestet, however, the rhyme scheme of the sestet is not different from that of the octet but rather interwoven with it, not only adding to the recurring rhythmic pattern we have already noted but also connecting assertion to conjecture, fact to imagination.)

The second assertion is: "The fact is the sweetest dream that labor knows."[46] It is clearly the mower's assertion and not the scythe's message, as we can see from the punctuation. It seems almost intrusive, coming as it does between scaring the snake and leaving the hay—it interrupts the narrative, but it is the continuation of the first assertion on the right to truth unadorned and unvarnished. As such it is an important statement, and it throws the weight of its authority onto the last line and *its* assertion (the third): "My long scythe whispered," as if to tell us: you may have been thinking that it was figurative whispering, but now that I have told you how factual this all is, you will believe it really whispered.

This poem, which contains no metaphors, no illusions, which rests only on fact, ends, after all, by turning ironically back on itself. The only fact we have a right to question is the fact *that* it *whispered,* and if we do question that, we find that what is like fact to the speaker is in fact part of the illusion and thereby lays open all seeming fact to the fertilizing power of imagination. If, however, we do not question the fact, we remain with the mower in his belief that *this* scythe whispered; we remain in the power of the scythe-whispering sound of the poem.

Perhaps Frost was right. Perhaps this poem goes about as far as one can go in creating correspondences without recourse to metaphor or any of the tools of analogy, in creating facts by means of sound. It is especially interesting in that it succeeds in blurring the distinctions between metaphor and thing itself. Where emotions or conflicts are involved, metaphor is a necessary bridge between explicable and inexplicable. What cannot be reconciled in fact seems reconciled by means of metaphor. This poem, however, is free of emotion and conflict; its subject is mowing, or poetry, or simply "making." It is a poem about making hay. It whispers, just as the poem says it does. Whatever else that poem is about is in identities, not analogies; it is in the mind of the reader, and if there is any illusion here, then facts themselves are suspect.

Of course facts should be suspect. So should denial of illusion and so should a poet's denial of metaphor. Even though "Mowing" approaches perfection in its fusing of fact and poetic act, the fusion cannot fully succeed. That it is pure fact is, of course, an illusion. The hay might "make," but the poem has been made—its existence attests to its making. The poem that denies metaphor is one. Frost plays humorously with this question in "The Rose Family," wherein he distinguishes between what one *calls* a rose and what *is* a rose. It is also a supreme compliment to the lady, who is also the genuine article. It is the fashion now to call pears and apples and plums roses, but of course the rose—and the lady—were always roses (CP 305).[47] Still the lady is not literally a rose either. The speaker says she is, for she shares "roseness" with the roses, and she is genuine, as they are; yet no matter how closely or how long she has been identified with a rose, no matter how strong the association, or the blurring within the poem between rose as metaphor and rose as lady, we cannot quite deny that the rose is a rose *and* a metaphor.[48]

The greatest illusion, of course, is that here there are no illusions, no fancy, no metaphor. The poem makes itself, a rose is a rose. The poem with no metaphors, the antimetaphor poem, is, in fact, a metaphor; and so the poem that denies metaphor but does so unsuccessfully illustrates the inescapability of metaphor. The poem that most tries to deny authorial craftsmanship (it was just left "to make") is one Frost most prided himself on having crafted, that most approached his notion of the sound of sense about which he was theorizing at that time. Look Ma no metaphors, no artifice, no making, no effort, the poems *say;* but as poems about poetry and making, they also say: see the sweat it takes to seem effortless, see how skillfully I have covered my traces of poetic making, even of poetic convention. In this duality we see again the conflict between the desire to make meaning, to reach a reader, the "read me" stance and the "don't read me" stance. Does a poem like "Mowing" close or open wider the space between reader and text? And further, we might ask, which way does Frost want it? There is the conflict once more, and never resolved, the hiding *of* the metaphors surely related to hiding *behind* them.

> I would be willing to throw away everything else but that:
> enthusiasm tamed by metaphor. . . . I do not think anybody
> ever knows the discreet use of metaphor, his own and other
> people's . . . unless he has been properly educated in poetry.
>   Poetry begins in trivial metaphors . . . and goes on to the
> profoundest thinking that we have. Poetry provides the one
> permissible way of saying one thing and meaning another.
> People say, "Why don't you say what you mean?" We never
> do that, do we, being all of us too much poets. We like to

talk in parables and in hints and in indirections—whether
from diffidence or some other instinct. (SP 36–37)

Of course one can hear echoes of Aristotle here: in the *Poetics* he had spoken of metaphor as an alien name applied by
transfer, by giving one thing a name that belongs to something else.[49] Although Frost has spoken of it as saying one thing
in terms of another, I find it significant—and characteristic—
that he should call it a "way of saying one thing and meaning another." The crucial difference, of course, is Frost's phrase
"meaning *another.*" For Aristotle, and other theorists of metaphor, the issue is how meaning is conveyed, transferred, in order
to mean more richly, more clearly, or in a way the language has
not yet provided (catachresis).[50] Frost seems to welcome metaphor as a "permissible" way to deceive, to veil meaning, or at
the very least to further the game of hide and seek he speaks
of in "Revelation" or the test for the right reader that he poses
in "Directive." How very Frostian: metaphor not only as lens,
filter, vehicle of transported meaning, but as possibly deceptive
veil that does not obscure but only veils, for behind the veil,
through the veil, one may have the privileged glimpse of what
lies behind it—maybe.

The notion of veiling—and veils have always combined mod-
esty with seductiveness—fits in well with the diffidence Frost
associates with hiding in one's metaphors or sense of humor, for
that matter, with the need to invite and withdraw, the crying
out of one's need and the self-deprecation for having done so,
the need to reveal and the need to conceal. All these opposites
create between their poles the gaps that attract, that draw the
reader only the nearer to the complexities of Robert Frost.

According to Hyde Cox, Frost had been fascinated by Jesus'
having said to his disciples: "Unto you it is given to know the
mystery of the kingdom of God: but unto them that are without,
all these things are done in parables: That seeing they may see,
and not perceive; and hearing they may hear, and not under-

stand; lest at any time they should be converted, and their sins should be forgiven them" (*Mark* 4:11–12). Frost "pointed out [to Cox] that it is the same as for poetry; only those who approach it in the right way can understand it." He alludes to these verses from Mark in "Directive" and, after its publication, said to Cox: "Not everyone can get saved as Christ says in St. Mark. He almost says, 'you can't be saved unless you understand poetry— or you can't be saved unless you have some poetry in you,'"[51] and that probably means being able to "come close to poetry" (SP 43), not only as a writer, but as a reader.

We remember Frost's saying: "That comes to this question of who has a right to do what with my poetry—the right kind of people can take it their way" (V 77). But we can never be quite sure whether we are among the "right kind of people." Frost wrote to Sidney Cox: "I have written to keep the over curious out of the secret places of my mind both in my verse and in my letters to such as you" (SL 385). A warning to interpret at one's peril, yet curiously an invitation at the same time to speculate, a frank admission that what he writes hides as well as reveals. Keep out! he says in that statement, but at the same time he says: it's very interesting in here. He concludes in "Revelation" that those "who hide too well away/Must speak and tell us where they are" (CP 27), but this is posited against the pity of needing to speak the literal, against the "agitated heart" that wants to be found behind those light words. "I'm never so serious as when I am [joking]," Frost wrote. (SL 139). Thus the reader and her imagination is also the butt of Frost's teasing and flouting. He says "Come In" but tread lightly. As he jokes, he says take me seriously; then when we *do* take him seriously, we are not quite sure whether we have been invited or we haven't been.

Metaphors open doors and close them, reveal and conceal. And the reader, like any curious individual, like the one who leans closer into the gossip circle—or the fairy tale hero who cannot resist finding the lock that fits the key, like Bluebeard's wife, who cannot resist opening the secret door—we take the bait, which, of course, is what the poet wants us to do. If he does not, or if we do not, that poet is left talking only to himself, hearing only an echo. If only *he* is allowed to look at his image, his own reflection is all he will see. It is this alternative, and its inadequacy to Frost, that we will explore in the next chapter.

3

"Me, Myself . . . Godlike"

Mirrors and echoes mock us with ourselves, mock not only our own images, but our very desire to see and hear ourselves, as if there were something in that reflection, those echoes, that we are not already in possession of. Literature is filled with echoes that mock,[1] but that mockery is sometimes haunted by the tragic Echo, the disembodied voice of the wasted nymph who could only return the words of others and whose love was never returned. The youth on whom her love was wasted—a figure of ridicule, or madness, not only because he was obsessed with himself, but because that self was only an illusion, a bodiless form—could also be considered tragic, were he not so mindlessly driven beyond his capacity to exercise choice or control of his situation. Narcissus was caught in a terrible bind that has such a powerful hold on our imaginations, as it did on the imaginations of Freud, Lacan, Ovid, and subsequent poets, because it reminds us of the impossible paradox of human fulfillment and unfulfillment. Narcissus is closed into a deadly circle of passion, which illuminates our ambivalence toward the conflicting needs of the self: the inadequacy we feel in our need of others and our fear of what that need costs, yet the even greater threat when there is no other save the self—the utter impossibility of self as Other. This is a conflict Frost felt and understood so profoundly: our inevitable yearning for a wholeness that is impossible to achieve either alone or with Others.

The need to remain inviolate can make one want to close the circle of self, an alternative that led Narcissus to death by starvation. To break out of that circle into dialogue with Others is to find other centers, which means that there can be no perfect circle, perfect closure, or reconciliation. Frost's poetry is filled with a profound recognition of the insolubility of this bind, the impossibility of resolving the conflict between the need to avoid the threat of encroachment, hurt, or claims on us by others, yet the even deadlier, more impossible alternative, where echoes mock our cries only to make us feel the more profoundly our need for counter-love, original response.

When Narcissus saw his image in the pool, a pool "to which no shepherds came, no goats, no cattle, / Whose glass no bird, no beast, no falling leaf / Had ever troubled,"[2] he fell in love with an "unbodied hope . . . only shadow . . . only reflection, lacking any substance." "What love . . . has ever been more cruel?" (421–22; 445) he cries, for this love always teases him with illusory counter-desire, the eyes, the outreaching arms reciprocating the look and action of Narcissus but escaping him always: "No barrier parts us, but a thin film of water . . . almost nothing keeps us apart" (453–54, 457–58). But of course to reach down toward the beloved is to blur his image, as it blurs when Narcissus weeps. To attempt to reach that self would be to drown—but not *in* the self, for the illusory, watery image would be destroyed before Narcissus could fully enter the water. Thus Narcissus could not even find refuge in drowning himself, for to have done so would have been to destroy his beloved, the image on the water. Therefore he was not even capable of willful, active self-destruction, only paralyzed, passive destruction by starvation and deprivation. Even when he recognized that the beloved was his own image, even when he saw his image wasting away, he was helpless, paralyzed into remaining immobile. Like the beautiful flower he was to become, he could only remain rooted to the spot, reflected in the pool.

That Echo returns his cries as if the moving lips in the pool were uttering them only fuels his passion the more, not for the nymph, of course, but for the self in the pool. Ironically, as auditory reflection, giving Narcissus back his own cries of "Alas," returning to him the sound of his beating on his breast, she might seem the perfect match for him, but actually she is the perfect complement for that other disembodied reflector, the visual image. It is this Narcissus loves—the illusion of self. Thus Echo ironically only reinforces the closedness of the self-circle. We will never know whether "original response" from the nymph might have saved Narcissus from himself.

But we will remember that it was because Narcissus was un-willing to engage in relationships with others that he was so cursed. A rejected youth had wished that "Narcissus / Love one day, so, himself, and not win over / The creature whom he loves." Tiresias had prophesied that Narcissus would only grow to old age "if he never knows himself" (405–7, 449), both statements implying that love of self, unredeemed by others, is a love that will destroy because it is the love of an unreconcilable, rejecting object. Inherent in the curse is the assumption of a divided self, with its object hating, rejecting, destructive. To know oneself, to love oneself as the youth meant it, is to suffer rejection and unrequited love. Our image is only beautiful if we do not get too close, or touch it, or disturb it. It may be the image of our-selves we prefer and wish we could preserve intact forever and for everyone, but to preserve that image means not to move, not to shift our gaze, not to attempt to come closer or reach it; and it results in starvation or, at best, transformation into vegetation, beautiful though that may be.

Paradoxically, we can only know ourselves actively, can only move or act or interact if we can face a face that will not nec-essarily cease to exist when we turn our backs; that, in its very otherness, will assure us that we—as other to *it*—have a separate, discrete existence. It is not only that we are lonely without others, it is that without a "not me" we cannot feel ourselves to be a "me."[3] The Other dramatizes, by its otherness, our own uniqueness.

True, mirrors can help us form a sense of who we are, what we look like, how we might appear to others; Lacan's mirror stage is a case in point. But, as Lacanians point out, though the mirror-stage experience of the infant's body image signals the beginning of a sense of identity and wholeness, it has still been found *outside* the body; our early experience of ourselves is dependent on relationship to others,[4] our maturation and sense of "wholeness," dependent on the continuing recognition and reflection of others (49).

Only by being reflected in and by another, of course, can there be difference in the returning image, difference that reinforces differentiation, hence, paradoxically, a truer sense of self. But such reflexivity is never possible within a closed, perfect circle having the self as its single center; it is at best elliptical—both geometrically and verbally—necessarily imperfect and asymmetrical, always dialogic,[5] and always in need of interpretation. Only in a dialogic mode can there be anything new or surprising or original. Any mode of encounter that fails to engage with some other in some kind of dialogue is like being stuck only in front of a mirror reflection of self—static and, if not deadly in its very stasis and inactivity, incapable of being fully alive, incapable of originality.

The one who wishes to remain inviolate is between the Scylla of Narcissus's immobile dissolution and the Charybdis of dynamism, with its attendant risk of change, entanglement, engagement, and asymmetry. Shoshana Felman writes of the subject becoming reformulated in the act of formulating (63), in other words, capable of change and activity, of being surprised, capable of something different and original, of activity, rather than stasis. Whether the object is a loved one, a tree, or a poem, this process goes on if we are to face the object in active, alive engagement. Such a relationship to what is viewed presumes that we are looking not just at a mirror in order to see ourselves but at some Other, with the possibility that it may have a reconstituting effect on ourselves; in addition it presumes that when we look at this Other, we are not seeking a mirror image of ourselves in it. And this is a risk. It reminds us of what Iser has said of reading: we may become shattered, but also reconstituted— for better or for worse—in the act of active reading, which we may take as reading the literal book, or the book of a loved one, or the "book" of nature. To "read" in this manner, whatever the "text," is to enter into a reciprocal relationship, which might threaten to blur subject/object distinctions owing to that very reciprocity and dynamism. Yet Iser would insist that the text on the page is *there,* that it is an Other to be engaged with, not a mere reflection of the reader, and I would agree. Certainly Frost would insist on such a difference.[6] The tree at his window, however it is related to the speaker, is still another head, still separated by the glass from the speaker, who, although he never wants the curtain drawn, needs to maintain the separation: he wants to see the tree, see reflections of himself in it, perhaps see it as metaphorically a part of himself but, in actuality, always apart. It belongs outside. (Encounters with nature—without and within—will be more fully developed in chapter 5.)

We remain, though, with the paradox that what threatens the separateness of self—the reciprocity and dynamism of engagement—is also what allows the self to be individuated. This brings us anew to the heart of Frost's conflict as lover, friend, or writer: the necessity of braving alien entanglements, of engaging with one's materials, conflicting with the fear of being subsumed, altered, swallowed up—the fear of what James spoke of as the uncertain outline of the self (313). Lacanians speak of the neonate's need to "build bridges between its 'helplessness' or boundarylessness and the outside world."[7] Perhaps what we most fear is returning to that state; perhaps that is the force for boundaries; and perhaps that is why we understand Frost so well as he maintains a constant dialectic, not only with the Other of feeling and perception, but between the notions of bounding and reciprocity, walls erected and walls eroded. It is the subject, of course, of "Mending Wall," where the "dialogue" is about walls, and erecting a wall is the occasion for dialogue.

Another human voice, unless it is a mere echo of ourselves, can only respond in dialogue. It is no coincidence that Echo is only found away from the noise and bustle of social life, as was Narcissus's solitary pool, so perfect a reflector because it was remote from other forms of life, untouched even by wind or leaf. Echoes live in caves and woods. One finds them in solitude, and then they mock that solitude as soon as the lone man raises a voice, tempt him to illusory satisfaction as soon as he stoops to take a drink. More terrifying to the poet is the mockery of language itself, words that do not communicate, sounds that cause other sounds but are not generative, merely repetitive. On one hand, echoes do not stop, and thus can potentially keep the words going ad infinitum, like reflections in a hall of mirrors; on the other, they never achieve closure or resolution—or answers. In this way, Echo underscores the impossibility of any genuine resolution, or originality, while keeping open the hope and the attempt. And she dramatizes the limits of solitude.[8]

Frost not only knew these conflicting needs and fears intimately, he also knew and loved classical literature. Echoes of Narcissus and Echo must have resonated at times in his own personal conflicts (they were surely felt on the part of people who came close to him, ample evidence of which is in Thompson's notes); they certainly resonate in some of the poetry, evoked not only by character or theme but also by reflexive imagery— visual or auditory. "For Once Then Something" and "The Most of It" are the most obvious examples, but there are others in which reflexiveness is more subtle.

Unlike the man alone in "The Most of It," solitary and demanding out of his need, is the speaker in "For Once Then

Something." A sort of Narcissus, he is ironically aware of the way his "always wrong" position is combined with his need to bend down and look all the same. He is also very conscious that his kneeling at well-curbs calls forth the mockery of others, but in that awareness of others and in needing to respond to them, he is showing himself to be social as well as self-seeking; in his seeking of truth, and in finding "something" that is not only himself back, as well as in seeking it, he also shows himself to be different from his Ovidian ancestor. John Hollander speaks of literature in which echoes serve as incentives to the hero to continue in his quest (45), and like those auditory reflections we call echoes, this reflection serves to motivate the speaker to keep looking for truth, or at least to reflect on what he sees. The poem is at once playful in the ironic self-deprecation of its speaker's ego and profound in its mature realization that we only ever see "through" the self—that self, if not the prime focus and motivator of our seeking and seeing, is at the very least a lens through which we see whatever else we are focusing on. The speaker attempts confrontation both with the self and with the unanswered questions; and when we arrive at the less-than-satisfied ending of the poem, we can assume, as we remember the "always" plus the present tense in the first two lines, that the quest for truth goes on.

We must wonder, though, if being "wrong to the light" will not predictively prevent "something more of the depths" from coming through, whether a position that can only yield the viewer's own mirror image, "a shining surface picture," will not necessarily block the possibility of seeing something deeper.

> Others taunt me with having knelt at well-curbs
> Always wrong to the light, so never seeing
> Deeper down in the well than where the water
> Gives me back in a shining surface picture
> Me myself in the summer heaven godlike
> Looking out of a wreath of fern and cloud puffs.

Once, when trying with chin against a well-curb,
I discerned, as I thought, beyond the picture,
Through the picture, a something white, uncertain,
Something more of the depths—and then I lost it.
Water came to rebuke the too clear water.
One drop fell from a fern, and lo, a ripple
Shook whatever it was lay there at bottom,
Blurred it, blotted it out. What was that whiteness?
Truth? A pebble of quartz? For once, then, something.
   (CP 276)

The taunt of being "wrong to the light" has been variously interpreted (YT 561–62). As a sort of Narcissus, the speaker feels
himself taunted for wanting repeatedly to see his own reflection,
being "wrong to the light" for truth, but right for his conceit
and self-seeking. This may explain the tone of self-justification,
or at least the speaker's need for it, but, more important, it sets
up the relationship between self and reflection, between mirrors
and echoes (aptly, for echoes are also found in wells).

The poem is filled with first person singular pronouns and
also with words echoing one another—six substantive words
are repeated at least once (curb, lines 1 and 7; water, 3 and 11;
picture, 4 and 8; well, 1, 3, and 7; once, 7 and 15; something,
9, 10, and 15). The poem does not rhyme, but there are three
pairs of identities (curb, water, picture), all of which reinforce
the mirroring. One wonders whether the speaker is replying to
the charge of kneeling wrong to the light, or trying too hard to
see deeper into the well, or persisting in this activity when he
always sees only his own reflection, or initiating it, really, for
the purpose of seeing himself once again. It is not that he puts
the image of God in heaven but that, by peering into the well
"wrong to the light," the speaker appears "in the summer heaven
god*like,* / Looking out of a wreath of fern and cloud puffs." The
absence of depth is implied in the two-dimensional quality of
the reflection. Heaven, cloud, fern, and "me myself" are reflected

as if they are all together, with no distinction between the proximity of one, the height of the other. Just as the mirror image is inadequate to distinguish height, then, it is inadequate to yield up depth. Reflection as mirror is shallow, two-dimensional, and unsatisfying.

The well as metaphor combines the properties of reflection and depth with those of water, on which we depend for life. It is a source, like those other sources in Frost, and as such it may contain truth in its depths. Frost, in a lighter, ironical vein, may have been thinking of the statement attributed to Democritus: "Of truth we know nothing, for truth lies at the bottom of a well" (YT 562), but we may ask what could have been behind Democritus's choosing that metaphor: he could have recognized that to seek truth at the bottom of a well is to encounter not only a source, or a necessity for life, but one's own reflection in the process, to be able to see it only through one's own reflection, through the self, that being a precondition to our seeing, accepting the vision of any truth. In any case, to try to reflect imaginatively (the speaker says: "I discerned, as I thought") while one reflects reality, to try to see deeply into the source of things, is to take this sarcastic taunt seriously, to try indeed to find something—perhaps truth—at the bottom of a well.[9]

He himself does not know what he is seeking, only that he wants to see more deeply—down below the surface of the well—more deeply than the reflection of what is above the water, more deeply than his own image. He never is certain of what he has seen—"a something white, uncertain . . . what was that whiteness? Truth? A pebble of quartz?" The important insight was that he saw *something,* that there was something "at bottom" (note: not at *the* bottom), and that, whatever it was, he lost it. It is as though he saw what he was not supposed to have seen. Nature cannot let itself give away the secrets that exist at bottom, and therefore "water came to rebuke the too clear water" and the ripple blurred the vision.

It was his own imagination, his own thinking, that made

truth of a flash of whiteness, possibly a pebble. Even the illusion that one has seen something rewards, if only partially, the seeking, and motivates further seeking. As in "The Most of It," it was not much, but something is better than nothing. The poem was originally entitled "Well," then "Wrong to the Light," and finally "For Once Then Something." "Well" can be ejaculated, or it can be said in a questioning tone, implying a tentative, unfinished expression. The change in the title throws emphasis on the finding of something: where the emphasis had been on the wrongness, it is now on "something," and something concrete, even a pebble, is necessary to serve as the basis for what we will build with our imagination. Very Frostian is the insistence that reality be combined with imagination if it is to yield truth that is more than just verifiable, palpable fact or irresponsible fancy. We can ask, in turn, how much imagination is affected by what we seek, what we want or need to see, what we bring to the confrontation with the "pebble."[10]

We must remember that he does not see the pebble instead of the reflection; he sees through it, beyond it. That vision which unites fact and imagination also unites mirror reflection and imaginative reflection. It also says that what is "at bottom" must be seen through self. That image, that "I myself," which recurs, is still fundamental to any other vision. It is at the very least a filtering lens that can affect the focus, range, color of what we see and, if the taunt of narcissism is correct, our motivation for looking as well. To see what lies "at bottom" in the universe, one needs perhaps to see what lies "at bottom" in the self, which, in turn, we only dimly discern as that self interacts with the not-self. But to remain at the level of surface reflection is to see *only* the self, and that is necessarily both shallow and predictable. Truth, or whatever that "something" represents, never bypasses the self, and we cannot seek outside the self but only through it; still, looking *through* is not the same as looking *at*; "through" implies that we can also seek beyond the self or deep within it.[11]

What is so moving and so powerful in "The Most of It" is that

the man on the beach is dissatisfied with having only the self;
he has brought a need so great it cries out, and the echoes that
seem to mock him [12] are thus mocking in the process his very
loneliness and his attempts to awaken response.

> He thought he kept the universe alone;
> For all the voice in answer he could wake
> Was but the mocking echo of his own
> From some tree-hidden cliff across the lake.
> Some morning from the boulder-broken beach
> He would cry out on life, that what it wants
> Is not its own love back in copy speech,
> But counter-love, original response.
> And nothing ever came of what he cried
> Unless it was the embodiment that crashed
> In the cliff's talus on the other side,
> And then in the far distant water splashed,
> But after a time allowed for it to swim,
> Instead of proving human when it neared
> And someone else additional to him,
> As a great buck it powerfully appeared,
> Pushing the crumpled water up ahead,
> And landed pouring like a waterfall,
> And stumbled through the rocks with horny tread,
> And forced the underbrush—and that was all. (CP 451)

This is a poem that eludes any definite interpretation or response. We feel the great loneliness, the need; yet when we
try to determine what response he gets—what happens in the
poem—we do not quite know. Maybe something, maybe nothing. We are told that "He *thought* he kept the universe alone,"
not that he *did* keep it alone. He thought so because ("for") he
heard no voice of "counter-love," of "original response." He has
not necessarily asked for something human, only for something
loving and responsive. By the end of the poem something, in
fact, appeared. And that is all.

If a phenomenon of which the narrator says "and that was all" turns out to be "the most of it," does that mean that man has been given precious little, or does it mean that this is "the most of it"[13] but not *all* of it—that some unidentified mystery remains, the *rest* of it? That there is something mysterious about the relationship between the man and the experience is borne out by the syntactical confusion in the poem, especially of reference, which creates a connection between the man and what he encounters as if one reflects the other. To what does the pronoun "it" refer? For the first "it" ("He would cry out on life, that what it wants / Is not its own love back in copy speech"), the antecedent is "life." Yet he is crying out on life, and we feel it is what the man wants and needs from life. There is some blurring, then, of the lines between his inner needs, *his* life, and the life "out there"—what he cries out on. What life "wants" can also be what life lacks, what he does not find there. But what of the possessive "its"? Here we are back to what it needs and does not need, not what it lacks. It needs original response, and thus we are returned to what this man's life needs and to his identification with "life."

The next time "it" is used as a personal pronoun—in fact, for the rest of the poem—the antecedent is "the embodiment," which is no help, because we may ask: the embodiment of *what*? Of the echo voice? Of life, of something mysterious and unnamed? Of "counter-love, original response"? Of nature? It is important in this connection that we are never told a *buck* appeared, but that "it" appeared *as* a great buck. The buck, then, is an embodiment of "it" or a symbol of something other than a buck.[14] And the experience has been "the most of it," whatever "it" may be.

The fact that it does not prove human could be disappointing if what the man needs is counter-love in human terms. If what he is looking for is something cosmic, some sign that *man* does not keep the universe alone, then this could have been an annunciation. Simply *that* "it appeared" would be the answer to his cry. Certainly this is supported by the mystery of reference, by the fact that the agent of "allowed" is deleted (allowed by whom or what), by the mystery of what the rest of it might be. But we feel no greater comfort, no greater oneness with life or universe for this man, even with this interpretation. It has not been enough. The *most* he knows is that he does not keep the universe alone. Whatever does so with him, God or nature, whatever the buck embodies, is not giving solace to that man. It is not stopping to communicate or to listen. It remains apart and silent. The only sounds are the pouring water, the forced-down underbrush, and, to add to the sense of insecurity, the "stumbling" of even this "embodiment."

Mirroring is implicit in the ambiguity created by the mingling of time levels used to express the man's voicing of his cries and needs. We wonder if the whole poem is not simply an echo of a man's cries and needs, cries and needs that come out of himself and back to himself. The implication of "some morning . . . he would cry out on life" is that he has not yet done this. This stands in direct contradiction to: "And nothing ever came of what he cried." He could have cried out but not yet cried out what he said he *would* cry out some morning, or maybe he never voiced outwardly that inner cry. This is reinforced by the echo effect of lines 2 to 4. He tries to awaken something into responding to him, but all that he wakes is his own echo. That this echo comes from the "tree-hidden cliff" and that the embodiment crashes "in the cliff's talus" later to pour like a waterfall is a visual effect of cliffs mirroring from one side of the water to the other. The sound of the words "mocking echo" is almost palindromatic. This and the confusion about whether "it" refers to life within himself or to life external to him has the effect of making this whole experience something that grows out of himself, reflects himself. There is undoubtedly a real cliff, a real body of water, and a real buck, but what these represent to the man depends entirely on himself, what has been "revealed" or refused, then, is simply a reflection of what the man needs. He remains, as he began, searching within himself and waking his own echoes with cries that may or may not have been voiced. The refusal to make of his crying out a specific act already completed in the past is surely deliberate on Frost's part, for originally he had written:

> At daybreak from the boulder broken beech [sic]
> He cried aloud on life . . .
>
> .   .   .   .
>
> And nothing happened from his having cried.

A comparison with the lines as they stand:

> Some morning from the boulder-broken beach
> He would cry out on life . . .
>
> .   .   .   .
>
> And nothing ever came of what he cried

shows that the changes have created the ambiguity we have seen regarding the man's actually crying out or not. "Ever" implies that whatever the nature of the cry, it has not been a one-time cry.[15]

Although more painful in this poem where the man recognizes his need for counter-love and original response, there is a sense in which unanswered, solitary reflection is wasting and diminishing this man, as it did Narcissus; he almost fades out of the scene. The poem begins with a man thinking and keeping. "He" is the subject of the first two sentences. By line 14, the only reference to the man is as object of the preposition relating the embodiment "to him." In the remaining five lines of the poem, there is no reference to him at all. The drama that he has opened ends by excluding him from the scene—further evidence of his alienation from the scene and, perhaps, from himself as well. Whatever has appeared, then, has not answered to his loneliness. The needs he brings to the scene—cosmic or human—are what are reflected in the natural scene: what is external reflects what is internal. In neither case has he found a response that is "additional" or "original" or "counter" to him.[16]

We cannot rule out that the man as human being is alone in human terms as well. The mythic quality of man alone in nature "keeping" the universe recalls, as we will see in "An Old Man's Winter Night," that it is not good for man to be alone.[17] In this view, counter-love, original response, is that of the human love and companionship we need. With this expectation, the lines "instead of proving human when it neared / And someone else additional to him" signal disappointment. It was only an animal, not another human being. But here, too, we must reckon with something, some force that appeared "as a buck," pushing, crumpling, pouring, stumbling with horny tread, and forcing. There is tremendous power and vitality in that rapid accumulation of verbs [18] and in the meaning of each word individually. In such a reading the buck could represent sexuality, also externalizing that which is within the man himself, in this case, "animal" nature within the man, reflected in the animal outside him. Still the phrase "and that was all" remains. For without "counter-love, original response, something else *additional* to him," sexuality is not enough for a human being. It remains *only* "nature" and not human nature. It is simply its own love back, insistently, flagellatingly forceful, but not enough, and not in itself an antidote against loneliness.[19]

We must keep in mind, though, that this was no Narcissus, content as long as he could gaze on himself; this was a man who recognized his need for Other and was willing to cry out. He thus risked disappointment but *maybe* accomplished something. He may have awakened that buck who might not otherwise have come, and that buck may have been an embodiment of something that did respond, however insufficiently, even though it was not the right response, or enough of one. At least he was not alone simply with the static scene. But, of course, if he was only going to seek response in a lonely, cliff-surrounded waterside, he might have realized that that is precisely the sort of place inhabited by Echo.[20]

The clearest contrast to the loneliness in this poem could be that earlier poem of encounter with a buck, "Two Look at Two." While that poem is basically optimistic and fulfilled, it shares with "The Most of It" the way in which the natural scene reflects what people bring to it: the deer couple reflect the human couple, and it is *as if* earth returns their love (only as if) because love is what they came with. This couple did not come to the natural scene to seek counter-love; they had it already. They came, in their love, to seek a "blessing" from nature in their affinity with it; but they also needed to establish their differences from it, the point beyond which "they must not go." And barriers are indeed what they found in the form of the fence, the oncoming unsafe darkness, and the realization that to have proffered a hand would have broken the spell of unscared affinity. They, more than the lone man, have risked entanglement—they are two-in-one—and they risked encountering nature—the sexuality that made them seem akin to the deer, with the snorting buck seemingly challenging them to more action.

In their refusal to deny either love or nature, the lovers are united not only with each other but with nature. "Two thus" they are unafraid of nature, just as the deer are "unscared" of them.

> Love and forgetting might have carried them
> A little further up the mountainside
> With night so near, but not much further up.
> They must have halted soon in any case
> With thoughts of the path back, how rough it was
> With rock and washout, and unsafe in darkness;
> When they were halted by a tumbled wall
> With barbed-wire binding. They stood facing this,
> Spending what onward impulse they still had
> In one last look the way they must not go,

On up the failing path, where, if a stone
Or earthslide moved at night, it moved itself;
No footstep moved it. 'This is all,' they sighed,
'Good-night to woods.' But not so; there was more.
A doe from round a spruce stood looking at them
Across the wall, as near the wall as they.
She saw them in their field, they her in hers.
The difficulty of seeing what stood still,
Like some up-ended boulder split in two,
Was in her clouded eyes: they saw no fear there.
She seemed to think that two thus they were safe.
Then, as if they were something that, though strange,
She could not trouble her mind with too long,
She sighed and passed unscared along the wall.
'*This,* then, is all. What more is there to ask?'
But no, not yet. A snort to bid them wait.
A buck from round the spruce stood looking at them
Across the wall as near the wall as they.
This was an antlered buck of lusty nostril,
Not the same doe come back into her place.
He viewed them quizzically with jerks of head,
As if to ask, 'Why don't you make some motion?
Or give some sign of life? Because you can't.
I doubt if you're as living as you look.'
Thus till he had them almost feeling dared
To stretch a proffering hand—and a spell-breaking.
Then he too passed unscared along the wall.
Two had seen two, whichever side you spoke from.
'This *must* be all.' It was all. Still they stood,
A great wave from it going over them,
As if the earth in one unlooked-for favor
Had made them certain earth returned their love. (CP
    282–83)

The reiteration of "this is all" and the conclusion, "it was all,"
recall the phrase "and that was all" in "The Most of It," but in

"Two Look at Two," the lovers, already fortified with "counter love," not looking for favor, nevertheless *find* favor and love. "This *must* be all"—that third exclamation—shows that *any* sign from nature, any communication, was more than they would have expected. Yet, in common with "The Most of It" is that mysterious "it" in "a great wave from it going over them." Surely, though, any "love" the earth returned to the couple was the love they felt for the earth, and the kinship they felt with nature. Even the tentative "as if" conjecture is mediated by their feeling of "certainty." We are never allowed to ascribe anything to the earth.

A difference in the use of the deer points up a fundamental difference between the two poems. In "The Most of It" the buck is called an "embodiment"—"something" appeared *as* a buck. In "Two Look at Two" the experience has not been with what appears as a buck but simply a buck, and this buck is not distant and unaware of them. Like his mate, he has made eye-contact with them. In their "two-ness" there seems to be some connection between "couples." To have tried to reach out to the deer, to have stretched "a proffering hand," though, would have been to break the spell, to cut the connection even more quickly than it was cut by the two deer's simple indifference to them. Parallel—analogous, but apart—there can be some relationship; in reaching out, in crying out, in ignoring the barriers, there can be only disappointment or dehumanization.

It is with a recognition of these barriers that the poem begins. The first "this is all" is a sighed "goodnight to woods," mixed with regret that this must be all, that the limits of humanity are such that to go further would be to render the way back "unsafe in darkness." Subtly we are reminded of the need for barriers (as we were in "Mending Wall"), for love and a forgetting might have taken them further. While we are told "they must have halted soon," the fact remains that "they *were* halted" by that wall from "the way they must not go,"[21] "But . . . there was more": the first additional experience was with the doe, who, incidentally, also sighed. The view they presented to her puzzled her but did not frighten her. She did not see a man or two people; she saw what "stood still, / Like some up-ended boulder split in two." In the darkening field, and in her darkening and limited field of vision, she saw what must have been a silhouette of an embrace, or at least of a couple standing so close as to seem one boulder split in two. "Two *thus* they were safe." "*Thus*" they would be no danger to her, she seems to discern mindlessly; but we can say that "two thus" *they* were able to feel safe.[22]

Eye to eye, doe and couple exchange views, reflections, and in a sense they reflect each other, an idea that is emphasized in the echo effect as well as the grammatical construction of "her in hers."

But this was not all yet. The buck introduces still another level of experience, that of challenge, almost contempt for their passivity. In case we might be tempted to see this experience as a mere repetition of the first, we are told that while the species and the spruce are the same, this is "not the same doe come back into her place." This is an "antlered buck of lusty nostril." Frost must have decided that we will understand well enough the more active sexuality that the buck represents, for he had deleted the line: "a click of horny footsteps."[23] There seems nothing cloudy about his vision; he does not find them a trouble to his mind, merely a puzzle in their stillness, and he almost dares them to "stretch a proffering hand."

Between the two couples, the greater harmony is with the human lovers, who are together throughout the poem in contrast to the deer who see the same view separately. "Two had seen two whichever side you spoke from," but the manner of seeing differed from side to side. The human lovers see everything together, not only at the same time, but in the same way. We cannot know which one said what in the quotes, but their reaction at the end is one. We are told that the deer, on the other hand, while obviously accompanying each other, see the same view not only at different moments but with different attitudes, different levels of perception, and different abilities to understand (lines 18–24). The respectful communication so necessary to human love is present in the human lovers and totally absent in the deer, where one does not expect "original response"—another difference even where there is reflection in nature.[24] And, of course, the lovers recognize their difference: they leave to go back to where they belong for the night. Originally, they had made an erroneous assumption that their "last look" at the woods would be all, then they are led, one encounter after another, to the limit of their experience with nature, to what really *was* all. They found an unlooked-for favor because they had come with it. " 'This *must* be all.' It was all."

But, of course, it was enough for the lovers, being two, having come with their own abundance. Even the man in "The Most of It" came with something—a need for otherness, a dissatisfaction with echoes. Because he does not even voice a need, the man in "An Old Man's Winter Night" seems to be living in the greatest emotional poverty of all. In this poem, reflection and echo effects also reinforce the lack of any Other:

All out-of-doors looked darkly in at him
Through the thin frost, almost in separate stars,
That gathers on the pane in empty rooms.
What kept his eyes from giving back the gaze
Was the lamp tilted near them in his hand.
What kept him from remembering what it was
That brought him to that creaking room was age.
He stood with barrels round him—at a loss.
And having scared the cellar under him
In clomping here, he scared it once again
In clomping off;—and scared the outer night,
Which has its sounds, familiar, like the roar
Of trees and crack of branches, common things,
But nothing so like beating on a box.
A light he was to no one but himself
Where now he sat, concerned with he knew what,

A quiet light, and then not even that.
He consigned to the moon, such as she was,
So late-arising, to the broken moon
As better than the sun in any case
For such a charge, his snow upon the roof,
His icicles along the wall to keep;
And slept. The log that shifted with a jolt
Once in the stove, disturbed him and he shifted,
And eased his heavy breathing, but still slept.
One aged man—one man—can't keep a house,
A farm, a country side, or if he can,
It's thus he does it of a winter night. (CP 35)

We do not know *why* the old man is alone, only *that* he is. We do not know whether the state he has reached in this poem is the result of his aloneness or the cause of it; it is with the state of his life as we find it that we must deal. We feel in this old man a shutting-out that keeps him more frighteningly alone. Here we find salvation neither in a human relationship, nor in communion with the outside world, nor in devotion to a task. There is no sense here of the old man's existing for anything or anyone at all. With his memory failing him, eroding his sense of purpose, the old man strengthens his ego by a stubborn taciturnity, and he protects himself by scaring away what frightens him rather than by inviting in what comforts him. Nowhere in this poem of terrible aloneness are we admitted to the man's feelings of loneliness. We are admitted only to his feeling "at a loss," to his concern with "he knew what," to his consigning of the snow to the moon, and to his falling asleep. If anything, the man seems more alone because we are not admitted into his feelings. Were we sitting in the room with him, we might not be admitted to them either, for in his concern with "he knew what" (and in that triple-stressed sound of the sentence), we feel a taciturnity, a stubborn unwillingness on his part to communicate and, more pathetic still, an unwillingness to admit, perhaps, that he did not know, could not remember what he was concerned with. Thus he not only keeps to himself in the sense of being without others, he keeps his ideas and his feelings to himself.

We are told he was a light to no one but himself—and a quiet light at that—"*and then not even that,*" possibly not fully in touch *even with himself.* He also *holds* a light, a light that prevents his "giving back the gaze" to the out-of-doors because he is tilting it back toward his eyes. The light he *was* unto himself and the light he *holds* unto himself work together to intensify the man's isolation: we understand that his aloneness is not simply the absence of another person in the house or the fact that no one is caring for him; it is that he means nothing to anyone. Moreover it means that he illuminates nothing for anyone else, and we have no way of knowing if he even wants to or was ever able to. This keeping of his light and his concern to himself seems to have some bearing on the man's relationship with the out-of-doors, for his very aloneness makes the world outside and the world in the cellar especially frightening.[25] He could use his light to look out by holding it at the window to do so, but he tilts it toward his eyes. While the tilting could have been involuntary, or for no conscious reason, the result is the same: he cannot see the outside. Had he wanted to "give back the gaze," he could certainly have done so. He may not have cared, or he may have feared what lies outside, in which case the tilt of the lamp prevents his seeing out, protects him from what seems to be "looking darkly" in. The two lights work together, for were he to have cast light outward in either sense, to have been a light to another, to have shone his light out the window, the out-of-doors would not seem to be "looking darkly in at him." With another he would be able to "keep house"—to have a home; this way the house is a "keep"—a fortress against hostile forces, but not a real home. As it is, he reflects only himself and his condition, haunted by what he imagines threatens from without. Even the conjunctive "where" contributes to the sense of his imprisonment in the self: it is not clear what we are to take as the reference of the relative clause "where now he sat." Is it the "light" he was sitting in—his own light, that is? Is "himself" the antecedent? But if we think about it, it is all the same, for he remains locked in that reflexive circle of self, the light he was only unto himself, the light he shone back toward himself, and the implied passiveness of that sitting.

What light he has will finally depend on the moon—late-arising, broken, chaste, cold, and undependable—and it is to her that he will consign "his" snow, "his" icicles. The moon, "such as she [is]," is better for holding his possessions, such as they are. She will fulfill his need, perhaps, to feel in possession of something, particularly of the snow and icicles on his roof, as if their very coldness, preserved as it would be by the moon, better at such a charge than the sun, was a part of him.[26] The "empty rooms" seem to have invited the stars—separate stars—of frost. The cold snow and ice seem all he has to give, all he has that he wishes preserved, both of which meanings are inherent in "to keep."

Yet in that dim and frozen atmosphere we hear noise, the noise he makes to scare the cellar and scare the outer night. We hear what must be his futile attempt to scare them *back*. The night "has its sounds, familiar. . . . But nothing so like beating on a box." Are we to assume that the poem means that nothing is so familiar a sound, nothing so hollow, nothing so "scary" by virtue of its loudness as beating on a box? We cannot be certain whether the man actually beats on a box, but we cannot escape the image of a man doing so to scare away the sounds, to drown them out, to *make* a sound when he cannot generate enough light, and the act of a man alone beating on a box seems even more frightening than noises from the cellar or the out-of-doors.[27]

The hollowness and the emptiness of the place and the life are reinforced by the auditory image of resonating sounds and further dramatized by repetitions within the poem—words and structures that echo one another: "Scared" appears three times, "light" "moon," "keep," "night," "one man," "clomping," and "what kept him" twice. (Notice, too, the visual effect on the page of lines 10 and 11, 4 and 6.) In this context of man alone, scaring the out-of-doors, consigning snow and icicles, creating voiceless sound by clomping, or maybe by beating, the echoes could seem mocking indeed.

Most telling, though, is the echo effect in the description of his disturbed sleep: he sleeps, and "the log that *shifted* . . . disturbed him and *he shifted* . . . but still slept" (italics mine). It is almost as if he is one with that log. Box-beating and clomping over, light put out, he sleeps like a log, moves when the log moves. It is almost as if in the man's aloneness, his connection with no one, no purpose, his lack of connection even with himself and his thoughts, he is less than fully human—not even connected with nature, for the log is no longer alive. It is another example of the deathward pull inherent in the unbroken circle of self. This is an old man's winter night, but we are not allowed to rest the blame for his condition simply on age. What kept him from remembering was age, but we are made to see, at the end, that not only can one *aged* man not keep a house, but that one man— any man alone—cannot keep a house, a farm, a countryside any better than this.[28]

In discussing a poet as conscious of form and sound as Frost always was, it seems entirely appropriate to notice the way formal features such as repetition and rhyme scheme, even sentence structure, relate to the content or theme. Echo is not mentioned in "An Old Man's Winter Night" but it is occurring in the sounds of the poem. Hollander points out that verse forms such as the sestina or the terza rima have an echoic effect in the ways they both echo past stanzas and point forward to what will be further echoing.[29]

In that loneliest of poems, "Acquainted With the Night," where the speaker's own footsteps, as the only sound at close range, must be resounding in a hollow manner that mocks his aloneness, Frost, significantly, has chosen Dante's stanza, the terza rima, even though it is not the usual rhyme scheme in a sonnet. He has resolved the problem of ending with an odd unrhymed line by means of repeating a line, as he had done in "Stopping By Woods." Here the repetition in the last line is not of the preceding line, but of the first line, as if, like Dante's characters, the speaker is going in circles bound at once by his particular circle of torment and by his inability to get anywhere even within it.[30] That he ends with the same line he begins with serves another function as well. "I have been one acquainted with the night" can be taken simply literally—night as a time of the twenty-four hour day—but by the time we have read the twelve intervening lines, we know that those night walks are also walks during some dark period in the person's life, some dark night of the soul in one way or another. By the final line of the poem, we understand the full anguish of the opening line. The incantatory nature of the repeated "I have" structure, in which he lists in brief sentences what he has done, and the repetition as well of other words, adds to the feeling of repeated, unending torment and to the "unearthliness" of the state of mind, the spiritual or emotional darkness.

Like the sestina, with its variously arranged repetitions of end words, "The Telephone," while not actually a sestina, has a similar intricacy and a similar echo effect. But as we saw in the difference between "The Most of It" and "Two Look at Two," the figure alone is mocked by the echoing return of his own voice, whereas the couple feel a kinship with their reflections when what is reflected is their two-ness. Whereas in the poems above, the formal features that create poetic echoes intensify the loneliness of the protagonists, the same kinds of features empha-size the unity of the two in "The Telephone," where the rhyme scheme is interwoven between the stanzas and where what "he" says rhymes with what "she" says. It is as if the speaker has so incorporated the existence and love of the other into his own being that these echoes are echoic sounds of the other, almost impossible to distinguish from his own words. This is very like the impossibility of distinguishing, in "Two Look at Two," which of the human lovers is speaking. In other words, in form as well as in situation, what is echoed is what is brought to the scene or the poem. Echo *in form* reflects what is there to be formed.

Less echoic but equally self-reflecting, or at least self-enclosing, is the syntactic form of "Into My Own," and the way the convoluted syntax supports the sense we have in reading the poem that, the further away the speaker runs, the more surely he runs into himself; the deeper he runs into the woods, the deeper he goes into the self, and that this is what he most fears.[31]

> One of my wishes is that those dark trees,
> So old and firm they scarcely show the breeze,
> Were not, as 'twere, the merest mask of gloom,
> But stretched away unto the edge of doom.
>
> I should not be withheld but that some day
> Into their vastness I should steal away,
> Fearless of ever finding open land,
> Or highway where the slow wheel pours the sand.
>
> I do not see why I should e'er turn back,
> Or those should not set forth upon my track
> To overtake me, who should miss me here
> And long to know if still I held them dear.
>
> They would not find me changed from him they knew—
> Only more sure of all I thought was true. (CP 5)

We wonder what exactly the speaker wants—more specifically, whether he wants to be lost or found. Even the title is ambiguous: Is this a description of a process by which the speaker comes into his own, a sort of maturing into achievement and self-confidence? Or is the phrase to be taken literally, implying that there is something of his, some noun, his own something, into which he goes? The poem hovers between the two possibilities throughout, expressing contradictory desires with regard to the dark trees, which, in turn, is reflected in the confusing syntax. One must untangle negatives to discover what positive statement is being made; one must distinguish between mode and tense in an attempt to distinguish actual from hypothetical, between "should" as a form of "shall" and "should" as a synonym for "ought to."

In the first stanza the speaker states *one* of his wishes: that those dark trees were "stretched away unto the edge of doom." His objection to their being a "mask of gloom" is not to their gloominess but to their being a "mere mask." He wants not a façade but a place with depth—endless depths of gloom. Were that the case, he would (ought to?) steal away, presumably within the depths provided by endless dark trees. The word "fearless" is strange: the line seems to mean "confident of never finding open land," in this case showing a desire for endless woods, a desire *not* to come out on the other side into a clearing. Fear seems a strong word in this context. Preferring to remain in the woods is one thing; *fear* of coming out is another. It seems that mixed with fear that one will come out onto the highway is fear that one will not, will never find open land.

The third quatrain is still more confusing: what is it that he does not see? For one thing, he does not see why he should ever turn back. More difficult to untangle is what he says about "those" others. Put in natural order, the sentence would read: I do not see why those who *should* miss me *here* and long to know if I still *held* them dear should not set forth upon my track to overtake me. This is a strange consideration for one who would not be held back from entering the endless woods, one whose fear is that they may end in open land, for it betrays not only the desire to be followed and overtaken but a self-consciousness about what they think about his feelings for them. They will not only seek him because they miss him, but because they want to know if he still cares about them. Whether or not they matter to him is less important than their worrying about it. The conditional "held" implies doubt that he would still hold them dear; they will seek him out, then, with little hope of being held dear.

The use of "should" for the third person hints of obligation. It is what he will expect them to do, what he assumes will be the case. His stealing away becomes not only an escape, but a test of the devotion of those who would set out to overtake him despite the doubts of his holding them dear, despite the vastness of the woods into which he has gone, despite his desertion of them by going in the first place. More important than getting lost, it seems, is getting found.[32] "I do not see why I should e'er turn back" betrays a doubt, a retreat from the firmness of this position in the previous quatrain. The use of "here" and "back" betrays a confusion about where he is and where he really wants to be. "Back" is from the vantage point of the woods; "here" is still in this place from which I have not yet gone, only I might, were those trees "stretched away unto the edge of doom."

With those words, of course, we are made aware that, woods or no woods, there is also a desire for a test of a "marriage of true minds"; that the speaker needs to go within himself, to steal away, to go beyond the "mask of gloom" to the depths behind it; but that he needs simultaneously to be missed, overtaken, and found. In this sense, what he thought was true would be the finding of him, the passing of the test. In another, it would be the renewing of self in order to remain constant, stable, consistent by going periodically within the self, by retreating.

It seems that the convoluted sentence structure is necessary to him to keep his motives better hidden, not just from the listener, but from himself; it obscures what he is not anxious to reveal.[33] It also takes speaker and listener on a circular path, suggesting once more the potential entrapment in a closed circle of self. But of course, as he says in "Revelation," those who love us will make the effort to untangle syntax, to catch nuances. They will find us. Only then is it safe to escape, to go into the woods or into one's own self.

Explicit in this poem is an analogy between self and trees or woods. So is the desire to escape. If we put these two ideas together, we find that to escape into those woods is to escape into self, and consequently that escape means withdrawal into self. Perhaps this is into the natural, wild irresponsible area of the self; perhaps only into solitude, seeking renewal from within, replenishing what has been eroded by contracts and obligations and the demands of others. Frost speaks of "the wild free ways of wit and art," which G. A. Craig interpreted as follows: "Not phony wildness just to be different [but] avenues through which he believes each of us discovers that he *is* different, that he *does* differ."[34] This, then, is the need to withdraw to self to repair self, to keep the self intact. This is consistent with the need for "strategic retreat" which he expressed in "The Drumlin Woodchuck."

The whole concept of escape is very complex in Frost the man and in his poetry. From childhood on into old age, he had his ways of escaping either in fantasy or in fact.[35] While he recognized that there are psychological dangers in withdrawal ("I sometimes think of those [Derry] years as almost a fade-out, an escape into a dream existence, as in *dementia praecox*" [EY 561]), he objected to the purely pejorative meaning of "escapist." "The point, he said, was: what are you escaping from? Possibly something that is strangling you. What are you escaping to? Possibly something you need and must have" (EY 561). But he recognized that "when you run away from a place it is yourself you are generally running away from and that goes with you and is the first thing you meet in the next place you turn up."[36] Thus to escape knowingly into self, or into a solitary place where one meets only self, requires courage. To escape distraction is to meet the self head-on, and it is sometimes necessary to escape distractions in order to renew wholeness of self and of purpose, or to be able to come into one's own.

In this sense, when asked whether poetry was an escape from the world's troubles, Frost answered: "No. Poetry is a way to take life by the throat."[37] To seem to escape can be to confront life and self in solitude, more agonizingly, more deeply. It can be creative and instructive, but it can also be immature and dangerous, and Frost is obviously aware of the ways in which escape is both.

Far more compelling in this poem is the fear that, once too deep inside, we will not be able to find our way out alone. To be drawn into what lies "out there" or within is also to be drawn into possible loss of control; to give in may be to be swallowed or annihilated. It may be to find oneself left with nothing. The need to give in to oblivion is thus countered by the fear of nothingness or the fear of death; the need to give in to wildness is countered by the need to preserve one's human dignity; the need to get away from people is countered by the need for people, both in society and in a relationship of love. There is being left alone, and there is being really alone. After Elinor's death, Frost wrote: "I shall be all right in public, but I can't tell you how I am going to behave when I am alone. She could always be present to govern my loneliness without making me feel less alone" (SL 470).

Both as person and as poet, Frost recognized the need to come out of the labyrinth, to transcend the mirror image—in the human domain of egoism, in the poetic domain of strict analogy or mimesis. The material he encountered and then fashioned had to be faced as Other, for what the encounter did to him and for what he was to make out of it. Such making was his surest "hold" on his individuated self, his way out of the entanglement that threatened to subsume him. It became his way of feeling himself validated rather than obliterated and his way of remaining in control. Of course, it was his most original response, which had to have been stimulated somehow out of the otherness of the encountered material to *him* and *to* which he brought the otherness of his imagination. We cannot forget that out of all this experience—hypothetical and imagined, or actually remembered—Frost made poems that include the illusions, the assumptions, the realities, and the necessary distance from it all. He was not the man on the beach or the man alone; he dramatized them. Narcissus only looked, only loved the reflection passively, and, passively got turned into a flower *by* other powers; Frost creates the beautiful object actively, by pulling back from reflection, by making with it and of it. His poem is an original response that invites *our* original response to what it opens up, invites us to, sometimes tries to shut us out of, but never fully closes off.

In the chapters that follow, we will examine the ways in which Frost dramatizes the encounter with the natural world as Other, or between a protagonist and a human Other. I would suggest that the many voices and roles of his speakers somehow comprise a diffused set of dramatizations of Frost's own need to grapple with the psychological, personal, and artistic questions that these poems raise. We will examine different kinds of encounter, both in relation to the natural world and the human one: the drama of person facing person, or person facing natural phenomenon, as Other. We will also see how experiences are "read" or interpreted; how they can serve the observer or participant as useful analogies, or, more powerfully, as projections or seeming identities—in both cases, reflecting the needs and views of that protagonist. Then we will step back, as Frost seems to do, trying to join in the poetic making as readers, asking what in any of these dramas also dramatizes the transformation inherent in artistic creation or models that process, what artistic concerns are reflected by the dramatic encounter in—or with—that poem.

4

Reading from Emerson
to Frost

"I have come [to the city] not to get excitement but
to get away from the excitement of . . . nature naturating" (LY
20). With this statement Frost reminds us that to him nature
could never be merely a scene or an ecological system viewed
only scientifically; it provided excitement that is both sensual
and dramatic. Encountering nature becomes the drama enacted
between the person and what he observes, as he feels himself
more the participant, less the uninvolved observer, or the drama
of recognition that natural process inspires or provokes. Any
American poet playing that role, especially one who, as Brower
says of Frost, "is playing a high game—as poet and worshiper—
in the presence of nature,"[1] must surely feel himself to be standing in the shadow of Emerson and Thoreau, or in their light. A
poet begins as a cloud of all the poets he has ever read, Frost
used to say,[2] the cloud image perhaps betraying the anxiety he
was not owning up to in the influence he *was* openly acknowledging. Perhaps he was able to acknowledge the romantic poets
and the nature poets, "Nature" and *Walden*, because he also
knew that he was doing something else, something that represented and expressed *him*, and that even while he showed rec-

ognizable affinity with traditions he inherited, he also showed himself to be something quite different—and more modern.

Brower locates his modernism in his consciousness of playing that high game. We can also find it in the insufficiency that nature presents to Frost's personae. Wordsworth finds a nature filled with "presences"; Emerson and Thoreau find satisfying correspondences; their writings bespeak their sense of sufficiency—morally or aesthetically—in the nature before them, but Frost will end a poem of encounter with nature by saying "and that was all"—only the most of it. The sort of satisfactions his predecessors express in their readings of the natural text is always qualified in Frost, who seems also to be more personally,[3] more deeply, and more psychologically affected by his readings than were Emerson and Thoreau, more fearful of the encounter than was Wordsworth. Nature as he reads it threatens to have a greater transforming power over him as reader/poet. It is this he tries to resist, as well as its power to reveal, or read, him. Moreover he insists that we enter the game: where Emerson may seem to protest too much, Frost openly challenges us; where Thoreau enjoins us to wander, still deriving positive morals even in his most brutal encounters with nature, Frost nervously erects fences in his fear of wandering, both leading us, and leaving us, to wonder.

Emerson taught Frost how to "read" nature, to see it emblematically.[4] As we have seen, what Frost calls synecdochism is really a way of reading the universe that Thompson called "metaphysical" and deriving from Emerson.[5] Even more important, Emerson validated Frost as a poet, exalting that reading function as a high calling, a necessary one, and suggesting that the writing function of the poet was a "reading" of nature for *his* readers, the implication being that the poet helps make poets of his readers, whose eyes would, by virtue of the reading, be opened, who, in the act of reading, would themselves become more poetical.

We remember that Frost's notion of correspondence was not quite the same as Emerson's: "Poetry is correspondence: it brings forth a response from the feelings and thoughts of the reader because the reader has similar feelings and thoughts. It goes back to the reader's performing his part in a serious engagement. It's *not* the correspondence that Swedenborg meant, or Emerson."[6] Frost thus sets up an empathetic relationship between poet and reader that has its analogues in the more personal way those poetic "readers" within his poems approach nature without and within. Frost is more vulnerable to those natural "texts" than Emerson ever shows himself to be, hence more fearful of what nature might do to him, more fearful of that nature in him that was always threatening to erupt. He is more realistically aware that, in the act of following a call to poetry, to nature, to climbing birches, he might get lost or changed from what he always knew. As we have noted before, at the same time that he was more aware of the blurring of the lines between what he was and what he experienced, more aware of what nature— or any encounter he was experiencing or reading—could do to him ("What the facts do to you despite your resistance transforms them to poetry" [I 21]), he was more aware of his need to maintain control, not only of what he might do, but of what he was, to retain his sense of self, the "I" at once so insistent and so vulnerable. He considered Emerson's "one of the noblest least egotistical of styles" (LU 166), perhaps because Emerson was so willing to be transparent and made one with the rest of creation, perhaps because Emerson's writing so often faced outward while Frost realized that his own faced so much more inward.

We have also seen that "nature" in Frost's poetry was a text made more variable by the ways it was seen. The more variable and "open" the natural texts, the more central *and* vulnerable the reader; the more vulnerable Frost-the-reader felt himself to be, the more cryptic the texts he would write, the more possessive he was of their meaning, or, to put it another way, the more their openness corresponded to the openness of the natural texts he was reading.

To the extent that Frost's temperament allowed, rather forced, greater personal involvement than did Emerson's, he felt himself and his texts to be less stable. He acknowledged more than Emerson did that there was risk in approaching nature, that to open oneself to experience and its texts had farther reaching implications than Emerson took into account. In these fears and differences—including, but not restricted to, Frost's well-known statements about Emerson's view of evil—lay Frost's recognition of Emerson's limitations. In those limitations, Frost would have been able to see further validation by Emerson, not only of his poetic calling, but of his passionate nature, his being the man Ciardi was to call Mount Frost, that magnificent volcano.[7]

James McIntosh locates the beginning of romanticism at the point where "the European man of feeling recognizes that he is alone with his imagination, with all the danger, fascination, and possibility for art, self-culture, and self-transfiguration that lonely recognition entails. . . . No longer related to [inherited social and cosmic ties, he has] to decide on 'an original relation to the universe.'"[8] He became aware both of man's separation from nature and his relatedness to it, even in its violence, and felt the tension that arose because, even while feeling human separateness, he was still trying to find peace in a relationship that was still thought possible. As McIntosh expresses the tension: "Romantic self-consciousness necessarily separates the romantic observer from nature, however much he may regret the separation" (20).

In Frost, moments of relationship, of peace and harmony, are not only rare *gifts* but, as we have seen, cannot be expected from nature, or from any force out there; rather they emanate from the person, his perception, his need, or what he brings to nature. Nature is more coldly alien, and man more conscious of his alienation in Frost. This will mean that encountering nature is

another braving of alien entanglement and that Frost, who fears
not only his own alienation but also his entanglement with alien
"others," will fear entanglement with nature as well. At the same
time, though, as we have seen in the previous chapter, he needs
such entanglement and such encounters (the risks of which we
will explore in subsequent chapters); therefore he finds himself
involved with, constructed into, and constructing out of nature
as well. A poem is a figure of the will braving alien entanglements, Frost says, and we have assumed that to be applicable to
reading a poem, too. Thus nature, as "text," invites the poet to
read as well as to write.

Emerson both invites and allows him to "read" nature—exhorts him to, in fact. To Frost, the unproved but determined
incipient *poet,* more specifically, the poet encountering nature,
surely nothing could have meant more than these words of
Emerson's: "We all stand waiting, empty,—knowing, possibly,
that we can be full, surrounded by mighty symbols which are
not symbols to us but prose and trivial toys. Then cometh the
god and converts the statues into fiery men, and by a flash of his
eye burns up the veil which shrouded all things, and the meaning of the very furniture, the cup and saucer, of chair and clock
and tester, is manifest. The facts which loomed so large . . . have
strangely changed their proportions" (W 2:311).

This poet would not be a decorator, writing pretty verses,
nor a self-indulgent idler, nor would he merely be giving solace
and beauty to others. He would do more than make the world's
natural beauty and reality manifest and noticed; even more than
being a legislator, he would interpret the world, as he gives the
universe tongue: "The world being thus put under the mind for
verb and noun, the poet is he who can articulate it. For . . .
though all men are intelligent of the symbols through which it
is named,—yet they cannot originally use them. We are symbols, and inhabit symbols; workmen, work, and tools, words
and things, birth and death, all are emblems. . . . The poet, by
an ulterior[9] intellectual perception, gives them a power which

makes their old use forgotten, and puts eyes, and a tongue, into every dumb and inanimate object" (W 3:20).

In addition, he would provide his fellows with ways to see better, and think better, for themselves: he makes of the natural world a lens (W 3:20); his poetry gives others heights and perspectives from which to view the world in new ways, "afford[s] us a platform whence we may command a view of our present life" (W 2:312). Since "every thought is also a prison . . . therefore we love the poet, the inventor, who in any form . . . has yielded us a new thought. He unlocks our chains, and admits us to a new scene" (W 3:33). In addition, the poet organizes and reorganizes our world: he "reattaches things to nature and the Whole,—reattaching even artificial things, and violations of nature, to nature, by a deeper insight" . . . puts even railroads into the order of the whole (W 3:18–19).

If this is what poets can do with the world, this not only places a terrific responsibility on poets but presumes a variable world, with every act of reorganization destabilizing a previous organization or coexisting with it as an alternative world, and with every act of organizing it anew, every new "reading," involving an act of reconstructing the reader within it. Emerson does not take this into account. Rather, he focuses on the function of the poet, who reads the universe as it was meant to be read—for its significance; it is not enough to see, appreciate, and study the universe. We need the poet to tell us what it means, but significance is always relative *to* someone, always within some personal, cultural, or historical context (even E. D. Hirsch concedes this). We could therefore put it differently: it is that very variability that requires poets and readers to teach us *how* to read and that reading is an interpretive act, that there will be as many meanings, or at least significances, as there are poets. Frost was to call a poem a momentary stay against confusion. Momentary. Stable and unconfused for the time and space of that poem. So we keep needing poems and poets who will read the world as only a poet can and will write it so that others can share his vision. In Emerson's view, the natural world is one language and needs to be translated into another; more than this, its ulterior significance needs to be made manifest to those who would know but have not that god's gift.

This had to have been terribly important to a young man who needed to justify to his family, his sweetheart/wife, but most of all to himself, the value of what it was he was sacrificing not only himself, but them, to do. One can only imagine how welcome was Emerson's validation of his enterprise, almost as if he could allow Emerson to answer his grandfather, for what could a Shelley or a Sidney, perfumed, profligate English noblemen, say to the Frosts—grandfather or Rob, those heirs of American earnestness, vigor, Puritan and democratic ethics that required hard work to build the New Jerusalem. One need go no farther than Hawthorne's Custom House chapter, where those ancestral portraits shake their heads, and Hawthorne imagines those persecuting divines punished at last by having a writer of stories, a teller of tales, as their ultimate fruit, if one wishes to understand what it must have meant to have one's poetic calling made sacred by the likes of an Emerson.

But it was not only the poet that Emerson validated; the poet's text was to be the natural world. He could be an exegete in the woods (and the symbolic forest so prevalent in American literature, a very important setting and symbol—a personal psychological one—for Frost as well, as we shall discuss in the next chapter). Of course Emerson was not advocating that men return to worshipping trees but that they see the natural world as symbolic, a view inherited from those early and earnest divines. Nature was a text to be read. Unlike those divines, though, he seemed to say one did not have to restrict oneself to church or Bible to read the word of God or, as he put it, the moral order, the law that the poet was extracting by means of his reading. We will see later that, when Frost reads the Bible, it will be through natural lenses.

It is not at all clear whether that god, that poet, will have to write publishable poetry, or any poetry. He is a poet by virtue of his ability to read, interpret, and organize the external world; of course, if he shows it in new images, resymbolizes what is already a symbol so that others may more easily and pleasurably comprehend it, so much the better. Not only is the natural world a text to be read, but Emerson, like modern reader response theorists, puts the "reading" human being at the center of the process[10] and makes reading itself a poetic act. "You love the boy reading in a book, gazing at a drawing, or a cast: yet what are these millions who read and behold, but incipient writers and sculptors? Add a little more of that quality which now reads and sees, and they will seize the pen and chisel" (W 3:66). While Emerson sees these boys as incipient and not the actual sculptors James later claims (see my chapter 1), he nevertheless sees the creative aspect of reading, and, like his forebears both among the Puritans and the eighteenth-century poets, makes of nature a book to be read.

A book to be read, of course, presumes a reader. Emerson seems to go as far as to say that, without that human reader, there is no text in this forest: "natural objects, if individually described and out of connection, are not yet known, since they are really parts of a symmetrical universe like words of a sentence; and if their true order is found, the poet can read their divine significance orderly as in a Bible" (W 8:8).

But that is assuming that there is a true order and a specially ordained poet and that it is the poet's job to *find* it and translate it—not to make it. To Emerson, reading is apprehending, ordering, and translating a text that already exists, complete. His reader, then, is less creative of the vision as well as less personally involved. The world is more stable and so is the integrity and wholeness of the poet, who also seems to arrive on the scene as a complete(d) construction.

To see every man and every reading as different is to point toward a Frost who sees the world far more provisionally,[11] to

realize his role in it as far more limited, and his writing it more
tentative *and* more open to interpretation, which could include
misinterpretation or, as we have seen, interpretations that "go
one better." Very useful to Frost was the notion of "the world
[as] an immense picture-book of every passage in human life.
Every object he beholds is the mask of a man" (W 8:9). To
Emerson this human reader is absolutely central: "[Because] the
whole of nature is a metaphor of the human mind" (W 1:32);
nature is there *for* man and his edification. Of this last, though,
Frost will not be so sure. Nature simply *exists.* What man makes
of it is his problem—or his glory. Also his text. Emerson finds
the human method to be that of organizing into relationships,
discovering analogies. Frost was to say later that metaphor was
the whole of thinking—putting this and that together, but as
we have discussed in chapter 2, analogy is far more limited and
limiting than metaphor. Emerson writes:

> Man is an analogist. He cannot help seeing everything under
> its relations to all other things and to himself. (J 5:146)

> He is placed in the centre of beings, and a ray passes from
> every other being to him. And neither can man be under-
> stood without these objects, nor these objects without man.
> (W 1:27–28)

> So every organ, function, acid, crystal, grain of dust, has its
> relation to the brain. It waits long, but its turn comes. . . . It
> would seem as if each [creatures and qualities] waited like
> the enchanted princess in fairy tales, for a destined human
> deliverer. (W 4:9)

Such deliverance, of course, is the *human* view, more specifically the view of a thinker who sees humanity as central to
creation. There is a difference between saying "nature is there . . .
for man" and saying "he cannot help seeing" the world this way.
It is the latter view that Frost will capitalize on and dramatize

(we will be discussing it in chapter 7 in connection with "The Aim Was Song"), how the world looks to a reader, a particular reader of a particular scene at a given time, in a given mood.

As we will see, Emerson himself says that mood affects vision, but he will locate any error or blankness in vision in that man's failure to see properly or in his moral poverty. He still seems to assume right and wrong, complete and incomplete readings. A mood does not change the world or its design; the world will merely look different through different lenses. Man and world are far less variable to Emerson. By the same token that we see man and his vision as central, and that we consider readings to vary from reader to reader, or from time to time even by the same reader, Emerson recognized, "The ruin or the blank we see when we look at nature, is in our own eye. The axis of vision is not coincident with the axis of things, and so they appear not transparent but opaque. The reason why the world lacks unity is .,. . because man is disunited with himself" (W 1:73–74).

In this idea is combined the understanding that the seen is affected by the eyes of the beholder—another validation of more relativistic views of reading and interpreting texts—with the overarching assumption that the universe is ultimately symmetrical and moral, that "those invisible cords we call laws" (W 8:5) bind it into a whole that includes the right reader in its unity, for the world is not an open book to just any observer. "A life in harmony with nature, the love of truth and virtue, will purge the eyes to understand her test. By degrees we come to know the primitive sense of the permanent objects in nature, so that the world shall be to us an open book" (W 1:35).

Still, it is amazing how close to modern reader response theory Emerson was, how willing to see not only what a "poet" can make of what he sees in nature but how relative and variable is what we see.[12]

Life is a train of moods like a string of beads, and, as we pass through them, they prove to be many-colored lenses which paint the world their own hue, and each shows only what lies in its focus. From the mountain you see the mountain. We animate what we can, and we see only what we animate. Nature and books belong to the eyes that see them. It depends on the mood of the man, whether he shall see the sunset or the fine poem." (W 3:50) [13]

. . . we suspect our instruments. We have learned that we do not see directly, but mediately, and that we have no means of correcting these colored and distorting lenses which we are. . . . Perhaps these subject lenses have a creative power; perhaps there are no objects. . . . Nature and literature are subjective phenomena." (W 3:75–76)

In the second of these quotations from "Experience," Emerson goes even further than the first in making literature of the natural world. From the more conventional book/nature analogy of the first example, he moves to the world as literature, closer to art and making, combined as it is with the creativity of the subject. It is not only that a mood can affect the way we see; we are not only wearing lenses, we are lenses—subject lenses that create. Those words could also imply that as subjects we are created, perhaps, by what we see, or we are subject to forces that mold our creating vision. Then, too, if we are lenses, and thus transparent, it is difficult to see whether we read objects or are read by them, whether we stand more revealed and revealed differently because of that transparency. If there are no objects, then our visions, or ourselves as instruments, not only distort but make. But Emerson does not continue along the lines he has opened up.

Once we begin to apply such questions to Frost, we have difficulty remaining philosophical and general; the theoretical paradoxes of romantic thinking become actualized in the modern poet. His poems at their best are dramas, with human beings in the foreground, as he has told us. We hear an individual voice of a particular kind, tone, and personality speaking. We sense a creating poet to whom such individuality matters a great deal, whatever the general scheme of things. We feel the drama of an encounter either within the poem or behind it. Norman Holland finds it sad that, in much recent literary theory, the person gets lost, that we have turned to philosophy and not psychology; we need to put people back into the picture.[14] In a way, that is what Frost does as his speakers encounter nature, and it is what we need to do in reading those poems.

We need to take Emerson's view of reading nature and wed it to psychology in an attempt to understand an individual's vulnerability in the face of a printed book, or a natural phenomenon, or a "reading" of that phenomenon as it becomes "text" to him. Frost could do just that, as he attempted both to fortify ego boundaries and to relate the phenomena of nature to his own fears, needs, questions, and ideas. At the same time that he shows us he is too versed in country things to expect anything from nature, he shows us the need that impels us to seek the most of it anyway and the inevitable frustration that results. The Frostian speakers not only see analogies but, further, feel themselves identifying with what is out there and analogous, project out onto nature what requires expression or displacement. The woodchuck that excites a savage thrill does not frighten Thoreau; the boy in the coonskin cap suggests all sorts of images that do not faze him. The battle between the red and black ants is fascinating and suggests human analogies, but the ants do not worry the observer.[15] He does not take personally a nature that can be savage, or cold, or steep, ascribes no malevolence to it, nor does he feel that it is creeping in, staring darkly in at him, or tapping at the windows.

It may be useful here to recall our discussion of Wimmers's reading theories (chapter 1), particularly her emphasis on self-interpretation, empathy, and identification in the process of interpreting texts and finding them significant. Especially relevant to our discussion is her moving on from empathy to the analogies set in motion once the reader-text interrelationship has been activated. We may remember as well her warning regarding narcissism and failure of critical distance. The phenomenon of resistance to reading—the need to stay "whole," to keep one's ego intact—such fears are not exhibited by Emerson and Thoreau, though the lack of personal engagement might be evidence of that resistance—or at least of its repression.

In these views I find not only fascinating applications to Frost "reading," and Frost as he needs to be read, but also crucial points of difference between Frost and both Emerson and Thoreau. In Frost we find the much more realistic recognition that there is indeed danger in losing the self in texts, nature, relationships, or even the self, and correspondingly the need to retain boundaries of self as individual, of humanness in the face of what is nonhuman or inhuman. Thoreau's lakes are pure, precious stones that contain no muck (TW 199), "the landscape's most beautiful feature . . . the earth's eye; looking into which the beholder measures the depths of his own nature. The fluviatile trees next to the shore are the slender eyelashes which fringe it, and the wooded hills and cliffs are its overhanging brows" (TW 186). True, the beholder's nature is mentioned but never developed or returned to. The eye is set into its physical analogy of eye:face :: lake:surrounding physical landscape. And that is all. The detailed description of what one sees in the water is reserved for its transparency, showing the fishes in its depth, or its reflective power, showing the surrounding trees. As in Frost, the very depths are symbolic ("I am thankful that this pond was made deep and pure for a symbol. While men believe in the infinite some ponds will be thought bottomless") (TW 287).[16] But in Thoreau we never see Narcissus himself, godlike. Emerson can ask: "Why should we fear to be crushed by savage elements, we who are made up of the same elements?" Because he exhibits such confidence in the face of a right sort of Nature: "Why should we be afraid of Nature which is *no other than philosophy and theology embodied*?" (W 6:49, emphasis mine).

The real test, for Emerson, comes not in fearlessness of savage elements but in the face of that other aspect of nature: death, and, ironically, it is here that his very equanimity in the face of nature is his burden. In the face of tragedy and grief, he feels himself unable to reach tragic heights because he cannot sink to its depths. Unlike Frost, who fears losing himself, Emerson bemoans his inability to do so.

Stephen Whicher finds Emerson's discussion of the "unreality" of grief to be protective of his hard-won security; only by refusing to conceive of life as tragic could he find the courage to live.[17] But one can question whether that "hard-won security" is truly being protected by Emerson's *words* that grief is unreal. The pain of experience seems to keep obtruding itself, especially in his exhortation to experience. The oppositions in "Experience," for example, between ideas and the pulses are left there for us to shift between; they are not resolved. Witness the following excerpt:

> I accept the clangor and jangle of contrary tendencies. I find my account in sots and bores also. They give a reality to the circumjacent picture, which such a vanishing meteorous appearance can ill spare. In the morning I awake, and find the old world, wife, babes, and mother, Concord and Boston, the dear old spiritual world, and even the dear old devil not far off. If we will take the good we find, asking no questions, we shall have heaping measures. The great gifts are not got by analysis. Everything good is on the highway. The middle region of our being is the temperate zone. We may climb into the thin and cold realm of our geometry and lifeless science, or sink into that of sensation. Between these extremes is the equator of life, of thought, of poetry,—a narrow belt. . . . A collector peeps into all the picture shops of Europe . . . but the Transfiguration, the Last Judgment . . . are on the walls of the Uffizi, or the Louvre, where every footman may see them, to say nothing of nature's pictures in every street, of sunrises . . . every day. (W 3:62–63)

Its mixed metaphors, its hopping from one analogy to another without much development of any of them or explicit connection between them, belie that affirmation Emerson so desperately wants. He leaves it to us either to create the connections or to discover that they are not really being made. Thus there seems to be a subtext of another human drama going on in "Experience": a person's inability to react with enough passion, enough rage of grief, or the failure of ideas and knowledge to seal out pain; his finding out, in other words, that pain does exist, and is real—these are the sources of disillusion and feelings of inadequacy. Job never lost his faith, but he certainly gave in to rage and argument. (Robert Frost, we remember, called himself an Old Testament Christian and wrote his own *Job*.) Emerson's life shows that he has managed the conflict, even if he has never resolved it, his writings and the act of writing them surely helping him to convince himself of the truth of what they were saying. He seemed to be able to find a way to deal with painful experience, but I do not believe he was able to deny its reality.

Whicher finds the tragedy in Emerson to be the chasm between what Heaven showed and what it gave—the hunger of desire left unsatisfied, a tragedy of incapacity, where five out of seven Lords of Life are weaknesses, but Whicher finds a quality of affirmation in the essay which we should be able to find if we sense the tension between faith and experience. He locates Emerson as teetering on the brink of the drop that could lead to despair while hoping for some sort of all-or-nothing assurance. Can tragedy *be* absence, though, or must it be a human drama of presence and action? Tragedy as chasm, and incapacity as the closest we come to defining what is tragic, is very like the view that our century is not capable of tragedy or heroism. Can a tragedy be a chasm, or a hero remain teetering at the edge of the pit? Whicher finds this to be a position that honest twentieth-century writers cannot hold: they start in the pit. He goes on to say that great literature requires us to break with extremist

Emersonian patterns and "find some means to face this world without either transcendence or despair."

Emerson's philosophic system worked against a genuine tragic sense; he suffered tragedy without being willing to grapple with it or with the suffering—often inexplicable—that it caused, seeming, in fact, to lack the requisite passions and the requisite acknowledgment of their power and importance. Thoreau was able to throw himself into experience, at least in nature, with passionate intensity; yet with all his vibrant sensuality, we find no evidence that other human beings were ever the objects of those passions or engaged with him in any significant way as part of his experiences; and without human conflict and suffering, there can be no tragedy. We find in Thoreau no hint of sexuality either. In Frost we find the stuff of tragic passion, conflict, and suffering; we find sensual appreciation of outdoor nature and the nature of human sexuality; we find the agonizing human questions of Emerson's "Experience," the acute sensual engagement with experience, and the capacity to rage. The combination was not always a pretty sight.

These differences between Frost's tragic sense and the lack of it in Thoreau, the failure of it in Emerson, can certainly be related to their various stances as "readers" and as writers: Frost, with his passionate nature and tragic sense, feared engagement even as he knew how unavoidable it was; he therefore had to protect himself from losing himself or becoming eroded, and he had to protect his writing. He was very conscious of the need to keep the obviously confessional and personal out of his poetry. In feeling himself more "involvable," he needed to maintain distance, and he did so in the poetry by means of irony, humor, and the use of other dramatic personae and speakers both close and far from himself. Emerson, who, in his reading, was far less apt to become reconstructed by his texts, who spoke as one far less vulnerable, paradoxically suffered from that very invulnerability. As we shall see in examining some of his texts, especially "Experience," more closely, he was painfully conscious of his inability to come close enough to people and to experience. Emerson exhorts us not only to look, think, and analogize but to live and to do. "Nature hates peeping" (W 3:59); "Man lives by the pulses" (W 3:68). Still, we are told that "all the facts of nature, of animal economy—sex, nutriment, gestation, birth, growth—are symbols of the passage of the world into the soul of man, to suffer there a change, and reappear a new and higher fact. . . . the poet . . . does not stop at [facts such as astronomy or chemistry], but employs them as signs" (W 3:21). Emerson tells us that even birth and death are emblems (W 3:20).

In juxtaposing these quotations from Emerson, we are able to see a fundamental conflict common to Emerson and Frost: what happens to the value of fact, experience, the real, when these are subordinated to their value as symbols, as vehicles of thought, or even as teachers? In Emerson, how do thought and idea weigh in the balance with material fact and experience? This seems to me the unresolved conflict of "Experience." We sense in Frost, on the other hand, a greater love for those real things in nature, more immediate and passionate engagement with the feelings and things of this world. More personally engaged with them, his conflict is not deciding whether they are real but how to live with their powerful reality—how to bear it and control it. As an artist, he seemed far less apt—or content—to maintain the separateness of analogy. But while Frost was never the idealist that Emerson was,[18] he always still had to balance his love of facts for their own sake, nature as actually experienced with what he was doing with those facts: the conflict between poetry that arises from what facts do to you and his knowledge that often he was doing the doing and using facts and the natural world. Emerson tells us "passion adds eyes; is a magnifying glass" (W 8:10), betraying his view of passion as additive and intensifying but not fundamental and inevitable, not essentially part of reality itself.

Seeing where Emerson places passion and fact in the scheme of his reality helps us to understand better the difficulties he had when they refused to remain subordinate to ideas, refused to behave in orderly fashion when they moved from his mind to his pulses. Montaigne, he tells us, "likes pain because it makes him feel himself, as we pinch ourselves to know we are awake" (W 4:169). We can only assume that if he so admires Montaigne, and quotes him without refuting such existence-validating experience, that it could be important to Emerson, too. It seems to assume more importance still when we see that Emerson is not exactly quoting Montaigne, for Montaigne spoke of different reasons for valuing pain.[19] Emerson, however, goes on to other thoughts and never really closes on the matter.

What seems apparent is that this very division of reality into idea and direct, physical sensation has the potential to cause him great difficulty when the pain is not physical. To come close to the Emerson of "Experience" is to ask the question of what Emerson—or anyone—is willing to call real and to see the problems inherent in separating material fact from mind, as if they were totally separable. The Thoreau of "Ktaadn" fears bodies, stands in wonder at "the solid earth [and] contact! contact!" (TS 525). In this regard James was far more useful to Frost. He had very little patience with Emerson at his most facile ideal but, significantly, paid the most serious attention to "Experience."[20] Frost insisted on the venture of the spirit into the material, even though he called it the greatest attempt that ever failed (SP 41). Emerson seemed to have great difficulty with that muddled, often messy, unclassifiable middle ground of emotions which assert their reality intangibly, but nevertheless relentlessly and undeniably. How can we talk about grief if it draws no blood? If we cannot locate a wound to bandage it, can we say we have a wound? Pinches are no help here. Emerson might concede that there never was a philosopher who could endure the toothache, but where in his scheme does a philosopher place the pain he feels at the loss of a son? How, exactly, does one separate the death of that son from the pain of loss, or from the idea of loss?

Emerson finds grief to have been sold cheap: we learn nothing

from it. On the other hand, he tells us that to be introduced into
reality, to be put in contact with it, "we would pay the price of
sons and lovers" (W 3:48). I am not so sure we would, or even
that he would. Frost was accused of having paid such a price
for his art; he professed admiration for Cellini's burning all his
furniture to finish casting the Perseus (LT 338). But furniture
is not sons and lovers, and one would have to be very callous,
indeed, to assume Cellini or Frost or Emerson would say yes to
the bargain were the price to be given in advance. In his essay
on Montaigne, Emerson writes: "Knowledge is the knowing that
we cannot know" (W 4:174), but the Montaigne he so admires
and quotes has written in *his* essay on "Experience": "There is no
desire more natural than the desire for knowledge. We try every
means that would lead us to it. When reason fails us we make
use of experience . . . truth is so great a thing that we ought not
to despise any medium that will conduct us to it."[21] Ironically,
even in the search for truth and knowledge, we are driven by
passion—the passion for "knowing." Montaigne refuses to deny
this passion or any other.

In Emerson's search for Reality, he may be bypassing reality in
the process—admittedly, not an ultimate, Platonic Ideal reality
or Ultimate Truth, but the intangible reality that does indeed
affect our pulses. Which brings us to another question em-
bedded in "Experience": what is the value placed on reality, not
simply as abstraction, but as *experience,* the title of the essay?
Far from devaluing experience, he seems to want more of it.
There has been too little. He does not bleed, and that is the
trouble. What can grief be, what can loss be, if "something that
I fancied was part of me, which could not be torn away without
tearing me, nor enlarged without enriching me, falls off from
me and leaves no scar"? (W 3:49). His disillusion is two-fold:
he has learned nothing, and he is still whole—body and ego are
intact—and he will not call an ache a scar. Obviously, then, the
grief must be only an illusion. Not even something imagined,
but only fancied.[22] That part of him, that "something," then,

could not *really* have fallen off, and the attendant grief, there-fore, cannot but be "shallow . . . [it] plays about the surface and never introduces me to reality." It teaches nothing; life sheds it. "Nothing is left us but death" (W 3:48–49).

Of course, no one alive has experienced death. In the con-text of an essay that cries out for experience, and almost rebels against thought, we are led to conclude that one cannot experi-ence death at second hand. If that is true, and if there is nothing left *but* death, then we are left with nothing—nothing real, that is. This deduction brings us face to face with the position of the Platonic idealist, but then what does one do in the world of experience with the pain of loss? What does one do with the desire to come into contact with the real, with even the thirst for Ideal Knowledge? Even the most profound grief at a death is still only death at second hand. "The nearest [anyone] can go to death, comes so far short / They might as well not try to go at all." It was what Amy in "Home Burial" could not bear, not realizing that the only alternative is death. "But . . . I won't have grief so" (CP 72). Such grief seems also what Emerson cannot come to terms with, although his problem, unlike Amy's, may be excessive calm in the face of grief. One feels that he may have felt more peace had he been raised in a society of breast-beating, hair-tearing wailing at the grave.

In this connection a few entries from his earlier journals are revealing:

> Look next from the history of my intellect to the history of my heart. A blank, my lord. I have not the kind affections of a pigeon. (J 1:134)
>
> What is called a warm heart I have not. (J 2:241)
>
> Sad is this continual postponement of life. (J 5:322)

Remembering his deceased first wife and brothers, he berated himself for his superficial coldness, asking himself why he could not be warm inside and outside as well, as if to acknowledge his capacity to feel but his inadequate capacity to express that feeling or show it (J 5:456). His comment after Waldo's death is also significant both in the context of failure of expressiveness and of the intellect: "Sorrow makes us all children again,— destroys all differences of intellect. The wisest knows nothing" (J 8:165).

If what he is calling reality cannot be found in life, it will require very direct experience to feel alive, and he has told us that nothing speculative or mental can substitute for experience. This must be a genuine conflict for an idealist. It seems that failure to be passionate enough, inability to commit himself completely, physically, emotionally to experience is what renders the experience of grief shallow and ultimately meaningless. If one has not received a treasure in knowledge for so high a price, and one cannot, on the other hand, experience fully with one's whole being, what then is life? Especially if man feels himself to be governed by Lords such as illusion, temperament, reality, dream, subjectiveness, who are propagated and founded out of his own human mind. "Dream delivers us to dream, and there is no end to illusion" (W 3:50). This seems to be an Emersonian version of the life-sapping circle of self. Is this what he means by private fruit? Yet, in other contexts, he expresses satisfaction with that private fruit, with knowledge and thought above experience. It is all very well to be an idealist, to say nothing is real, that all is illusion, but when reality impinges on the Ideal, when it throbs, then we remember Emerson's telling us that Montaigne appreciated pain. Emerson might say—and even believe—that the knowledge that we exist is our Fall (W 3:75); on the other hand, he may acknowledge firmly that experience, and the need for more of it, seems to be in conflict with thought and philosophy, thus creating a difficult conflict indeed. He writes: "Intellectual tasting of life will not supersede muscular activity. If a man should consider the nicety of the passage of a piece of bread down his throat, he would starve . . . do not craze yourself with thinking, but go about your business anywhere. Life is not intellectual or critical, but sturdy" (W 3:58–59). The Lord Temperament, though, has rendered him incapable of living as he advocated.

Thus, as we have noted, in "Experience" Emerson validated for Frost the importance of being able to experience passion, the value of a passionate nature.[23] Frost has in abundance what Emerson calls for but does not find. Frost surely refers to Emerson when he writes in a notebook: "He never knew the pretensions of the unintellectual lords of creation were not absurd—because he was brought up in the New England professor [sic] aristocracy."[24] By contrast, that difficult volcano, Frost, could have felt that even the danger of behaving badly, of losing control, was better than this anguish Emerson cannot quite express over a pain he cannot quite fathom or accept because of inability—philosophically or temperamentally—to reconcile realities whose planes can never meet.

"Life is not dialectics," says Emerson (W 3:58). "Life is that which can mix oil and water . . . all a man's heart is a bursting unity of opposites," said Frost (EY 427). In Emersonian terms, dialectic does not refer to life as it is lived but to philosophical debate, to thought. Emerson here opposes experience, life lived and felt, to dialectic, but to Frost, the dialectic is between forces *in* life and experience, dialectic of the passions. Herein lies the drama of his attempts to reconcile opposites and his failures in the face of the irresolvable—conflicting needs and passions, psychological conflict, physical and emotional pulls and pushes.

Emerson may thus have provided Frost a way of validating the passions in this essay that tries so hard to find the Real in reality, knowledge in experience as well as further proof that one must encounter life out there: whether in the form of other people, nature, or the unwelcome and unfamiliar self. An important validation that would have been, too. Openly, though, Frost has acknowledged his appreciation of Emerson for "supply[ing] the emancipating formula for giving up an attachment for an attraction" (SP 115); yet, when it came to attraction to nature, one does not feel it in Emerson as one does in Thoreau, whose hands get dirty, whose feet get wet, who wants, in fact, to wedge his feet through the mud of reality until he comes to hard rocks (TW 97–98), whose Nature is never mere beauty, or mere shadow; it draws him in, and it excites the sort of passion and poetry that Emerson seems incapable of. Thus it is that Frost spoke of Thoreau as his passion.[25] Thoreau, too, approaches nature as reader and as artist, but he approaches it with all his senses and with his muscles. Still, like Emerson, he keeps remembering his role as analogist, finding correspondences, finding, or needing to insert, his confirmation of a moral order in what he sees, even in the violent and destructive.

> We can never have enough of Nature. . . . We need to wit-
> ness our own limits transgressed, and some life pasturing
> freely where we never wander. We are cheered when we ob-
> serve the vulture feeding on the carrion which disgusts and
> disheartens us and deriving health and strength from the
> repast. . . . [Thoreau then goes on to refer to the dead horse,
> its inconvenient smell; yet the] strong appetite and invio-
> lable health of Nature was compensation for this. I love to
> see that Nature is so rife with life that myriads can be af-
> forded to be sacrificed and suffered to prey on one another;
> that tender organizations can be so serenely squashed out
> of existence like pulp . . . and that sometimes it has rained
> flesh and blood! The impression made on a wise man is that
> of universal innocence. Poison is not poisonous after all, nor
> are any wounds fatal. (TW 318)

We are given ugliness but not *as* ugliness; pain and suffering are simply unacknowledged, and unrelated to analogous human pain and mortality. Natural process is shown to us as exact- ing its price from within nature, but unlike the tone of "Spring Pools," this voice holds nothing accountable; rather, the tone is one of exultation in the life force that is made so evident. That this universal process is part of the glorious scheme, and that compassion cannot be generalized into natural law, excludes the death or suffering of any individual being. While Frost would not have sentimentalized a dead horse either, he would have implied an analogy to process and its price as it also impinges on individual, human life, for he never seemed able to forget *that* in the scheme of the universal. Life was too individual, too dramatic, and therefore so capable of giving rise to tragedy. One remembers that tragedy was a phenomenon born in the individualized West and never took root where life was seen as part of the whole, the timeless and universal, as in the philosophies of the East. Keats made the distinction in his "Ode to a Nightingale" between the generic immortality of a bird and the always individual, suffering mortality of a human being, and in this Frost more resembled Keats.

Frost would have sympathized with "work[ing] in fields if only for the sake of tropes and expression, to serve a parable-maker one day" (TW 162), and he certainly would have felt, as Thoreau did, that "it is something to be able to paint a particular picture, or to carve a statue, and so to make a few objects beautiful." But he would not have continued to Thoreau's conclusion: "But it is far more glorious to carve and paint the very atmosphere and medium through which we look, which *morally* we can do, to affect the quality of the day, that is the highest of arts" (TW 90, emphasis mine). At least we never get the moral relationship overtly expressed, or even ratified, in Frost. Nor does Frost ever conclude his encomia to nature in this manner: "What a delicious sound! It is not merely crow calling to crow, for it speaks to me too. I am part of one great creature with him. If he has voice, I have ears. . . . Ah, bless the Lord, O my soul! bless Him for wildness, for crows that will not alight within gunshot! and bless Him for hens, too, that croak and cackle in the yard! (TJ 7:112–13), nor by saying: "There needs no stronger proof of immortality" (TW 317). Frost's strong are saying nothing.

Frost would "read" the crow for its blackness, as in "Dust of

Snow," or for its wildness although he may have been less ready
to bless God for what was so mixed a blessing to Frost, that wildness at once so inviting and inspiring, yet so threatening. We
need only contrast Thoreau's fact cum exaltation presentation
of "rawness" with Frost's to see where there is guilt and fear:

> Do or say my dambdest [sic] I can't be other than ortho-
> dox in politics love and religion: I can't escape salvation. . . .
> And I try not to think of it as often as I can. . . . The con-
> viction closes in on me that I was cast for gloom. . . . I have
> heard laughter by daylight when I thought it was my own
> because at that moment when it broke I had parted my lips
> to take food. *Just so I have been afraid of myself* and caught
> at my throat when I thought I was making some terrible
> din of a mill whistle that happened to come on the same
> instant with the opening of my mouth to yawn. But I have
> not laughed. . . . *I have neighed at night in the woods* behind
> the house like vampires. But there are no vampires, there
> are no ghouls, there are no demons, *there is nothing but me.*
> And I have all the dead New England Things *held back* by
> one hand *as by a dam in the long deep wooded* valley of Whip-
> poorwhill. . . . I hold them easily—too easily for assurance
> that *they will go with a rush when I let them go.* (Frost, SL
> 221, emphasis mine)

Compare Thoreau's view: "I was also serenaded by a hooting owl [by means of which Nature seems] to stereotype and
make permanent the dying moans of a human being—some
poor weak relic of mortality who has left hope behind, and
howls like an animal, yet with human sobs. . . . It reminds me
of ghouls and idiots and insane howlings. . . . I rejoice that there
are owls. Let them do the idiotic and maniacal hooting for men"
(TW 125).[26] Thoreau's displacement of our fears and insanities
was surely welcome to Frost, but Frost seems less sure that the
owls can do it for us, more afraid that we may begin hooting like
them. In another reference to wildness and its effect on sanity,

Frost wrote: "Very few people that leave the good old folkways can keep from getting all mixed up in the mind. We can make raids and excursions into the wild, but it has to be from well kept strongholds" (LU 193).

To cite another example, Thoreau is far more accepting of his propensity to wildness:

> I grow savager and savager every day, as if fed on raw meat, and my tameness is only the repose of untamableness. I dream of looking abroad summer and winter, with free gaze, from some mountain side, while my eyes revolve in an egyptian slime of health,—I to be nature looking into nature with such easy sympathy as the blue-eyed grass in the meadow looks in the face of the sky.[27]

> [He writes of] a wildness whose glance no civilization can endure,—wild as if we lived on the marrow of antelopes devoured raw. (TJ 2:171)

> I caught a glimpse of a woodchuck stealing across my path, and felt a strange thrill of savage delight, and was strongly tempted to seize and devour him raw; not that I was hungry then, except for that wildness which he represented. (TW 210)

Perhaps because Thoreau can also say, "I found in myself, and still find, an instinct higher, or as it is named, spiritual life, as do most men, and another toward a primitive rank and savage one, and I reverence them both," he can more easily acknowledge that savage thrill. He can wish sometimes to "spend [his] day more as the animals do" because he has more confidence—or says he does—in that "higher law" (TW 210). True, the animal in us "which awakens in proportion as our higher nature slumbers . . . is reptile and sensual, and perhaps cannot be wholly expelled" (TW 219). But then the proportion can change in the other direction. McIntosh writes that Thoreau used "wildness" in various ways, its meaning changing. It was also fecund—a rich source to inspire literature and religion; gentled, humanely and properly guarded, it turns into good, and nature turns into spirit.[28] Frost would also see that fecundity as nourishing, wild freedom and chaos as necessary to inspiration, but he seems to stay more afraid, perhaps because more driven by his passions than was Thoreau, or more fearful of losing control of them, or perhaps because, like Goethe, he includes sexual love in his view of Nature[29] and insanity in his view of wildness. He needs to keep the sash in place.

For more profoundly than either Wordsworth or Emerson acknowledge in their writing, Frost, like Thoreau, understands that we are *of* nature as well and that the forces of nature do not just oppose us or lure us from without, but they drive us from within.[30] Thoreau writes: "Shall I not have intelligence with the earth? Am I not partly leaves and vegetable mould myself?" (TW 98). He also shows us the boy whose woodchuck cap represents the complex combination of man using nature, even in its wildness, toward his domestic ends, the combination of innocence and bloodshed, "the human parents' care of their young in these hard times," and that unforgettable image of the boy's head in the woodchuck's belly (TJ 13:166). We are reminded of Thoreau imagining his own head as an organ for burrowing in the earth (TW 98). There are no tigers in Thoreau's woods, and so he does not use tiger imagery, as does Emerson when he reminds us that the snap of the tiger is part of the system—our system (W 6:7). Thoreau uses woodchucks because he has skinned real woodchucks, smelled and seen real dead horse feeding its guests.

One can believe Thoreau because in the midst of extolling solitude and the wildlife surrounding him, he can say: "But once . . . for an hour, I doubted if the near neighborhood of man was not essential to a serene and healthy life" (TW 131). And because he recognizes the excitement and attraction of the wild, even as he does our need to keep it in its place: "Our village life would stagnate if it were not for the unexplored forests and meadows which surround it. We need the tonic of *wildness* . . . at the same time that we are earnest to explore and learn all things, we require that all things be *mysterious* and unexplorable, that land and sea be infinitely wild, unsurveyed and unfathomed by us because *unfathomable*" (which can also remind us of "Neither Out Far nor in Deep") (TW 317–18, emphasis mine).

He has the courage to say: "I love the wild not less than the good" (TW 210). We cannot picture Emerson saying this. Frost does but fears it. Thoreau says it with no apologies—another example of his joy in the real, the factual, even at its most incorrigible, combined with his unconcern with (or backing off from) the implications that Frost attaches to these realities. Frost fears that he will be too drawn in or too closed out. He needs to fill the cup to the brim, past the brim, but without spilling a drop— an exacting and precarious balance.

Thoreau also writes of his willingness to be lost: "Not till we are completely lost, or turned round . . . do we appreciate the vastness and strangeness of nature . . . do we begin to find ourselves, and realize where we are and the infinite extent of our relations" (TW 171).[31] McIntosh points out that in such situations we may not know where we are but that, in the possibilities inherent in such willingness, Thoreau goes beyond Emerson in dramatizing over and over the loss and recovery of the self in nature and the open-ended discovery this allows (301). We have only to remember the ambivalence in "Into My Own" to understand how akin Frost was to Thoreau's wishes, yet how fearful he was of enacting them. It will not be until "Directive," and a very different kind of getting lost, that we sense willingness to go it alone on the journey, and then it is not quite alone.

Still, as we have seen, Thoreau, with all his sensuality, "fear[s] bodies"; his dramas lack human conflict and passion. Emerson has experienced human love and tragedy but, as he complains, not feelingly enough. He tries too hard to find resolution where life simply does not supply it. For example, having painted an admiring and engaging portrait of Montaigne—the man and his skeptical stance—Emerson concludes with a series of up-beat exhortations ("Let a man [him] learn" three times in a few lines) and a fine moral that simply has not been sufficiently earned (W 4:186). No pat conclusion he draws has the force of what almost immediately precedes it:

> Young and ardent minds . . . accuse the divine providence of a certain parsimony. It has shown the heaven and earth to every child, and filled him with a desire for the whole; a desire raging, infinite; a hunger as of space to be filled with planets; a cry of famine, as of devils for souls. Then for the satisfaction,—to each man is administered a single drop, a bead of dew of vital power, *per day*,—a cup as large as space, and one drop of water in it. . . . In every house . . . heart . . . soul this chasm is found,—between the largest promise of ideal power, and the shabby experience." (W 4:184–85)

Even though the subject is a generalized power, or thirst for understanding, power could also be referring to The Power; furthermore, no matter what else is being expressed by means of the hunger metaphor, that haunting image of famine remains and overpowers any facile generalization that follows. In a superb metaphor of his own, Parini has said of Frost that he is "deflating the Emersonian balloon but not relinquishing the string."[32] In the essays under discussion, we could almost say the same of Emerson. It might have seemed more true to himself to have said the strong are saying nothing; even if the secret sits in the middle and knows, men sit in a ring and suppose, only suppose.

"Too Platonic about evil," Frost said of Emerson (SP 118), suggesting with respect to the line "unit and universe are round" that "ideally in thought only is a circle round. In practice, in nature, the circle becomes an oval. As a circle it has one center—Good. As an oval it has two centers—Good and Evil" (SP 118). As a poet, he would have subscribed to the encouragement to "Build . . . your own world" (W 1:76), but he also knew that there is always something—sometimes mysterious, sometimes obvious, sometimes outside us and sometimes within—that does not leave a stone on stone. Nor would Frost have believed nature to be simply the metaphor of the human mind. It is far too powerful, its facts too pressing and real to be only symbol. Yes, the poet reattaches, organizes, and finds meaning, but if he "disposes very easily of the most disagreeable facts" (W 3:18–19), how can we trust him? What Frost seemed most to value in Emerson, according to his remarks "On Emerson," was the Emerson who admired the visceral language of the "rude" he wrote of in "Monadnock" and of Montaigne: "Cut these sentences and they bleed" (SP 112–13), and the Emerson who left "dark sayings [one] must leave the clearing of to time" (SP 114)—an Emerson who left dark gaps he himself seemed not to be aware of. Those gaps that attracted Frost to Emerson are the sort that attract us to Frost. Frost teaches us how better to read Emerson, because in *his* poetic "readings" he went one better.

As a see-er, as a reader, and as a writer, Frost shows himself to be the pupil who has learned a great deal from his master and then goes further, pushing ahead by recognizing, and more fully exploiting what the Master was just beginning to imply. One example is metaphor: Emerson's *Nature* must have been a great influence on Frost. What Emerson says in *Nature* about unpoetic savants, about science and poetry (W 1:66), shows up in "Education by Poetry," but in that same essay Frost goes on to show how metaphor breaks down. One can reverse the process and read Emerson back from "Education by Poetry," observing that Emerson's method of elaborating by means of brilliant and effective metaphors—adding another, or hopping from one to the next, while dazzling us with their brilliance—must break down. We will see this if, as Frost advises, we have been "properly educated in metaphor."

While Thoreau also feels the need to draw moral lessons from his observations in nature, as McIntosh points out, he goes back and forth among contradictions, giving both sides expression even though he retains idealism at the core of his work.[33] McIntosh finds polarities left open and unreconciled in Thoreau (36) and suggests that he used them to provide "a structure for his self-presentations without the simplemindedness of straightforward argument or the factual distortion of fiction" (45).

Such polarities are the very stuff of Frost's work: dualism, formulae that do not quite formulate, facts with no conclusions drawn. Correspondences will be what the reader finds or creates. "The Onset" presents a speaker whose confident tone is undermined by his imagery; designs are not simply imperfect but deadly. Facts are presented, and we either see the ironies or we do not; maybe there are none, and the doubts are all on our side. Morals are not drawn for us, or, if they are, we ask who is drawing them. It is not that Frost is some sort of lapsed or diminished Emerson, a falling off from Emersonian greatness as Waggoner seems to imply.[34] He pushes farther what Emerson implies but tries to deny and what Thoreau tries still to imagine possible. Frost at his best shows, dramatizes as one can only when human protagonists and human emotions are engaged, but does not attempt to solve.

What places Frost more squarely in this century is his dramatizing, not only by means of his situations, but his poetic method, the impossibility of closure and resolution.[35] Openings that will not or cannot close, whether in the sureness with which one can interpret a text, the clear correspondence of a metaphor to its referent or "significance," or the inconsistencies in an observation of nature, create the sorts of "gaps" that, as we have already observed, draw us in. Readers are thus drawn into texts and poets into nature and experience, not necessarily to find the ultimate solutions, or even to close the gaps, but to find in that space ways of seeing possibilities, ways, even, of entering them and emerging with some greater understanding of ourselves as readers. And Frost did this, too, as he "read" nature.

Frost as reader combines in very important ways the New

England tradition with the views of reading discussed earlier. Both Emerson and Thoreau validated his seeing nature as a text to be read and helped him learn how to do it; they validated the process of finding analogies between nature—the world of fact and experience—and the questions that only humans can pose. They helped him see the importance in all thinking, as Frost was to say in "Education by Poetry," of "putting this and that together." But they stopped short, at least in their writing, of that narcissistic posture, of relating their very personal fears or needs as terms in that analogy. Frost did so, and to read by appropriating the text, by identifying with it, is to be at once more deeply attracted to what one encounters, to feel more threatened by what it will reveal or how it may break down the boundaries between the perceiving self and the object so closely identified with it. The trancelike state that reading theorists describe [36] is delicious escape, but one can fear it. And is not the fear cum attraction in "Stopping by Woods" a perfect description of beauty that induces a trancelike state from which the speaker is rescued (if indeed he is) by that practical, home-bound nonhuman, the horse? Even in the distance that obtains in analogy, the Frostian speaker sees decay and death in analogies to natural process. How much more attractive and threatening are those situations in which he goes beyond analogy, toward identification and identity.

What saves Frost as a poet, and very often his speakers, is that distancing that Wimmers reminds us of: in Frost's case, the distance of irony, humor, and the diffusion as well as catharsis in creating a variety of personae. Most important is the act of creating—making—as the surest means of controlling visions and analogies, or participating in process.

In subsequent chapters we will focus on poems of encounters both with the nonhuman world of nature and the human one of relationships, of encountering nature within us. In the following chapter we will explore various stances toward nature in the poetry—as Other, as analogous, as dangerously us—and that in nature which demonstrates a saving creativity.

5

Nature and Poetry

Encounters with nature, of course, are not always contemplative or symbolic. In "Storm Fear" the person encountering nature is not just fearing what it may represent, nor reading the storm for its significance; rather he expresses genuine fear of annihilation prompted by actual circumstances—a nature unleashing dangerous and untamed forces that have the power to destroy him and that, consequently, dramatize his helplessness and render him subdued and fearful.

When the wind works against us in the dark,
And pelts with snow
The lower chamber window on the east,
And whispers with a sort of stifled bark,
The beast,
'Come out! Come out!'—
It costs no inward struggle not to go,
Ah, no!
I count our strength,
Two and a child,
Those of us not asleep subdued to mark
How the cold creeps as the fire dies at length,—
How drifts are piled,
Dooryard and road ungraded,

Till even the comforting barn grows far away,
And my heart owns a doubt
Whether 'tis in us to arise with day
And save ourselves unaided. (CP 13)

This is a nature hostile to human beings which pursues them even into the fortresses they have built against it. Just as Frost's poems of nature's indifference prove to be less concerned with nature and more with a person's unsatisfied needs, so this poem is more concerned with a person's fears—fear of annihilation, of the cold and dark, of his own helplessness and his own isolation. Even though the danger is real enough, it is the speaker who has turned an unthinking storm into a malevolent beast, "working against" him in the dark. It whispers, barks, and creeps. The "pelting" snow adds to the visual image of the beast that even doors and windows cannot shut out, for as the fire dies out, the cold advances inside. The strengths of the house as physical protection against the cold, and home as spiritual protection— two and a child, love and family—seem increasingly inadequate. The fear is one that antedates buildings and institutions. We are in the grip of a primitive, elemental fear—back in a world in which fire gave temporary security against the cold and the dark and frightened away the beasts—until it went out.

We have, then, the solid strength of the man-made and the strength of human love and companionship against the wild strength of the storm. But as the snow obliterates gradations and distinctions, it makes all other buildings, and by implication all the rest of humanity, seem farther and farther away. Piling drifts spin a cocoon from which the family will draw no comfort, for this is not an isolation that protects and shuts out evil. This is being shut in with the enemy, isolated from anyone who can help in the battle. Eventually the speaker doubts whether it is in them to arise with day and save themselves unaided. In one sense the fear is very real: it is possible that they will not survive the night; it is because of this that they remain awake, mark how the cold creeps, and, for this reason, feel subdued by it. In another sense, the fear is hypothetical and points to the fact that a person—even one who is not alone—still needs more: perhaps society, perhaps God, perhaps a benevolent nature, to save him from nights like this.[1]

Such storms are a fact of life, especially life lived close to nature and far from town and neighbors. What is imagined and projected, however, is enmity on the part of a nature that does not seek to destroy any more than it seeks to invite. The storm is as unaware of the speaker as is the spider in "Range Finding." It is the person who supplies intent as a reflection of his own feelings.

Intent or awareness notwithstanding, it is the person who has his life at stake and needs, therefore, to retreat to his fortress and barricade it as well as he can. In "Spring Pools," on the other hand, it is the human speaker and, behind him, human experience and knowledge that makes the poem something more than a simple description of a natural scene:

These pools that, though in forests, still reflect
The total sky almost without defect,
And like the flowers beside them, chill and shiver,
Will like the flowers beside them soon be gone,
And yet not out by any brook or river,
But up by roots to bring dark foliage on.

The trees that have it in their pent-up buds
To darken nature and be summer woods—
Let them think twice before they use their powers
To blot out and drink up and sweep away
These flowery waters and these watery flowers
From snow that melted only yesterday. (CP 303)

What to the casual observer might be a scene of tranquil and delicate beauty—spring pools reflecting sky and flowers— becomes in this poem a struggle without struggle, a devouring of the weak by the strong, the process and development of the mighty at the expense of the fragile. The first line, with its qualifying "though in forests" and "still," signals the transitoriness of what will follow. Only now, when snow has melted and trees are still bare, can a forest pool reflect the sky. In reflecting the flowers, the pools become one with the flowers—they share with them the "chill and shiver" and share with them the source of their pending annihilation. Watery flowers and flowery waters seem interchangeable, as do substance and reflection.[2] Since they look the same at the present moment and will also share the same future, it is not the distinction between substance and reflections which determines what is real. Rather it is the distinction between the present scene and its future which determines "reality." The statement of the first stanza, which is the statement of the poem—the substance, is simply: "These pools . . . will . . . soon be gone." Everything else in the poem is a further reflection upon this. We are shown the beauty of the present and consequently the price that the future exacts, and this is the "reality" of the scene. But it is a reality that is perceived by the human speaker because of his awareness of the meaning of cyclical process; it is not a "reality" that the scene itself conveys.

It is the warning tone of the second stanza which makes this distinction between scene and speaker's view of the scene absolutely clear. The sentence is a strange one: "The trees . . . let them think twice before they use their powers." It is almost as if he began to speak about the trees and ended up exhorting them.[3] It is at this point that the metrics show a pronounced irregularity. Line 9 is the only one that begins with a stressed syllable. It seems to emphasize that giveaway, the use of the pathetic fallacy—let the trees think. The man who wrote "Range-Finding," "Come In," and "The Need of Being Versed in Country Things" is not the man to commit it. This use of the pathetic fallacy surely underlines for us that it is the human observer who erroneously attributes thought and intent to these trees. We are witnessing a play within a play wherein nature plays out its drama of the fragile against the mighty; but we are witnessing still another drama—a person's "dialogue" with nature, or rather, as we can see it, a monologue with a nature that neither listens nor answers.

The process under discussion is certainly "natural": winter snows melt into spring pools, which nourish spring flowers; sap will rise in the trees, utilizing all the moisture its roots can carry up toward trunk and then toward leaf, until the forest is green. The scene of the poem is, after all, still at the stage of bare trees. We normally look forward to leaves budding and opening; yet in this poem the trees seem sinister, menacing, and destructive. They "have it in their pent-up buds" to harm the pools. We usually think of the destructiveness of pent-up fury, for example, but what is actually pent up in the bud is the compressed flower or leaf, the potential beauty. To "have it in them" implies unleashed strength: they will "darken nature." We normally think of foliation as beautifying nature, not harming it. Neither do we think of trees as "using powers," here to blot out, drink up, and sweep away—again, greedy and destructive, and appropriately expressed in angry spondees.[4] In another uniting of pools and flowers, we are told that the water will not go out "by any brook or river"—in other words, to enlarge its own medium. It will be *used* and used in the transformation to something else. The method of its annihilation will be "up by roots," a term that brings to mind the uprooting of a flower. But in this context, it is the water that will be "up by roots"—the roots of the trees which will drink it. This poem, incidentally, is an excellent example of the way sound can function to reinforce content: the first stanza in particular is filled with the liquid "l" sound, which appears, appropriately, not in "brook" or "river," but in "foliage."

Yet if the process is indeed "natural," if we do want those trees to be leafy in summer, we wonder why they are made to seem so sinister. The answer, once again, lies in the fact that the human observer brings something of himself to the scene, that what is natural process in an uncomprehending natural universe is process at a price to the comprehending human being. Because he is human and aware, he will see implications in natural process which threaten him; because he fears death himself, he fears those trees in a way the flowers have not the wit to do.

Thus while the poem is about spring pools, fragile flowers, and foliation, it is also about a person's fear of nonbeing, his own destruction in the process of ongoing life. It shows a thinking human incapable of seeing the present without envisioning the future as well. As in "Acceptance," we are shown the difference between wishing that "the dark night be too dark . . . to see into the future" and acknowledging our human inability to ignore the future and our fear of it. In "Spring Pools" we have one person's view of a scene—his own distortion (nowhere, for example, are we told that the pools reflected branches as well), the perspective he alone brings to it. Still, he seems to be representing a human view of natural process, man the analogist, as Emerson would tell us, finding in nature the lessons we can apply to our own vulnerability in the face of process; and the poem, in leaving even such analogy implicit, also leaves more for the reader of the poem to do.

"The Drumlin Woodchuck" is at once more simple and more personal: simple, in its explicit analogy; personal in that a very individualized voice speaks of his own personal need, and thus we move from nature representing larger philosophical or cosmic concerns to something specific in nature which illustrates a personal, psychological one. Certainly not one of Frost's complex poems, its very simplicity, its clear-cut analogy, helps us to understand the more complex Frost of unspecified or multiple referents. As we have noted, clear-cut analogy is the easiest and most comfortable relationship we can find with nature. To choose a point, or limited points, of comparison with an object in nature and to ignore all the other possibilities that are inherent in close identification is to keep a comfortable emotional distance. While the poem explains much, its tone remains light and jocular. What could have been made of the sinister psychological possibilities of subterranean retreat, for example, is simply not present in this poem. A woodchuck is no threat; here, it is not even a temptation to wildness as it was for Thoreau. The short rhyming couplets reinforce the patness and easiness of the emotional position.

More explicitly tied to personal emotion are poems in which the speaker finds analogies with nature because of his mood or his state of mind. Some aspect of nature corresponds with what he is feeling at the time, and for the moment he makes the connection between mood and nature. In "Bereft" the mood of the speaker affects his view of wind and wind-blown leaves.[5] Although there is far less actual danger in the situation of this poem than there is in "Storm Fear," the malevolence is even more pronounced. His aloneness and his grief cause him to see himself as a natural target for a sinister wind that roars animal-like, and for snakelike hostile leaves.

The motive he projects on the wind and the leaves is a projection *because* of his mood, not *of* his mood.[6] It is a temporary mood—one that is occasioned by a desertion, a being left alone. While his emotions are engaged, the speaker is clearly separate from those leaves. He feels no lasting affinity with them.

When we see leaves or trees, however, become more closely identified with more fundamental, more on-going traits, fears, or needs of the speaker, we lose the distance and separateness of clearly drawn analogy. It becomes more difficult to pinpoint the exact element in nature that corresponds to a precise element in the person. In a more open-ended way the leaves and trees are shown akin to the speaker in such nonspecifics as "darkness" or "dream"; in such nonleaflike gestures as flight or wanderlust, the fears that these trees express are lasting and fundamental to the speaker.

There is no specific comparison or identification made between the hill wife and the tree in "The Oft-repeated Dream." As in "Bereft," sinister motivation is projected onto the tree, yet we feel a connection between person and tree in this poem which we do not feel in "Bereft":

> She had no saying dark enough
>   For the dark pine that kept
> Forever trying the window-latch
>   Of the room where they slept.
>
> The tireless but ineffectual hands
>   That with every futile pass
> Made the great tree seem as a little bird
>   Before the mystery of glass!
>
> It never had been inside the room,
>   And only one of the two
> Was afraid in an oft-repeated dream
>   Of what the tree might do. (CP 161)

Perhaps because the hill wife seems obsessed, perhaps because the experience is "oft-repeated," because it comes out in nightmare, we feel a genuine, lasting fear in this poem. That "dark" modifies something for which she did not have the words, and then also modifies "pine," adds dimensions to the darkness of the pine which go beyond color and light.[7] Not only is nonliteral darkness established, but a connection between that darkness she cannot express and that tree. The hill wife does not reach the level of perception that the speaker in "Afterflakes" does as he poses the possibility that the darkness is in him; she does not relate the tree to her "darker mood" as does the speaker in "Leaves Compared with Flowers." She is only bothered by the tree, and by her inability to verbalize its motions and its darkness.

Once the nonphysical is attributed to the tree, so can voluntary, purposive motion be: it tries the window latch with its "hands"; therefore it is to be feared for what it might do.[8] The hill wife feels herself pursued by the tree (we could label the fear paranoid); yet to be pursued by a tree is tantamount to being pursued, victimized by one's own fears, one's own darkness, and thus, while there is no overt comparison made, we feel that somehow that tree has become, in its darkness and its persistent tapping on the window, a representation, or an extension of, something dark and urgent in the hill wife. The identification between them seems borne out by the phrase "only one of the two."

The immediate antecedents of "two" are the "one" who is afraid and "it," the tree. Thus we could assume that "two" refers to the hill wife and the tree. Since, however, there is a reference in stanza one to the fact that she is not alone in the bed ("the room where they slept"), "two" seems also to refer to the two in the bed, and read this way, it is the husband who is unafraid. So easy is it to miss the reference to him that we can only deduce he is not in any sense a help in the drama that is taking place between his wife and the tree. Probably unaware of it, probably asleep, he does not help her to "find a saying" for it; in his unawareness of her need, he leaves her alone with her fear. Neither is his physical presence any company, the opposite of the situation in "The Dream Pang," wherein the dreamer's anxiety is resolved solely because of the physical presence of his wife in their bed. One could, on the contrary, see sexuality as a source of the anxiety.[9]

The tapping of the branches is ineffectual and even seems birdlike before the "mystery of glass." In this poem, as in "Tree at My Window" and "Now Close the Windows," it is a window that provides a necessary barrier between person and nature, but here glass is called mysterious, probably because it creates the illusion of accessibility. One can only see through it, not reach through it. It also acts as a lens—a way to see and "read" the natural object without allowing complete (and frightening) entanglement with what is seen. It reminds the viewer that the identification is both made possible and controlled by means of that lens. In "The Oft-repeated Dream" one can as easily attribute to the tree the power to see as the power to manipulate the window latch, the power to "do." Therefore she feels exposed to the tree even though she is protected by glass, for glass is both transparent and fragile.

In "Tree at My Window" the speaker makes a distinction between window sash and curtain—he will lower the sash as it grows dark, but he insists that no curtain be drawn between himself and the tree.[10] While he is cautious about projecting human vision onto the tree ("*if* you have seen me when I slept"), he feels that he and the tree have their "heads together." While he goes on to show how he and the tree are different, it seems that those differences are complementary, a necessary balance to him. Therefore between what he sees as similar and what he sees as complementary, he needs the sight of that tree enough to say, "But let there never be curtain drawn / Between you and me." Both of them are "taken" and pushed about by "weather." Both use their "tongues" to articulate their condition. Thus the tree, in one sense, externalizes and represents what is of major concern to the poet—dreaming, articulating, and being tossed by some force more powerful than tree or person. At the same time, the tree is so refreshingly external, so unselfconsciously physical. Its dream-head does not create dreams. Rather it is lifted out of the earth by the force and growth of nature. It seems dreamlike by virtue of its diffuseness and its looseness, not its subconscious mental activity. Its leaves seem to talk but cannot be profound.[11] The tree has height, but the man has depth. Likewise the tree's concern is only with outer weather, for only man can suffer "the tempest in [the] mind." The tree at the window becomes the window tree—part of the man's home, though safely outside it.

In these poems, and also, for example, "Misgiving" and "The Wind and the Rain," Frost has shown the human protagonist identifying in some way with the trees, feeling somehow related to them because of mood, emotion, fear, or desires that are being projected onto the trees, creating relationships that are more than analogy, that approach an expression of identity. "Leaves Compared with Flowers" explores a more complex association of trees with various stages and needs in human life and a progression, within the poem, to a closer and closer identification with the natural object. The poem moves from valuing and pursuing objects "out there" in nature toward recognizing affinity with objects in the natural world. The speaker does not deny the value of flowers. Nowhere does he say that leaves and bark *are* enough, only that they *may* be. He shows the same tentativeness about his own feelings and values: "I *may* be one who does not care." If one does not concern oneself with the particulars of beauty, with visual aspects such as color, shape, and form—or with perfume—if one is satisfied with a tactile discrimination that only distinguishes between smooth and rough, not concerning oneself with softness, for example, one may find leaves and bark enough. If one does not care about bearing, and prefers not to have the additional burdens of concern with yield,[12] then one will find reasons to be satisfied with leaves and bark.

There are three basic contrasts in this poem, the most obvious one introduced in the title: leaves as opposed to flowers. Related to this contrast are the contrasts between "once" as opposed to "now," "late in life" and its implied opposite, earlier in life; then there is night as opposed to day, dark as opposed to light. Flowers, then, are associated with youth ("petals I may have once pursued") and the light of day. Leaves, on the other hand, are preferred at night, and *seem* to be preferred at this time of life. It is never really so stated, and an examination of the last lines shows that the speaker does not end with leaves and flowers in exact opposition. Before he may have *pursued* flowers; now leaves *are* his darker mood. The first real difference between the two clauses lies between pursuing and being; the second between a subject/object relationship (I pursued petals) and a predicate nominative, renaming, therefore an identity relationship (leaves are my mood). To pursue is to go after something outside, removed from self. To be is to remain with self. Pursuit

of anything is no defense against, or escape from, what is within;
Frost has stated his recognition of this fact, but it is not a part
of this poem. One can see in it, however, the difference between
the need to *pursue* (the object in this case remaining extraneous,
apart from the self) and the need to *identify* with something
outside the self (in this case the object becoming related to the
self), especially if the object seems to express what is within.
The relationship then becomes a confrontation with self rather
than an attempt to escape self in the pursuit of something outside and unrelated to self. The confrontation now seems part of
the greater maturity, part of the spirit of resignation to realities that we noted in the preference for leaves. It illustrates once
again that the way the natural object is "read" has everything
to do with what the "reader" brings to the encounter, what he
needs to see or sort out, or express.[13]

Whatever we have said of trees, whatever attraction, identification, fear, and invitation are associated with them, can simply
be multiplied in woods, which are, after all, composed of trees.
There is still another dimension to woods: not simply a multiplication of objects, individual trees, they create a place, and the
place, composed as it is of so many trees growing densely, is
dark; growth is wild and untamed—and often beautiful. It is
inviting, but dangerously seductive,[14] an excellent hiding place,
but at the same time a place in which one can become irretriev-
ably lost.[15]

Even if we had never read any Frost poems of leaves calling
a person to join them in flight, or threatening him, or trying
to carry him deathward, never seen trees as representing one's
darkness of mood, or woods as frightening or attractive, we
would find in "Stopping by Woods on a Snowy Evening" the
basic conflict between attraction toward these woods and conscious resistance to that attraction—to use the verbs of the
poem—between stopping and going:

Whose woods these are I think I know.
His house is in the village though;

He will not see me stopping here
To watch his woods fill up with snow.

My little horse must think it queer
To stop without a farmhouse near
Between the woods and frozen lake
The darkest evening of the year.

He gives his harness bells a shake
To ask if there is some mistake.
The only other sound's the sweep
Of easy wind and downy flake.

The woods are lovely, dark and deep,
But I have promises to keep,
And miles to go before I sleep,
And miles to go before I sleep. (CP 275)

The speaker of this poem is recounting a particular incident that takes place at a clearly specified woods on a clearly specified evening. Yet the title of the poem refuses specificity and concreteness. "Stopping by Woods (with no article, no noun marker) on *a* Snowy Evening" generalizes the experience to imply that this is not only one man's particular and peculiar experience: this is the way it is when one stops by woods on a snowy evening. This is the nature of stopping at such a place in such circumstances. Snowy woods can *have* this effect.

What, exactly, is the effect? So moved is the traveler by the sight of woods filling up with snow that he stops. Conscious first of all of the owner whose house is in the village, safely and sensibly away from snowy woods, he seems to need to assure himself that the owner will not see him stopping there. For one thing, he would presumably prefer that the owner not see him trespassing;[16] but for another, sensitive as he is to the mentality of the horse, he would probably feel foolish were he seen by another man—especially by a man whose house is in the village. It would be difficult to explain why he is stopping on such a night at such a place. This need not to be seen adds to the feeling of isolation that the poem has already provided in showing the man's aloneness. Not only does he happen to be the only person on the scene, but he is doing what someone more sensible would not do, or what a less sensitive person would not do—stop at the worst possible time simply because a scene is so attractive.[17] In this sense the traveler welcomes his solitude, luxuriates in an experience he need not share or explain.

The judgment of "queerness" is his own, as he projects it onto his horse, and this further isolates him. Not only might he be judged by the man in the village, but even his horse thinks he is queer. Robert Penn Warren makes a very apt distinction between man, who is capable of dreaming and appreciating, and the horse, who is not. There is, however, another set of contrasts. The man in the village would judge him based on standards of sensible if unimaginative practicality. This traveler, though, chooses, for the moment at least, the world of nature, of snowy woods as opposed to the village. Why then this imagined judgment on the part of an animal? An animal, a creature of no imagination, will do what is instinctive for its safety. Wanting to get home, out of the snow, dictates the shake of the reins. A deer would have run into the woods. This horse, however, has his place of rest in a barn. Tamed, domesticated, this animal stands somewhere between woods and civilization. And the man, between horse and woods, stands there as well. Human though he may be, he is drawn toward those woods, just as that horse, animal though he is, is drawn home to the barn.

The woods are dark and deep. Not frightening, this dark, not nightmarish, this unknown, but lovely, attractive even in the depth of its darkness, perhaps because of it. Because this lovely darkness is so quickly counteracted by "promises," it has been easy to see the lure of this darkness as the lure of whatever dark and lovely thing stands in opposition to promises, with its overtones of obligation (perhaps to society, family, self, a higher power, or moral code) and which requires something as strong and binding as "promises" to break the spell and call the traveler back to the road.

We could name many things, but they would probably all have in common some version of freedom from that which binds us to promises, to obligation or duty, to a sense of right and wrong— a freedom from awareness of the boundary between woods and road, or of any boundaries at all. Fundamental to all aspects of the contrary pulls, even the literal one of going as opposed to stopping, is the sense of responsibility that obtrudes itself at the end, probably winning over the impulse to irresponsibility, or perhaps the more specific irresponsible impulse.[18]

Lawrance Thompson takes John Ciardi to task for inaccurate and unfounded theorizing on the composition of this poem.[19] Ciardi knew that Frost had written it after having worked all night on a long poem that he thought had never been completed; he did not know that the poem was "New Hampshire." What Thompson objects to is Ciardi's willingness to "stake [his] life that . . . that work sheet . . . would be found to contain the germinal stuff of 'Stopping by Woods,' that what was a-simmer in him all night . . . offered itself in a different form, and that finding exactly the right impulse proceeded to marry itself to the new shape in one of the most miraculous performances of English lyricism." In correcting Ciardi's errors, Thompson states: "There is no connection between either the themes or the subject matter of 'New Hampshire' and 'Stopping by Woods.'" The biographer proves himself to be the more reliable on the facts, but the poet seems better equipped to understand germinal ideas,[20] for "New Hampshire" has many ideas, many themes, many subjects. Among them is Frost's nonanswer to the question put to him by the "pseudo-phallic . . . New York Alec . . . 'Choose you which you will be—a prude or puke.'"

I wouldn't be a prude afraid of nature.
I know a man who took a double ax
And went alone against a grove of trees;

But his heart failing him, he dropped the ax

. . . .

He had a special terror of the flux
That showed itself in dendrophobia

. . . .

He knew too well for any earthly use
The line where man leaves off and nature starts,
And never over-stepped it save in dreams.
He stood on the safe side of the line talking;

. . . .

I'd hate to be a runaway from nature.
And neither would I choose to be a puke
Who cares not what he does in company. (CP 210–11)

He has not really chosen; and pressed again for a choice, he
will *choose* to be a farmer—a resolution that seems to evade but
really does not evade the issue. He will work with nature, but
with some measure of control over it; he will live in the country
near the woods, not in the woods; he will not go *against* a *grove,*
he will cultivate it. If he does use his ax, it will be on one tree at
a time, and when he "oversteps the line" he will remember his
promises.

"New Hampshire" is the poem in which Frost calls himself
a "sensibilist," a word that can mean one who is sensible, has
common sense, but it also can mean one who is sensible *to* the
world, and it reminds us of the word "sensualist."[21] The teasing
statement "the more sensibilist I am / The more I seem to want
my mountains wild" was not in the original manuscript, which
reads "the more I seem to want my mountains awful."[22] Whether
he meant bad or awe-full (which would certainly fit into the context of the discussion on wanting to make the people shorter and
the mountains higher) or both, the substitution of wildness to
complement sensibility seems apt, especially when he goes on to
discuss pukes, prudes, overstepped lines, and cultivated farms.

The word "wild" does not appear in "Stopping by Woods,"

but because wildness stands in opposition to cultivation and tameness, to restraint, order, and predictability, it also stands in opposition to the boundaries, duties, and rules that are represented by "promises." We have seen that the wildness in Frost seems to have frightened him on occasion. He had also spoken of "wildness" in poetry in "The Figure a Poem Makes," opposing it to the steadiness that comes from theme and subject: "to have . . . wildness pure, to be wild with nothing to be wild about . . . [is] giving way to undirected associations." At a later date Frost related this passage to his own nature: "I lead a life estranged from myself. . . . I am very wild at heart sometimes. Not at all confused. Just wild—wild. Couldn't you read it between the lines in my Preface nay and in the lines?"[23]

Wildness in poetry linked to wildness in his nature, which is linked in turn to deep woods, appears in the letter, written five years before this poem, which was quoted from in the previous chapter. Underlying everything he speaks of, from conservatism to gloom, seems to be a fear of dangerous irresponsibility that waits to erupt chaotically if it can find an unguarded spot to break through. He expresses explicitly the fear of being "a party to the literature of irresponsible, boy-again freedom . . . there is nothing but me. And I have all the dead New England Things held back by one hand as by a dam in the long deep wooded valley of Whippoorwill . . . I hold them easily—too easily for assurance that they will go with a rush when I let them go" (SL 193). In another reference to wildness and its effect on sanity, we remember Frost wrote that "we can make raids and excursions into the wild, but it has to be from well kept strongholds" (SL 193).

One thinks of the "two and a child" watching the snow from their stronghold, the closed farmhouse, hoping for aid against the beast of a storm creeping up—and in. "Come out!" it says, just as the lovely woods filling up with snow seem to say "come in." It is ironic that we feel a greater danger in the one invitation—the quiet, restful beauty of the woods in "Stopping by

Woods"—than we do in the other. The major point of contrast between these two poems of inviting snow lies in the nature of the appeal and consequently the response. In "Storm Fear" there is no temptation to say yes to the invitation: "When the wind works against us in the dark . . . It costs no inward struggle not to go, ah no!" But there *is* a tacit recognition that there might, under different circumstances, be an inward struggle, that the "beast" saying "come out" might find a kindred spirit wanting to come out, or get out. It is only when the invitation comes from what is obviously "the beast," when it pelts, barks, creeps, and poses a threat of physical pain, that it becomes no struggle to refuse. The very ferocity of the beast that can kill physically can also save psychically and spiritually. It is significant that there is no fear expressed in "Stopping by Woods" of what is potentially a dangerous situation.[24] The woods are dark, deep, and filling with snow. Whereas in "Storm Fear" the threat of annihilation comes from the man's being overcome by nature, in "Stopping by Woods" it comes from his giving in. What causes the man to go on comes from within him, not from the woods. He remembers his promises, and these promises exert a pull that works in opposition to the attraction of the woods—against their beauty, against his desire to stop there and to relax.

Ease and relaxation are among the most remarkable features of this poem. Like those snowy woods, the poem can lull us into an unaware acceptance only of its loveliness. The linked rhyme scheme draws us on from one stanza to the next, culminating in the repetend this scheme demanded, the perfect repetition that simultaneously soothes, concludes, and opens up further extensions of meaning.[25] The rhyme contributes to the lulling effect, for this poem is a rare example in Frost of near-complete regularity—strict iambics with no caesuras, no pauses. The only exception occurs in the last stanza where we pause slightly at the comma after "lovely," as if we are being prepared for the slight jolt of "promises"—that decisive word on which the poem turns, and the man turns. One can read the line with metric perfection, but to do so is to violate what Frost considers so important: the tones of real speech. This line is an excellent illustration of "the possibility for tune from the dramatic tones of meaning struck across the rigidity of limited meter" (CP 18), and the tension between the two reflects perfectly the tension that "promises" exerts on the man and on the experience.

Were it not for the turn because of "promises," we too might forget what snow is associated with in other poems, and how cold it is in reality, for we are told nothing of this. Besides the harness bells, "the only other sound's the sweep of easy wind and downy flake." The softness of the repeated "s" and "n" sounds adds to the "ease" of the wind, the softness of the snow-flakes. They are downy, like a bed, and the man is thinking of sleep. The temptation to give in is not only to give in to relax-ation of rules—to abandon—it is to give in to rest, to cessation, to stopping, and surely by now the snow has obscured the clear lines that divide road from woods.

When asked in a television interview what he thought of this poem's having been interpreted as a suicide poem, Frost re-plied, "That's terrible, isn't it?"[26] The question may have referred to Ciardi's article, which was widely circulated and very well known. Ciardi called it unmistakably a "death wish," a statement he has since wisely revised to a question.[27] Thompson, however, only suggested that Ciardi recognize that the death wish is re-sisted, a rather obvious point. Indeed, the biography shows a great deal of evidence that Frost toyed with the notion of sui-cide throughout his life, perhaps most often during the Derry years. There *was* a frozen pond he used to pass coming from the village, and he did tell Elizabeth Sergeant of a "black 'tarn' . . . (for convenient suicide), and what a pang it cost the poet not to have chosen it" (EY 548, 267). Even more telling are two poems he chose never to publish: "Despair" is about suicide by drowning—a poem he knew by heart in his old age;[28] the other is "To Prayer I Go," about which he wrote to Louis Untermeyer at one time: "That is my last, my ultimate vileness, that I cannot make up my mind to go now where I must go sooner or later. I am afraid." And at another time: "I decided to keep the matter private and out of my new book. It could easily be made too much of. I can't myself say how serious the crisis was and how near I came to giving in." Whether the reference in these letters is to prayer or to death seems almost irrelevant, for the two go together in the third and final version of the poem, a going down to a crucified and penitential death in prayer.[29]

So much for expecting Frost to admit on television that "Stopping by Woods" is a "suicide poem." We must ultimately judge by returning to the poem, where once again we wonder how much can be loaded onto a delicate lyric.[30] Of course, as we have noted elsewhere, Frost has us, the readers, both ways: if we see nothing but snowy woods, we have been lulled by it; if we see every possibility, we have been lured by it into weighting it with possibly unwarranted meanings, or into exposing ourselves in our readings. It is precisely here that we see once again the artistry of Frost; while remaining the simple and beautiful lyric poem that it is, it opens itself to extensions of meaning that are possible—but only possible.[31] That dark, deep woods can be dangerously lovely, dangerously wild; that death is the ultimate relaxation, the ultimate destination, and the ultimate escape from the world everyone knows. Whether these are the subjects of the poem no one knows. We have no right to say that this poem is about suicide, or moral or psychic wildness; only that it *might* be. We *can* say that it is about resisting an attractive invitation extended by the beauty of nature, an invitation to forget promises.

In the same way we can only conjecture whether the speaker feels any kind of identity with those woods, whether the pull they exert on him to enter corresponds with something within him that demands withdrawal into self and away from promises. In "Desert Places," however, the traveler explicitly relates the snowy scene to himself.

Snow falling and night falling fast, oh, fast
In a field I looked into going past,
And the ground almost covered smooth in snow,
But a few weeds and stubble showing last.

The woods around it have it—it is theirs.
All animals are smothered in their lairs.
I am too absent-spirited to count;
The loneliness includes me unawares.

And lonely as it is that loneliness
Will be more lonely ere it will be less—
A blanker whiteness of benighted snow
With no expression, nothing to express.

They cannot scare me with their empty spaces
Between stars—on stars where no human race is.
I have it in me so much nearer home
To scare myself with my own desert places. (CP 386)

This later poem makes a fitting companion piece to "Stopping by Woods." Even the rhyme scheme (aaba) is the same, although in this poem, the poet has not chosen to commit himself to the greater difficulty of linking his stanzas by means of rhyme. This speaker too is traveling through falling snow at night fall. The woods are present in this poem as well, though we are more conscious of their darkness in "Stopping by Woods" and more conscious of whiteness here. While the opening line sounds soothing with its repetition of "s," and "f," and "o," we know as early as the second line that this speaker does not stop, even for a moment—the fields he describes are those he is "going past." What is not presented as frightening in "Stopping by Woods" is frightening in this poem. Nothing here makes one feel that the speaker finds this snowfall attractive, nothing draws him in, for this snowfall does not present a relaxing oblivion; it presents a concrete blankness. Because it is with blankness that he identifies, it presents no escape, only a reminder of self, a self that is not a welcome haven or wellspring. Withdrawal would not be "strategic" and self-preserving. It would be facing a desert.

The open space is surrounded by woods that "have it." They claim it, and the speaker willingly relegates it to them—willing not because of a decision he has struggled to make, but because he is too apathetic, "too absent-spirited to count." The structural ambiguity in this line and its seeming carelessness emphasize his absent-spiritedness, his apathy. We cannot be sure whether "count" is being used in its active sense (to count, to tell what is happening, to reckon up woods, animals and fields) or in its passive sense (to be counted, to count to anything or any-one else). The following line is also enriched by its apparently careless use of "unawares," which could modify "loneliness" or could modify "me." Again, the ambiguous use of the word illus-trates that very unawareness, that carelessness that causes us to associate absent-spiritedness with absent-mindedness.

In the third stanza loneliness is in apposition to snow, and just as the snow will cover more and more, will leave nothing uncov-ered to relieve its smooth unbroken whiteness, so the loneliness will become still more lonely and unrelieved. That same white-ness—snow or loneliness—is what makes desert of a field, helps the woods to "have" the fields in that it obliterates clear bound-aries between field and woods, raising, as it does in "Stopping by Woods," the dangerous prospect of boundarilessness. Even when the journey is into one's *own* desert places, one's humanity or identity is threatened, and loneliness, the apposition sug-gests, can do this too. What terrifies him so much, however, is not the fact that he is alone, without other people, but that alone with himself he may find nothing—no one and nothing within. Whereas "Stopping by Woods" presented an invitation to the solitude and inertia of snow, this poem presents the attendant fear that once giving in to the self, or going into the self, he will find that the journey has been for nothing. That there is nothing but loneliness, blankness, and absent-spiritedness in the sense of absence of spirit.

The "nothingness" that Frost fears is not the metaphysical void, it is the void he fears in himself. In relating this personal void to the spaces between stars, he suggests that a personal void can have—or seem to have—cosmic proportions, that it can seem at *least* as important, as vast and as frightening, as anything "out there." This speaker fears the void, but he does not seem, like Wallace Stevens's snow man, to be "nothing himself"; he is capable of beholding what is not there. He is not a man of snow because he has enough feeling to be afraid. His is not yet a "mind of winter," for he can still think about having one, fear that he might discover it if he explores inside himself. He has it "in him"—again, as in "Spring Pools"—the threatening potential of what lies within. The man with the "mind of winter" does not think, but to Stevens there are two kinds of nothingness—"the nothing that is" and "nothing," which is the absence of something. The greater lack is the latter—the absence of imagination in the man who "beholds nothing that is not there." In "Desert Places" the speaker fears blankness "with no expression, nothing to express." There is a difference between "nothing to express" and an expression of nothingness, as Stevens has shown us. The fear in the poem is of the former, but the act of the poem is the latter.

For the poet there is an additional terror in identifying his own "desert places" with the blank landscape: it is a "whiteness . . . with no expression, nothing to express." If there is nothing there, nothing showing or growing, if there is no spirit, what will he have to say? This fear of nothing to say was a constant one to Frost. To Untermeyer he once confided "a very damaging secret. . . . The poet in me died nearly ten years ago. . . . The calf I was in the nineties I merely take to market. . . . Take care that you don't get your mouth set to declare the other two [books] a falling off of power, for that is what they can't be. . . . As you look back don't you see how a lot of things I have said begin to take meaning from this? . . . I tell you, Louis, it's all over at thirty. . . . Anyway that was the way I thought I might feel. And I took measures accordingly. . . . I have myself all in a strong box"

(SL 201–2). Having nothing more to say was what he assumed lay behind Hemingway's decision to commit suicide—a motive and a decision Frost defended (LY 294).

Even worse than having nothing to say, perhaps, is emotional poverty—feeling used up, both by the pain of events in life and by the demands of his art. He once wrote: "[poets] are so much less sensitive from having overused their sensibilities. Men who have to feel for a living would unavoidably become altogether unfeeling except professionally" (SL 300). Whatever the basis, the poem ends with the fear of one's own emptiness, one's own nothingness. To traverse these spaces inside the self is to traverse the barren.[32]

At the same time, though, and characteristically, the fear is expressed with a kind of bravado: "they can't scare *me!*" The comparison between the interstellar spaces and his own desert places also serves to aggrandize the speaker and the importance of his personal desert. Then, also characteristically, Frost undercuts both the bravado and the self-importance, mainly by means of metrics. Where the speaker tries so hard to show strength the lines end weakly: they are the only feminine rhymes in the poem; the three rhyming lines of the last stanza all have an added, unstressed eleventh syllable: /əz/. The effect in lines 13 and 14 is to undercut the tone of confidence. By the last line, where bravado gives in to fear, the unstressed ending reinforces the fear by sounding weak in the face of what is feared. The ′ ˘ rhyme concluding the poem also works against a feeling of closure and resolution.

While the whole final stanza has its metrical bumps, line 14 jolts us the most and alerts us to other tensions with and within that line. For example, whereas "spaces" and "places" are both noun objects of prepositions, rhyming what is also structurally parallel, "race is," as a noun subject and verb, seems out of kilter with the other two. To focus more closely, though, on these words is to notice the possible pun "where no human races" and the tensions *that* produces between the two possible meanings: in one sense, the contrast between a place where people do not race—no rushing, no competition—and a world where the need to go forward quickly and competitively obtains even in one's private desert. Following on this contrast is another: the active verb of one reading—"races"—contrasts with the static "is" of the other, which creates further tensions. Grammatically, the two would be awkward together, as we do not coordinate an active verb with a stative one. Semantically, the difference is related to two conflicting needs: going, doing, rushing to compete and simply being. Such stasis, though, is located where there is no human life (a concept we will take up in another context in chapter 7). Seen this way, the poem presents another version of the conflict between going and stopping, motion and stasis. While in this poem the outward action is not stopping but going *past* the field (he races?), what inner desert it represents, of course, goes with him, and, as "Stopping by Woods" reminds us, we must go—move, do—if we are to be.

An obvious contrast in a similar setting is the poem Frost chose to end his final collection, "In Winter in the Woods Alone." Here he crosses the fields to go against the grove of trees and, as if realizing that one man cannot conquer an entire grove at once, fells one tree and promises himself to return "for yet another blow," with "yet" leaving open the possibility that there will be yet another and another until life or strength gives out. The need is to act *upon* those trees and that frozen landscape even if the action can make no great immediate difference. This need to act and exert some form of control in the face of destruction dominates "The Leaf Treader" as well:

I have been treading on leaves all day until I
    am autumn-tired.
God knows all the color and form of leaves I
    have trodden on and mired.
Perhaps I have put forth too much strength
    and been too fierce from fear.

I have safely trodden underfoot the leaves
  of another year.

All summer long they were overhead, more
  lifted up than I.
To come to their final place in earth they
  had to pass me by.
All summer long I thought I heard them
  threatening under their breath.
And when they came it seemed with a will to
  carry me with them to death.

They spoke to the fugitive in my heart as
  if it were leaf to leaf.
They tapped at my eyelids and touched my
  lips with an invitation to grief.
But it was no reason I had to go because
  they had to go.
Now up my knee to keep on top of another
  year of snow. (CP 388)

The leaves have invited him deathward, and he will not find it
adequate simply to refuse the invitation (as does the speaker in
"The Wind and the Rain"). He needs to act, to demonstrate, and
in so doing he makes a futile attempt to obliterate what he fears.

In this poem, as in others, the speaker identifies with the
natural objects, even feels invited by them, but when he perceives that their invitation is "to grief," he becomes "fierce from
fear." He resists, at the cost of draining his strength. In this case,
self-preservation is precisely this strong resistance to continuing
identification and to the invitation: "But it was no reason that I
had to go because they had to go."[33] In retrospect the summer
rustling of the leaves has become "threatening" and endowed
with will and intent to carry him to death. They tap at his eyelids and touch his lips as if they were caressing him, seducing
him deathward. It is not in the leaves but in the speaker's resistance that there is violence. The threatening quality of the

leaves is what he *thought* he heard all summer; the relationship between speaker and leaves, flight and death is as the speaker/ reader of the scene perceives it, and it is this perception of the meaning of that deathward flight and invitation which impels his strong and angry, if futile, reaction.

The leaves stand in three basic positions with relation to the speaker: they are above him in the summer, they are level with him, touching him, in their fall flight; and as they land, they are on the ground, under foot as eventually they will be under snow. The present time of the poem is the time of flight, land- ing, and treading, and in the speaker's saying: "To come to their final resting place in earth they had to pass me by," he estab- lishes a connection not only between himself and the leaves, but between time and those leaves. All summer long they seemed to be threatening, a verb that carries implications of futurity—a threat is what one says he *will* do at some future time. At present they are falling, passing the speaker by, but trying to carry him along. Those that reach the ground have already passed the speaker. He represents what is past to them; yet their state in their final place in the earth is the future to him. Flight and position, which occupy space, are in this sense representative of the passing of time, and it is as if to conquer time itself that the speaker is treading on those leaves.

His achievement has been that he has "safely trodden under- foot the leaves of another year," but what is it to stand on top of a pile of leaves—or even on top of what it is those fallen leaves represent? He has remained alive another year—he is on top in that he has outlived them; he has demonstrated that fact in grinding them under his feet, rather than allowing them to carry him off. They are the "leaves of another year." Another year victorious is also another year older, another year closer to death, locked captive still within the scheme of time. This idea may help to explain the curious final line of the poem. It makes sense as a grammatical sentence only if "up" is an imperative verb, an exhortation to continue the battle. The introduction of snow seems totally out of place here; yet in the context of passing time, we are reminded that winter follows autumn, that snow will cover the leaves. The snow, however, is not acting as an ally to the speaker, helping him conquer the leaves; rather it is another challenge to him, another threat that he must "keep underfoot." As in "They Were Welcome to Their Belief," there seems to be a connection between "all the snows that clung to the . . . roof" and "the one snow on his head," the conclusion of the poem being that neither grief nor care, but time was "the thief of his raven color of hair" (CP 390).

Both treading on snow and treading on leaves can be futile in that both are soft; one often treads *in* not on them. Despite the fact that the leaf treader ends by saying "up my knee to keep on top," one cannot quite escape the image prompted by a phrase so similar to this one as to obtrude itself upon it: up to my knees to keep on top.[34] The final image of the poem is a combination of that man stamping furiously on leaves or snow that will not stay "safely down," that cause him to keep sinking, and the fighter who will keep fighting, keep winning every battle until the final one that will lose him the war.[35]

Of course, all the man is doing is obliterating the sign, trying to kill the messenger, with no control whatsoever over the reality of the message that winter is coming, time is passing. In the absence of control over time, he works very hard to exert some control over the signs of its passing.[36] We can see at once the futility of the act on time, the glory of the attempt, and the possible meaning for a poet. If language and poetic reading and writing are the only means we have to exert any control over reality, or accommodate it to us, then acting on the metaphor is a saving act, a poetic one, illusory though that may be. It is at the very least a refusal to be passive.

But acting on or with nature need not be fighting or resisting it. There are poems in which a poetic speaker finds in nature a partner in creation, more than simply the artist's raw material but cooperating in creation. True to the convention of nature as teacher, nature is also a model for artistic transforming and creating. In "The Freedom of the Moon" the moon represents nothing; it is the artist's raw material, and as in "Now Close the Windows," the "freedom" lies in the ability of the observer to change his position and thereby his perspective and to form analogies if he wishes:

I've tried the new moon tilted in the air
Above a hazy tree-and-farmhouse cluster
As you might try a jewel in your hair.
I've tried it fine with little breadth of luster,
Alone, or in one ornament combining
With one first-water star almost as shining.

I put it shining anywhere I please.
By walking slowly on some evening later,
I've pulled it from a crate of crooked trees
And brought it over glossy water, greater,
And dropped it in, and seen the image wallow,
The color run, all sorts of wonder follow. (CP 304)

The poet/observer is free to compare the moon to a jewel, as he is free to compare the branches to a crate. The point of the poem is that it is the artist who *does* by seeing and varies the arrangements by varying his modes of seeing. He cannot touch the moon or approach it, much less control it; yet he is the subject of every active verb and the moon their object for eleven out of the twelve lines. Even the exception that occurs in the last line and a half is not really an exception for the subject is the *image* of the moon—an image that he has arranged. He says of the moon: "I tried it . . . I put it . . . I pulled it . . . brought it . . . dropped it." He combines it with a star and watches its image in the water—noting that in the reflection of the moon there are still further possibilities for change of shape, color, consistency. Thus in viewing a part of nature, in arranging and composing with it, in playing with its reflection and in applying his own imagination to it, he, as artist, feels himself to be in control of an object that in natural fact is obviously impossible. The moon is as "free" of his control as he is "free" to create with it.

The speaker in "Evening in a Sugar Orchard" wants the fire-man to "give the fire another stoke, / and send more sparks up chimney with the smoke." More interested in the view of the sparks than in the maple syrup, he watches the play of sparks tangled in maple boughs and watches them rise toward the moon. The moon—here the means of illumination—shows the trees and shows the snow around them looking like a bear-skin rug; it remains superior to the sparks, higher than they are. Yet the sparks are "content to figure in the trees / as Leo, Orion, and the Pleides" (CP 289). They are not content to be sparks, nor do they aspire to being celestial bodies; somewhere between the two conditions lies the figurative condition: sparks seeming like stars. For them it is enough.

Being stars as opposed to seeming like stars is much more sharply drawn in "Fireflies in the Garden," wherein the "emulat-ing flies" who can "achieve at times a very star-like start . . . of course, can't sustain the part"[37] (CP 306). No more can sparks. The difference in the two poems—that of praise and the con-tent awarded to sparks and the disdain pointed at fireflies— lies in the attitude of the speaker and, indeed, his part in the illusion. The figure trying to be the real thing is doomed to fail-ure. The figure content in being figure, and figure, of course, of an observer's imagination, has its own value, a value created in the mind of a human observer. Whatever will be "sustained" or made permanent lies in what the observer will remember, what the artist will create.

In all these poems, we do not deal simply with "figuring" but with creating that figurative view. The artist in all of them is very consciously arranging his figures, stimulating them. He is aware that his imagination plays a large role in the way he sees and in what he does with what he sees. Only slightly less conscious, and consequently slightly more self-deceptive, is "A Boundless Moment":

> He halted in the wind, and—what was that
> Far in the maples, pale, but not a ghost?
> He stood there bringing March against his thought,
> And yet too ready to believe the most.
>
> 'Oh, that's the Paradise-in-bloom,' I said;
> And truly it was fair enough for flowers
> Had we but in us to assume in March
> Such white luxuriance of May for ours.
>
> We stood a moment so in a strange world,
> Myself as one his own pretense deceives;
> And then I said the truth (and we moved on).
> A young beech clinging to its last year's leaves. (CP 288)

The only direct quotation in the poem—" 'Oh, that's the Paradise-in-bloom' "—is the false statement, the illusion. The truth, "a young beech clinging to its last year's leaves," stands as a fact of the poem. It concludes the poem in a one-line phrase that is punctuated as a sentence[38] but is merely a visual image; we are not given a statement about anything. We are merely shown the object as it *is*: the truth. Still the fact that it is not *stated,* that it is self-evident but undeclared, can show a lack of faith in the fact or lack of commitment to it. The "he" of the poem is struggling between his thought and his knowledge of March, "and yet ready to believe the most." His receptiveness seems absolutely necessary to the "lie" that the "I" of the poem verbalizes. That receptiveness to illusion and pretense must be there because neither one of them is ever truly deceived. The poem shows no discovery; "had we but in us to assume" is in the conditional, the hypothetical, not the actual. The word "as" in line 10 gives away the fact that his own pretense could not really deceive him. This has been not the passive reader's "suspension of disbelief" but the active courting of the imagination by one who wishes to cultivate his illusion—to make a moment "boundless" by removing for that moment the bounds of time and fact.[39] As this is Frost, however, we are not allowed to be boundless in this manner for more than a moment. The poem ends with the truth.

In "A Hillside Thaw" nature herself rearranges and transforms, and the observer sees melting snow as analogous to live animals; yet before we reach the end of the poem, we feel that there is an interplay between nature, its transformations, and the artist/observer's thinking about *his* transformations of material. Nature models the creative process. Melting snow is compared to lizards, but the sun and the moon cooperate in their creation, and this creativity is obviously analogous to the various facets of the artist's creativity—the manner in which necessary conditions work now together, now against one another, to mold between them the finished work. The artist watches what the moon has done and despairs of succeeding as she has succeeded in "transfixing," in "holding" the lizards in her spell.

The poem begins in sheer exuberance at the beauty of a natural scene:

> To think to know the country and not know
> The hillside on the day the sun lets go
> Ten million silver lizards out of snow! (CP 293)

Inseparable from the appreciation of the scene's beauty, however, is the emotional effect of the thaw and what has loosed those lizards. That emotional response looses the imagination as well for, as Emerson says, "the quality of the imagination is to flow and not to freeze."[40] The human observer is thawing in response to the thaw. Warmed by the sun, he feels enthusiasm letting go commensurate with the snow's letting go, but it would be no use to try to catch these "lizards."

> It takes the moon for this. The sun's a wizard
> By all I tell, but so's the moon a witch.

From the high west she makes a gentle cast
And suddenly, without a jerk or twitch,
She has her spell on every single lizard

. . . .

. . . the swarm was turned to rock
In every lifelike posture of the swarm,
Transfixed on mountain slopes almost erect. (CP 293)

What is let loose by "the magic of the sun" is held by the spell of
the moon. The rush of life, the "breeding" of the animals out of
snow, is checked by the coldness of the moon, and these "animals" are preserved only during the sovereignty of the moon,
who "held them until day, / One lizard at the end of every
ray" (294).

That the speaker compares his abilities to "hold" or catch a
lizard with that of the moon encourages us as readers to compare him with the moon. He "can't pretend to tell the way it's
done" (293), that turning of the snow into lizards which the sun
achieves; he knows that no matter how he tried, even throwing
himself "wet-elbowed and wet-kneed / In front of twenty others'
wriggling speed" he would "end by holding none." That takes
the moon, and in comparing his ability to hers, he concludes:
"The thought of my attempting such a stay!" (294).

It is only because these are not real lizards that he cannot
catch them. Like the sparks and the glowworms they are "figures" and such illusions must either vanish or be transfixed,
either by the moon on the hillside or by the artist in the work
of art. This poem seems to be Frost's "cold pastoral," presenting as it does the paradox that only in freezing can we hold,
and only in holding can we preserve. The continuing onrush of
warmth—either the sun's or the hands of the speaker—would
end by melting the forms, destroying the illusions. It takes the
opposite, the cold, to mold, to transfix, and to hold.[41]

Yet there would have been nothing to hold had the sun not
used its warmth to generate those lizards in the first place. Like
Antony's "fire that quickens Nilus' slime," the sun breeds lizards

in the snow, and it lets them go as well so that the moon-made sculpture captures a scene in which the lizards may be frozen, but frozen into "lifelike" postures—"across each other and side by side they lay" (293). Thus in this scene we feel not lifelessness, but frozen life and motion. As in "To the Thawing Wind," Frost seems to recognize that the artist and his work must be turned outside, melted, swung and rattled and scattered (CP 16), but that this emotion, this enthusiasm, this creative life force is not yet art, for that takes the transfixing power of the moon. Both sun and moon work mysteriously—the sun is magic, the moon casts spells; the sun is wizard, the moon is witch. It takes both to create the sculptured lizards out of snow. The sexual connotations of the language reinforce the creativity of the process, of uniting mind and scene to create a poem.[42]

Whereas the speaker in "A Hillside Thaw" is overtly concerned with how things are transformed and transfixed, the speaker in "Hyla Brook" seems to focus on the brook itself, especially on its diminishing into nothing. The poem does not speak *about* transformation; rather, transformation takes place within the observed natural context:

By June our brook's run out of song and speed
Sought for much after that, it will be found
Either to have gone groping underground
(And taken with it all the Hyla breed
That shouted in the mist a month ago,
Like ghost of sleigh-bells in a ghost of snow)—
Or flourished and come up in jewel-weed,
Weak foliage that is blown upon and bent
Even against the way its waters went.
Its bed is left a faded paper sheet
Of dead leaves stuck together by the heat—
A brook to none but who remember long.
This as it will be seen is other far
Than with brooks taken otherwhere in song.
We love the things we love for what they are. (CP 149)

We are not coaxed by the speaker into forming comparisons; therefore we do not necessarily grasp this poem as working analogically. The brook is a brook. The "drama" of the poem— everything that lies between the "our" of the first line and the "we" of the last line—is the change of the brook as it dries out and either gropes underground or flourishes in jewel-weed. It could be another poem about process, and indeed the actual facts of the poem resemble those of "Spring Pools." Yet how different the two poems are, for we feel in "Spring Pools" that the overriding concern is fear of annihilation. In "Hyla Brook," there is no overriding emotional concern; nothing acts on the brook, the brook acts. Whatever the change has been, it is not feared but accepted: "We love the things we love for what they are."

But something in that last line rings hollow. We may ask: What is it that they are? What is it that we love them for? Is it the fact of diminishment and nonexistence? Is it whatever things have become that we love, like the jewel-weed? Do we love them *for* being what they are or despite it? The line is so pat, so platitudinous, and it seems to stand in direct opposition to the fact that this is a brook only to those "who remember long." Rather than being an acceptance of the present reality that grows out of the poem, it seems almost like a non sequitur, like an "oh well," a resignation dutifully and gratuitously tacked on. It even stands as line 15 of what would have been a sonnet without it; nevertheless, we cannot remove the line, for the rhyme scheme depends on it.

These questions send us back into the poem to find out what *is,* and we find not only brook-into-jewel-weed but "a faded paper sheet," which is no longer a brook. The "paper sheet" is a brook only in memory, but it stands as a record of what *was,* and that is one of the "things" that "are." The paper metaphor need not be belabored; it seems obvious, but what is interesting is that what it records is accessible only by means of memory. The most beautiful and most memorable line in the poem—in fact one of the most beautiful in the Frost canon—is also "only" a memory: "Like ghost of sleighbells in a ghost of snow."[43] There is more beauty of sound in this line than we usually attribute to real tree toads. The haunting, evocative quality of the line seems to result from the perfect fusion of repeated sounds (an appropriate "s" for ghosts and snow, for example) and the image— both visual and auditory. Ghost not only evokes the white and mysterious, but remains unseen, merely suggested. The rhythm of the line contributes to the feeling of sound coming on and retreating:

The stress pattern shows that, from the center of the line outward, the spondee followed by two unstressed syllables, every syllable is likewise paired in exact opposition with regard to stress. This seems born out by the fact that the line reads "[like] a ghost of snow" but *not* "like a ghost of sleighbells."

It is not actually sleighbells, but a ghost of them in a ghost of snow; the suggestion is that we are not certain of really hearing them or really seeing the snow, or perhaps we are not certain when the reality faded into memory—the heard sound became "aftersound" in its wake. The snow itself is ghostly because it obscures vision, and therefore we may hear the bells without being able to see the sleigh.

Of course we are not even speaking of sleighbells; we are speaking of tree toads. In a poem almost shorn of metaphors, presenting only the facts (the way things are?), the two metaphors stand out: paper sheet for the brook's bed and ghost of sleighbells in a ghost of snow referring to the sound of the Hyla breed "in the mist a month ago." The point of the comparison in the latter is sound whose source is difficult to see. Thus even the actual tree toads were audible and not visible. The sound is now a memory, expressed by a metaphor of sound obscured by snow, aided by a subsidiary metaphor, "ghost," with all that "ghostliness" evokes. This is a good example of the way in which metaphor works associatively.[44] As we apply ghostly sleighbells back to tree toads, we find heightened the quality of disembodied sound, no longer actual, but still haunting us in memory.

This evocation by means of memory, and the combination of "memory" with the "faded sheet"—the "brook to none but who remember long"—brings us anew to the questions regarding the last line: What are these "things"? *This* brook does not go "otherwhere" (a word that seems to underscore Frost's contrast between the romantics' ever-singing brooks and his remembered brook). This brook either gropes its way underground or flourishes in a transformed state; or perhaps the groping must precede the transformation. At the same time, its leaving has made memory of factual reality, and it has created "paper sheets" of dead leaves. Nowhere is there an analogy between this process, this transformation, and artistic transformations; yet so interrelated are the present, the memories of the past, the wisps of imagination, and the concept of transformation that the connection seems unmistakable.

The connection between memory and reality and the attendant questions of what we love when we love things as they "are," how these things relate to the record of what was, and the understanding of the change by which things present have become something they formerly were not—all these considerations are stimulated by the last line and its opposition to line 12: "A brook to none but who remember long." The original draft, however, ends at line 11. We cannot know conclusively that the poet considered the poem finished, but the prospect is a fascinating one. In its original form, it stands as an example of process and transformation:

> By June our brook runs out of sound and speed
> Sought for much after that, it will be found
> Either to have gone groping underground
> And taking with it all the Hyla breed
> That shouted in the mist a month ago

Like ghost of sleighbells in the ghost of snow
Or flourished and came up in jewel weed,
Pale foliage that is blown upon and bent
In memory of the way its waters went.
The bed is left a faded paper sheet
Of dead leaves struck together by the heat.[45]

Memory is named within the context of the process, and the relationship of present reality to a very different past reality is simply not in question. Accordingly, in the first four lines of the poem the verbs are in the present—the transformation going on for the duration of the poem—to be completed by line 11. (In the copy book, above the poem, the initial false start reads: "our brook has run," which becomes "runs.") As it stands published, of course, the brook is no longer a brook except in memory. Many readers would still find the last line unacceptably platitudinous.

Frost, who loves the facts for their own sake, sounds for their own sake, and nature for its own sake, nevertheless sees art as fact remembered, transformed, and combined with imagination or thought into a new, more powerful reality. What *is* is inseparable from what was and from the associations our imaginations bring to it to give it new form.

Ultimately, the lessons of creating our realities, of seeing the lessons of transformation in the processes of nature, coach us also in the best answer an artist—or any human—can bring to that Socratic "teacher," the Oven Bird, when he asks what we can make of a diminished thing. We reply: we *make* of it.

6

Bond and Free:
The Human Encounter

If the text of nature can seem threatening for what we see in it or read from it, if an external nature whose beauty threatens to seduce us can swallow us or make us forget where we belong, how much more threatening might it be to encounter nature within ourselves; how much more might one need to retain clear divisions between the self and a powerfully inviting or demanding human other? ("No artist should have a family!" Frost once wrote [LU 204]). In most of the "nature poems" the human speaker stands as a spectator who is making something of the scene. True, he may feel a connection with it, as we have seen, ranging anywhere from observing to forming analogies to feeling a pull so strong or an identity so close that he fears it. Still, it is usually as a reader of a scene that he approaches it or makes something of it. Sometimes his reading is more visual, sometimes more visceral, but it is as an object outside the speaker that it exists and is first experienced. What the fact in nature becomes is what the speaker or poet makes of it, what he reads into or creates out of it.

In poems of human encounter, on the other hand, the speakers or the protagonists are actually participants in the drama.

This is certainly true in the love poems, but not only in the love poems. What gets read or made is experienced as human drama, with the speaker or the protagonist playing a role. The making requires involvement in or empathy with the drama, and it also demands extrication from it. There is always this double (or triple) role: actor in the drama, and reader/writer of it. As Ciardi explained the inevitable division of the poet, one feels the grief, and yet with one side of the mind asks how will I treat it, because a writer has to treat it. "Frost was [a passionate man with a certain darkness and certain confusions in him] plus a master poet forever in the presence of his medium."[1] The need then to extricate himself from the entanglement of human drama and involvement was two-fold: first of all, as discussed before, to protect the integrity of the self, to remain whole, and free to create; and then to achieve the distance necessary to "make" out of the encounter, to read it as an observer, and to write it. At the same time, without the involvement there would be no art. Without involvement in the experience, he would not, in Dewey's sense, be having an experience, nor would he be capable of creating an expressive object that would provide an esthetic experience for the reader of the poem. "No tears in the writer, no tears in the reader" is Frost's way of saying very much the same thing. It does not matter that speakers and protagonists are not Frost. We know his personae could be diffusions and protections, masks of the various Frosts; they could be characters he has created or modified for his dramatic purpose. We empathize with them as their creator must have done, but most important for this discussion is the way they illustrate within the poems the conflict between involvement and distance, keeping and spending, engaging and withdrawing.

In any case, whatever we have said with respect to entanglement, the need of it and the fear of it, becomes that much more dramatic, difficult, or glorious when the "object" is another human being. To the extent that the participant feels himself or herself becoming uncomfortably entangled with another, or with some alien or disturbing force within, the reaction can be conflict over boundaries and over possession, whether of self or of the other: how to "read" and participate in a situation without destructive and obliterating entanglement; how to maintain control and possession of what one is and what one has (in the face of the terrible cost that avoiding the not-me exacts); how to maintain dividing lines. We remember that, of the line between good and evil, Frost said that we are the line ourselves. He understood entanglement profoundly.[2] These questions and conflicts form an important subtext of Frost's oeuvre—of poems concerned explicitly or implicitly with sexual relationships, surely, but not exclusively.

In these poems we confront the distinction and the relationship between binding and bounding, bounding and boundaries and, in so doing, confronting Frost's arch-poem of boundary-building and tearing down, where walls are not only erected to separate men but to "wall in" and "wall out" we are not sure what. While the speaker tells us "it comes to little more than an outdoor game," this game seems governed by rule and ritual, played at a proscribed time; it even uses "spells" to repair gaps no one has seen or heard made. The neighbor is not simply following his father's saying; he goes back further, to some primeval ancestor—some *mutual* ancestor—who is not building with stones but destroying with them, or at best defending himself in a stone-waged battle that existed before stone-placed walls.

A serious kind of game, this, whose rules—one on a side, to each the boulders that have fallen to each, walking the line, keeping the wall between them as they go—insure the separation between the men, the fairness of the division of labor, and the integrity of each man's person and property. Where two can pass abreast, they do not; they erect a wall between them. It is possible to do this job alone, we notice, for the speaker tells us that he has come after hunters and repaired damage by himself which is far worse. But *this* task, at *this* time, necessitated by whatever mysterious force that does not love walls, this annual "game" must be shared. It is only fair, for one thing; it is a game, for another; and of course, it is a chance to spend the day with the neighbor, even if only to put the fence between them.

The poem is filled with such contraries: Frost begins with the pun on his own name[3] and continues with a speaker who heaps scorn on his smug neighbor's "Good fences make good neighbors"[4] even as he himself takes the first step toward mending the wall ("I let my neighbor know"). Thus he teases us into playing his game as his speaker and the neighbor play theirs. Something there is that makes the speaker initiate the communication, call the neighbor to come and play the game, even though the neighbor has nothing original to offer, is totally rigid and predictable, and cannot meet the poet in any act of imagination.[5]

At the same time, the speaker resists the need to mend the wall. He would go behind the saying to ask "*Why* do good fences make good neighbors?" but in supporting the validity of his question, the "mischief" of it, he fails to distinguish some fundamental differences, combining into one what really should form separate questions requiring separate answers. He asks why fences make good neighbors, a very general question, and proceeds to illustrate with a particular example: "He is all pine and I am apple orchard. / My apple trees will never get across / And eat the cones under his pines . . . here there are no cows" (CP 47–48). Very well, then *here* we may not need a fence. He has already said, "There where it is we do not need the wall," but in saying this he still leaves open the need somewhere—perhaps elsewhere—for walls.[6] "Why walls?" is not answered by saying, "We don't really need *this* wall."

The ritual quality of the wall mending fits in well with the primeval quality of the vision at the end, the man "moving in darkness . . . not of woods only and the shade of trees." Darkness of what, then? Fear, ignorance, the darkness that caused such fear because it was so dangerous an unknown to that mythic savage ancestor?[7] Correspondingly, we ask of his modern heir: what is he walling in, what is he walling out, and whom might he offend? First of all, there is a great difference between "what" and "whom." One offends a person whom one walls out, that is true, but when one asks *what* he is walling in, what he is walling out, the answer is not likely to be people. Is it something in nature we are walling out—and furthermore is there something in nature we are walling *in*? We are reminded of the precarious damming in of "The Flood."

Neither he nor his neighbor really goes behind what they say or think. The neighbor will not test his father's saying nor will the speaker test the validity or the implications of his own questions. The neighbor remains secure in repeating his father's traditions; the speaker, in being able to criticize the neighbor. Ambivalence toward walls and perhaps their unfortunate necessity is really all we are left with. Perhaps what we need are fences with gates. We need our territorial sovereignty and our individual privacy, but we do not want to shut nature, or spring mischief, or neighbors out of our lives completely. Neither do we want to go out too far or in too far. Walls, for better or for worse, can offend, can inhibit, and can protect. This ambivalence extends to any human relations, where we too may ask: *why* do good fences make good neighbors? Even more difficult questions are: do we need fences between friends? between lovers? between man and his own inner being? Something there is that wants them down, but something also keeps erecting them again, thereby inviting once more that mysterious spilling over.

Our need for communion—put simply, our need not to be alone, and our need to share feelings and ideas—will always insure that spilling over, just as our need to remain individual will cause us to keep the walls between us. Also basic to the communion of shared feelings and ideas is the relationship between a person's integrity of self as an individual and the capability of giving of that self for and to another. This was a balance that Frost always struggled with: how conscious must one be of the self and the extent to which one retains or gives of the self to another. The corollary, how conscious should one be of the same needs for the self, the same giving and retaining on the part of another human being as the relationship becomes reciprocal. On his need he explains himself most openly, almost apologetically, in "The Drumlin Woodchuck." Like Erich Fromm,[8] he seems to feel that self-love is not the same as selfishness; but this means that one must also respect that integrity of the other "self" in any human relationship. Both success and failure in this regard are illustrated in the poetry.

The pathetic woman in "A Servant to Servants" is completely selfless in both senses of the word: she will make no demands on others, she only serves; at the same time she is without a sense of self, sinking closer and closer toward the oblivion of insanity, welcoming it, in fact, as a final release from consciousness and its attendant fears, hopes, and desires. Hers seems an erosion of self by wear, a tiredness (broken only by a too occasional conversation or view of nature) that drains the mind and dulls it like an opiate. She has nothing left to give; she can only serve, only be used.

The question of respect for one's own needs despite an apparent selfishness is raised in "Two Tramps in Mud Time." Because the speaker has had no previous relationship with the tramps— they are "two strangers"—the question can remain the abstract one of what one owes to one's fellow man, what one must give of one's self to the claims of another if the claims conflict, even if there is no obligation to that person, no claim by right of anything except common humanity, human kindness, or guilt in the face of another person's need.[9] One issue in this poem, then, is simply that of selfless giving up as opposed to keeping something for oneself. It is a question relevant to the artist's need to hoard himself as opposed to his human obligation to give himself; it illustrates the kind of conflict in Frost that was generated by his mother's hero tales of self-sacrifice and his opposite need to work for himself in asserting his creative originality (EY 377, 578–79). Like the question in "Love and a Question," this poem too asks how far one is supposed to go in self-sacrifice, how one is to draw the line between personal rights, property, or needs and some other's right to make a claim on his sympathy, to make him feel guilty, or to make him give up something that he need not have given up.

In this case the conflict is further complicated because it seems to be between something that is of little consequence to the speaker, yet vital to the tramps. The claims are not of equal weight: they are work as opposed to play, need as opposed to love. The last stanza, which declares the necessity for uniting vocation and avocation, love and need, work and play as the ideal way of doing a deed, does not resolve the dilemma of who should be chopping the wood. There seems to exist a separation between love and need, work and play.

Yet there is need and need: there is financial need and there is emotional need. There is also right and right—the right of a man to expect sympathy for his need to earn a living and the right of a man to chop wood—especially if it is on his own property—if he wants to do so. In fact the recognition on the part of the speaker is a generous and an unselfish one:

Nothing on either side was said.
They knew they had but to stay their stay
And all their logic would fill my head:
As that I had no right to play
With what was another man's work for gain.
My right might be love but theirs was need.
And where the two exist in twain
Theirs was the better right—agreed. (CP 358–59)

The claim on his conscience may not have been valid or fair, but it worked all the same. Their "logic" did fill his head as they had counted on its doing, and whether he gives up the task or not is irrelevant,[10] for once their logic had filled his head, the pleasure in the task would be gone. At first their claiming the task simply intensified his love for it ("The time when most I loved my task / These two must make me love it more / By coming with what they came to ask"); but then that was before their logic filled his head. The resolution of the poem will depend on whether feeling wins out over logic, and then the question is *which* feeling—sympathetic feeling for another or feeling about the task that unites work and play, love and need. The separation the speaker sees between work and play, love and need, is, after all, the separation he assumes the tramps to see—it is *their* logic, and he shows himself to be very sensitive in assuming it. If the conflict is resolved on his terms, we must assume he will give up the task should these claims remain separate; that he will continue to do it should they be united. "Theirs was the better right" only "when the two exist in *twain*."

Here, as elsewhere in Frost, we are shown the seriousness of "play,"[11] for this activity was "play" as long as one did not do it from motives of gain. Pay then was what defined it as work rather than play, that made it vital and "right." That it was hard work in either case is beside the point; that there was something at stake—pride in the quality of the workmanship and the aim—is beside the point. The crucial question is what will be the gain. Of what importance is it to the chopper? At least that becomes the question once the speaker feels himself to have been "caught" in the act (a tacit admission of guilt), which leads him to consider the wood "unimportant" despite the fact that he was loosing his soul, giving vent to whatever was pent up—"the blows that a life of self-control / spares to strike for the common good" (357). Loosing his soul in spending these blows on the wood is an important activity whether the wood is important or not.

In the inability of the tramps to understand *his* needs, Frost proves them inferior to the speaker who sees theirs. It is, once more, a matter of how one is reading the scene and what one brings to the reading. Frost reads them better than they read him. They see what their agenda permits them to see, a criticism we could level at the socialist critics who made the poem—and

Frost—a target on their agenda, often unfairly, certainly missing rich possibilities of interpretation and maybe missing the
point or mistaking the resolution.

Another need that the task answers is for a physical connection, muscular exertion, pitting oneself against an earth, a tree, a
nature that shows crystal teeth, that moves capriciously between
March and May and back in a moment:

> You'd think I never had felt before
> The weight of an ax-head poised aloft,
> The grip on earth of outspread feet.
> The life of muscles rocking soft
> And smooth and moist in vernal heat. (CP 358)

A deed done "for . . . future's sake" must exert weighty grip
and muscle in the face of so uncertain and capricious a future.
It must require poise and balance as surely as does that boy
mastering birches.

In this poem, as in "Birches," "love" is introduced where it has
not seemed to be the subject: love of the work, love of the feel
of the earth, and "the life of muscles, rocking soft / and smooth
and moist in vernal heat"; love as it relates to labor, love as it relates to need. We see that only in uniting these will the speaker
be entitled to make a claim that equals the claim of the tramps,
for love must be related to need and to effort. Only in applying
this union to any relationship, any task, or act of creativity does
the last stanza seem to be genuinely a part of the poem and
not simply the gratuitous nonresolution of Frost's poetic career,
which it is so often taken to be.

> But yield who will to their separation,
> My object in living is to unite
> My avocation and my vocation
> As my two eyes make one in sight.
> Only where love and need are one,

And the work is play for mortal stakes,
Is the deed ever really done
For Heaven and the future's sakes. (CP 359)

In two separate letters, Frost relates this poem somewhat curiously to love of a woman. In his famous assertion that Elinor had been the unspoken half of everything he wrote, he went on to add: "and both halves of many a thing from My November Guest down to the last stanzas of Two Tramps in Mud Time" (SL 450). In writing about his view of imperfection, he said: "I am not a Platonist . . . one who believes . . . the woman you have is an imperfect copy of some woman in Heaven. . . . I am philosophically opposed to having one Iseult for my vocation and another for my avocation; as you may have inferred from a poem called Two Tramps in Mud Time . . . a truly gallant Platonist will remain a bachelor . . . from unwillingness to reduce any woman to the condition of being used without being idealized" (SL 462).

Love and need, then, must be one, or the relationship, whether in marriage, in friendship, or in art, is exploitation. But there is another factor in a love relationship—in a relationship with any other human being or with one's task—which distinguishes love and need from exploitation, and that is "spending" oneself rather than merely spending another: "be it art, politics, school, church, business, love, or marriage—in a piece of work or in a career. *Strongly spent is synonymous with kept.*" The speaker in this poem speaks of the soul-loosing blows he "spent on unimportant wood," and if anything entitled him to "keep" the task rather than to give it up, it is the effort, the love with which he spent himself on the task. In the above quotation from "A Constant Symbol," Frost had been speaking of writing poetry: "Every single poem written regular is a symbol small or great of the way the will has to pitch into commitments deeper and deeper to a rounded conclusion and then be judged for whether any original intention it had has been *strongly spent or weakly lost* (SP 24; emphasis mine). Peculiar to relationships of love and creativity is the opposition of spent and lost. In commerce, one is short by what one spends; in love and in creation, one only keeps by spending, saves one's heart with losing it; one only fulfills oneself by giving oneself. In "Two Tramps," strongly spent, *being* strongly spent, is the only real justification for keeping.

The question of respect for self, of integrity of self as opposed to giving up of self, is posed in two ways in "Two Tramps in Mud Time," for there are two relationships: the relationship between the speaker and the two tramps, and the relationship between the speaker and his work. If the relationship between himself and his work is one of love, need, and spending of himself for his task and the perfection of the job for its own sake, then that may take precedence over a relationship with two strangers where there is no love, no pride in work, no effort, no mutuality of give and take. The self *and* its labor of love are united and preserved, kept, in the face of claims that would separate that unity. If, however, the task separates love and need, if nothing further will be "spent" on it, then the job is exploitive. It had better be given to those who can use it for gain.

While the drama of the poem is more overtly social than sexual, the relationship between love and need, keeping and spending oneself, respect for the needs of the self and the other, and willingness or unwillingness to surrender to it are clearly also applicable to a discussion of love, especially as the poet has drawn attention to this poem in such a connection. If we see the sexual undertone of "outspread feet. / The life of muscles rocking soft / And smooth and moist in vernal heat" it would not be the only poem, as we shall see, to conflate earth and love, the act of earth-labor with the act of love.

In "The Gift Outright," as in "Two Tramps," while the subject of the poem is the relationship of people to land, the theme of possession and its relation to giving of self is as applicable to love between people as it is to the love of a people for its country.

The poem speaks of "possessing what we were still unpossessed by," of the weakness inherent in withholding something "until we found it was ourselves . . . and forthwith found *salvation in surrender*" (CP 467; emphasis mine). But not all surrender is saving. If there is to be "salvation in surrender," there must be mutuality of surrender, not the selfless submission of the servant; there must be a balance between surrender and "keeping."

While we may feel the balance tipping uncomfortably in "Devotion,"[12] or in "Bond and Free"—where the thralldom is gendered by grammar and personification as female—loving, slight "bondage" is idealized in that magnificent tribute to woman-in-relation, "The Silken Tent":

> She is as in a field a silken tent
> At midday when a sunny summer breeze
> Has dried the dew and all its ropes relent,
> So that in guys it gently sways at ease,
> And its supporting central cedar pole,
> That is its pinnacle to heavenward
> And signifies the sureness of the soul,
> Seems to owe naught to any single cord,
> But strictly held by none, is loosely bound
> By countless silken ties of love and thought
> To everything on earth the compass round,
> And only by one's going slightly taut
> In the capriciousness of summer air
> Is of the slightest bondage made aware. (CP 443)

This poem is not about a personified love, as is "Bond and Free," but love as it is seen and felt in a loving woman, and thus the poem is a tribute to the kind of woman who, because of her loving and thoughtful ties to others, becomes proud, erect, and beautiful even as she exists as a shelter, creating a home, or providing a haven of privacy and emotional protection.

The silken tent swaying gently at ease presents an image not only of beauty but of dignity and free movement—the tent

swaying "in guys" sways also in the "guise" of freedom of movement. But one guy going taut, a summer breeze, or increased
moisture remind her occasionally of "the slightest bondage." Because these ties are ties of love and thought, however, because
they are "silken ties," the slight bondage is not undesirable. What
is necessary and positive about such bondage only becomes fully
apparent when we realize that in giving she receives; that those
"ties" to others are what keep her erect;[13] that were those ties to
snap, the tent would collapse; that heavenward pinnacle signi-
fying the sureness of the soul would fall, for nothing emanates
simply from the pole. The pole stands only in relation to the
guys.[14] It is important, too, that the ties are many, for that very
diversity is what keeps the pole balanced at the center. In the
relationship between heavenward pole and guys, it is almost as
if the ties of love and thought are in fact her claim to heaven.[15]

This poem of loving bondage and of an existence based upon
it is a perfect example of form and words, form and idea, "em-
bracing."[16] It has been observed that the entire sonnet is a single
sentence, but what seems so remarkable is the way in which the
structure of this sentence is analogous to the metaphor itself
and to the relationship that the metaphor expresses. The single
sentence construction provides, even more firmly than the sonnet form, a unified tightness which corresponds to the tightness
of the single image and the tightness of the ropes controlling
the very existence of the silken structure. At the same time, the
sentence comes perilously close to going out of control with its
multiplication of subordinate clauses (a guise of freedom).[17]

When one identifies the subordinate clauses, their subjects,
verbs, and antecedents, one discovers that the sentence raises
some real syntactical questions: for one, what is the main clause?
For another, if "as" is used as a conjunction of comparison, it
must introduce a clause—a subject and a predicate. Assuming
the tent to be the subject, what verb completes the clause—
what verb that is not inside another clause and governed by its
own subject? We find that "tent" actually governs no verb in

the poem. For example, the subject of "sways" in line 4 is "it"; the subject of "seems" and "is loosely bound" is really "pole." The "and" clause of the final three lines refers to "tent' as an implied subject of "is . . . made aware," but since the clause is a coordinate, not a subordinate clause, since "and" creates a compound sentence, we are still left with the question of what the verb should be of which "tent" is the subject in the "as" clause, that is, in the first half of the compound sentence that is contained in the larger complex one. It is interesting that the subtlety of control that is a subject of the poem is also carried out in the syntactic structure of the poem. Just as "tent" is the implied subject of "is . . . made aware," so is it the antecedent of "it" as the subject of "sways." Thus what the word "tent" does not do directly, "tent" as implied subject, as antecedent, does do indirectly—another "guise" of freedom, here freedom from the grammatical control of "tent" as subject.

One might so easily be tempted to identify "seems" (line 8) and "is loosely bound" as the verbs completing the clause whose subject is "tent," rendering it: "as . . . a silken tent . . . seems to owe naught to any single cord, but . . . is loosely bound by countless silken ties of love and thought." But then we run into problems of another kind in such a structure. The whole sentence would then essentially read: "She is as a tent seems to owe naught to any single cord, but . . . is loosely bound," which makes no sense. Even were we to insert "which" before "seems" we would still be left with an uncompleted clause. Were we to reverse the sentence—"As a tent seems to owe naught to one . . . but is loosely bound to many, she is"—we still have not solved the difficulty. The parallelism is faulty.

Further examination, of course, proves that it is not "tent" but "pole" that is the subject of the verbs under discussion. We find, too, that the "and" of line 12 really coordinates *within* the clause whose subject is "pole." The sentence reduced to simpler terms would read: "and its pole seems to owe naught to any single cord, but is loosely held by countless ties to earth, and only by one's going taut is of the slightest bondage made aware." What then is "made aware"? The pole, it seems; yet because of the word "its" we are forced to make the connection between pole and tent. What keeps up the pole—or binds it—is keeping up and binding the tent that it supports. Somehow the existence and erectness of the tent has become identified with the uprightness of the supporting pole, as if one cannot syntactically separate the pole from the tent any more than one can separate "sureness of the soul" from "her." Indeed we are forced back to "her" because there must be more than grammar operating in a sentence: there must also be sense—semantic sense—and this sense tells us that a pole cannot "be made aware." Just as a distinction is sometimes made between the grammatical subject of a sentence and its logical subject,[18] so we find that a distinction must be drawn between a grammatical subject—even a logical subject—and an "emotional" one, one that we *feel* to be the subject, the dictates of grammar notwithstanding. "Pole" is the grammatical subject of "seems to owe naught," and as such it is logical as well; "tent," while it is not the grammatical subject, is also a logical subject of the same verb. When we get to "is made aware," however, we must reject both "pole" and "tent" as logical subjects. Only "she" can be made aware. The logic of our feelings has supplied the human subject, grammar and logic have supplied "tent" and "pole," and the operation of all three has forced the metaphoric fusion.

What of the original questions of main clause, though, and of verb to complete "tent"? They seem resolvable only if one can insert an implied "is" so that line 1 would essentially say: "She is as is . . . a silken tent in a field at midday" and on to the end.[19] The parallelism then is one based on existence—analogous existence. And we must see this in relation to Frost's choice of "as" over "like."

The first line lends itself to two possible readings:

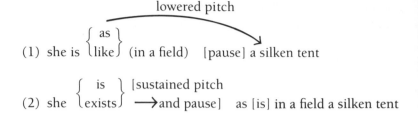

(1) she is $\left\{\begin{array}{l} \text{as} \\ \text{like} \end{array}\right\}$ (in a field)   [pause] a silken tent

(2) she $\left\{\begin{array}{l} \text{is} \\ \text{exists} \end{array}\right\}$ [sustained pitch —→and pause]   as [is] in a field a silken tent

At first glance, (1) seems to have been intended. This would presume that "as" is being used for the preposition "like," a function that it actually does not have.[20] Version (2), on the other hand, uses "as" correctly as a conjunction, and the result is the emphasis on existence and the necessity for assuming an implied "is." The whole grammatical problem would not have existed at all had Frost allowed the sentence to read: "She is like a silken tent in a field at midday, when a summer breeze has dried the dew, and all its ropes relent." It would make perfect sense, better sense, even, all the way to the end. By using "as," and thereby forcing us to supply the missing "is" for "tent," Frost has created a subtle distinction between "like" and "as." He has rejected the easier comparison between woman and tent and forced the comparison, not of nouns, but of relationships. She is not like a tent; she exists in the same manner as a tent does, by means of the same conflicting, balancing pulls. So the main clause can only be "she is"; and highlighting this clause at the very outset creates a compelling relationship between the fact and the manner of her existence.

As we have noted, only when one guy goes taut does the tent pole seem tied down; only when affairs are not proceeding smoothly, only when one "tie" of "love" pulls in an unusual way, is the woman made aware of "bondage" that she never feels when her "ties" are smooth and in balance. These countless ties, of course, are only countless when we apply the term to the ties of love and thought binding the woman, for surely actual tent guys *can* be counted. Once more, we have been deftly moved from a concrete tent to qualities and feelings that the tent as meta-phor makes clear. Once more we are reminded that it is in the balance, in the manner of existence, that we find the analogy.

There is another aspect to the relationship between tent, pole, and guys. The tent depends for its uprightness, in fact for its very existence, upon the relationship between pole and guys. We are told that this "supporting central cedar pole"[21] is "its pinnacle to heavenward / And signifies the sureness of the soul." We are not only told that these things of the spirit are bound by ties of love and thought but that they are bound by these ties "to everything on earth the compass round."[22] Such a connec-tion only serves to reinforce the relation of spirit to matter—in other words, that the spirit is dependent upon matter,[23] that the spirit must rest on earth, that love is bound to earth or else its spirit cannot rise heavenward, cannot remain erect, and finally that the tent, and what it signifies as a loving woman, remains beautiful and erect by virtue of both the heavenward pole and the ties to earth, ultimately "the right place for love."

The one remaining problem involves the word "seems" ("seems to owe not to any single cord"), which raises the ques-tion: seems to whom? The fact that tent and pole are incapable of perception rules out these possibilities. The remaining possi-bilities are: (1) the casual observer of the scene, (2) the woman who has been metaphorically connected with tent and pole, or (3) the reader. If the reference is to the tent, then this is the way it seems to the casual observer; if it is to the woman, it may refer to the way it "seems" to her—the nature of seeming thus related to the "guise" of freedom that is, in reality, a complicated bondage. Psychologically this can refer to her self-delusion, her unawareness of bondage when there is no tension or pulling of a guy. In looking at the implications for the poem itself, how-ever, "seems" reminds us of the manner in which we as readers are finding it difficult to keep tent, pole, and woman apart, the way in which metaphor works on us, and the way in which we depend upon illusion and manipulate illusion as metaphor ourselves. We can imagine the way in which the metaphor, once conceived, continued to work on—and for—Frost as he was working it into a poem, the ways he may have needed that metaphor, the needs he brought to his reading of the metaphor, and his reading of the relationship that created it. One need may have been of that very relationship. To be one of the guys is to play a relatively safe role, as the tent will not collapse if only one goes slack, for it is not dependent on any *one;* at the same time, if the guy does not slacken, it remains "tied" to the tent and benefits from the spiritual sureness of the pole, even as it contributes to its erectness. Because the dominant image is that of woman in relation, we tend to lose sight of how important the relationship is to the guys.

This need for relationship, for balanced, mutual support, makes even more dramatic its failure in a poem such as "Home Burial"; the need to keep by spending is best illustrated by the *un*willingness of either partner in that poem to give up any part of the self. Fierce possessiveness of one's feelings, of one's sense of who and what one is or should be, of one's self-conceived role, plays a large part in that disaster, the marriage in "Home Burial." So does a frustrating unwillingness on both their parts to respect, along with an inability to understand, what the other partner is feeling. "Who is that man? I didn't know you" (CP 71), the wife said of her reaction to his digging of the grave. Indeed she did not seem to "know" him, not in any sense of the word, but then he did not "know" her either; neither did he know himself, or she, herself. The husband's offer of "some arrangement / by which I'd . . . keep hands off / anything special you've a mind to name" and his recognition that "two that don't love can't live together without [such restraints] / but two that do can't live together with them" (70–71) is exactly to the point. What he may not understand, however, is that what she wants his "hands off" are not peripheral possessions but what is fundamental to a love relationship—her person and her feelings. His plea, "Let me into *your* grief," is at the same time acknowledgment of this very separateness that he claims two who love cannot live with. It is as if this grief, "*your* grief," is a prized possession that she needs to feel exclusively hers, but he has allowed her to feel this way, letting it be *her* grief, never shouting, "This grief is *ours, not yours*," in just those words. Now is the one time, by saying "twice over *before he knew himself*: 'can't a man speak of his *own* child he's lost?'" (70), that he names the loss as his as well. He has been moved to speak out of character, an indication that this verbalizing of the loss has only just now come for the first time. He too can see it only as "his own," as if to imply the loss is his, the grief is hers.

She will not allow him the right to speak of the loss because of this distinction; one who does not *feel* the loss has no right to *express* the loss, and it is not only he but "any man" who cannot be allowed to enter the grief of a woman. He asks for help but seems to agree with her stereotypic view that to be a man is to fail in this arena of human emotions:

My words are nearly always an offense.
I don't know how to speak of anything
So as to please you. But I might be taught
I should suppose. *I can't say I see how.*
A man must partly give up being a man
With women-folk. (CP 70; emphasis mine)

Deeper than the misunderstanding of each other's words and motives lies this fundamental misunderstanding about what manhood should be. It would require a woman of greater sensitivity and larger feeling than she to be the teacher of that verbal expression he requires, for to teach a new language, the teacher must try to understand the broken and sometimes incomprehensible attempts of the inarticulate learner.

It is here that gesture and action could potentially have bridged the gap in verbal communication. One of the horrors of this poem is that, when action takes the place of words, it is as inadequate as the words, and just as misunderstood. Action is used to reject communication, as in her silent stiffening of her neck, or in her "fingers mov[ing] the latch for all reply." He uses action in a mistaken attempt to force communication, mounting until she cowers under him. "I will find out now—you must tell me, dear" (69–70), that "dear" so incongruous and out of place with the forceful five consecutive stresses of "I will find out now"—and just as futile. As futile, too, is the threat of force in the last line: "I'll follow and bring you back by force. I *will!*" (73). It is just as clumsily that he used action to vent his feelings when he dug the little grave. We have her account of it:

> I saw you from that very window there,
> Making the gravel leap and leap in air,
> Leap up, like that, like that, and land so lightly
> And roll back down the mound beside the hole.
> I thought, Who is that man? I didn't know you.
> And I crept down the stairs and up the stairs
> To look again, and still your spade kept lifting. (CP 71–72)

He did the "manly" thing in digging that little grave himself, and "manly" too was his ability to "sit there with the stains on [his] shoes / Of the fresh earth from [his] own baby's grave / And talk about [his] everyday concerns." (We could contrast him at this point with the unmistakably manly Macduff, who, dazed at the news of the death of "all [his] pretty ones, all," must reject Malcolm's appeal to "revenge it like a man" until he has had his opportunity to "feel it like a man." "He has no children," Macduff says of the man who thinks first of action before he allows for grief.) It is a very limited self-respect and a carefully circumscribed view of "manhood" that requires that a man's self-respect *as* a man deny feeling, deny verbal or emotional giving in to grief.[24] Now the husband is ready "to laugh the worst laugh I have ever laughed," seeing himself as "cursed. God, if I don't believe I'm cursed" (72). He must mean a laugh of bitterness which could be at the irony of the way she saw that grave-digging, or it could be at himself for his emotional limitation.

Her view of his action must have been as literal-minded as her understanding of what he had said as he had come in from the digging of the grave:

> I can repeat the very words you were saying.
> 'Three foggy mornings and one rainy day
> Will rot the best birch fence a man can build.'
> Think of it, talk like that at such a time!
> What had how long it takes birch to rot
> To do with what was in the darkened parlor. (CP 72)

It has, of course, a great deal to do with it. It is ironic that she, who faults his inability to phrase questions, to "see," is herself totally unable to "see" and "hear"; that she seems capable only of understanding literal exclamations but is totally unable to understand metaphor; that he, nonverbal man that he is, finds expression in metaphor that she cannot interpret.

With all the grievances out on the table now, one could hope for the understanding that may come out of it to save the marriage, but the opportunity is irrevocably lost, again because of his inability to come out with a genuine expression of feeling, or his inability to understand or tolerate her grief. His assertion that she overdoes it a little is not necessarily untrue, but at this moment it is so tactless, so wrong. Worse still is his failure to explain why he shall laugh the worst laugh he ever laughed, his failure to explain what that rotting birch fence had to do with the little body in the parlor, his acceptance of her accusation, "you *couldn't* care!" In this revealing dialogue, he has finally noticed what it is she always looks at out there. He has finally found words to ask her for some explanation, and then, ironically, having found his tongue, he "think[s] the talk is all" (73).

Of course, as a man of action, he could have let his actions speak, but even his actions serve more to hide his feelings than to reveal them, assuming he *is* feeling grief or love. In his being more preoccupied with someone's seeing his wife crying than he is with the crying itself ("Amy! There's someone coming down the road!"), he has lost his last opportunity. The opening and closing of the door at the end, like the crossing of the stairs at the beginning, are actions that lead nowhere in the relationship. They are the empty gestures which throw into relief the crossing that took place rather than the meeting that should have; she responds to the plea to "let me in" by opening the door— not to let him in but to let herself out, for the home entraps her not only in marriage to this man but within a reality she tries desperately to escape.

In his digging the grave he demonstrates his acceptance of the death, his instinctive acceptance of the fact that he buries much as he plants. He accepts his own hard and bitter role and responsibility, rather than having anyone else take the burden from him. She, who cannot accept death, who "won't have grief so," cannot accept his acceptance. Her saying "the world's evil" is more extreme than saying the world is sad or unbearable. She introduces evil where there is perhaps only a hard fact of nature and life.[25] She won't have grief so *if she can change it,* but of course she cannot change it; to see this she would have had to see that her own grief could be changed only by her ability to transcend it, to allow it some healing.

We can only assume that he does not explain or discuss these things because they have not formed as ideas in his mind. Rather he acts instinctively; he fails to understand that she cannot do the same, because he is not thinking of these things; he only lives by them. It is the husband who compares the graveyard to a bedroom in a smooth and calm speech that contrasts strongly with the nervous, staccato irregularity of the wife's speech rhythms:

'The wonder is I didn't see at once.
I never noticed it from here before.
I must be wonted to it—that's the reason.
The little graveyard where my people are!
So small the window frames the whole of it.

Not so much larger than a bedroom is it?
There are three stones of slate and one of marble,
Broad-shouldered little slabs there in the sunlight
On the sidehill. We haven't to mind *those*.
But I understand: it is not the stones,
But the child's mound—'
        'Don't, don't, don't, don't,' she cried. (CP 69–70)

Surely without understanding the implications of what he has just said, he nevertheless instinctively grasps the relationship between the bedroom and the grave—the place of love, the place of birth, and the place of death as they all relate to each other in the process of life, which includes death as well as birth.

He can easily incorporate that physical fact of life into his own life by virtue of his own physicalness. This translates itself into his ability to dig without being emotionally paralyzed by what has necessitated that digging. It also shows in the physicalness of his responses to his wife's perverse stiffness. He *checks* his actions, he promises not to come down the stairs, then threatens again: "You make me angry. I'll come down to you / God, what a woman!" At the end, there is his inability to see any recourse other than brute force: "If—you—do! [26] . . . I'll follow and bring you back by force. I *will*!"

Her cowering beneath him at the beginning of the poem suggests her fear of his brute force. Yet a moment before this, her face had "changed from terrified to dull"—dull as she faced him, terrified as she still was from having looked "back over her shoulder at some fear." The view that frightened her was that of the mound in the graveyard. Terror was probably compounded of this fear, fear of her husband's seeing it, and also, perhaps, fear of her husband's anger or strength, as we have already seen in her cowering. Still the realities of life and death are the sources of terror, and fear of him is only a part of this. It would seem that we have here still another example of failed communication, missed opportunity, and misunderstanding of manliness. The marriage is, among other things, a combination of a woman who seems unable to accept the hard facts of life and death and a man who is too completely physical, who feels that to express himself in words to womenfolk is "partly [to] give up being a man." Perhaps to express tenderness or gentleness physically may have been equally compromising to his perception of manhood. We cannot know, but it would be consistent with his mode of action and with her response. Just as she cannot meet him half way to help him express himself, just as she refuses to understand his mode of expression, so he cannot understand her needs in her grief or her inability to accept the brutal realities of life and death. Their home has been buried as surely as that child has been.[27]

We have seen that Frost's poems often show a speaker identifying uncomfortably with aspects of nature which he wishes were not so reminiscent of his own inner nature; he may find in scenes of dissolution, disintegration, and destruction that which is too close to his fears of his own physical and psychic destruction. But binding humans even more closely to nature "outside" is an element in nature that he can recognize, not as analogous to him, but *within* him. In love, birth, and death, for example, we are one with nature, participating in the natural process, which operates within us as surely as in nonhuman nature, and it is here that we are not separate from nature but *of* it.

While in some poems Frost demonstrates the need for human beings to see themselves separate from nature, he also demonstrates the folly of being unwilling to recognize not only the similarities we share with nature but the actual connections. As John Lynen has put it in his discussion of "puke," "prude," and "runaway from nature," the real prude, the real escapist, is the person who cannot face the fact that our physical being connects us with nature.[28] To deny and reject what is "natural" and physical, to reject this in ourselves and our relationships, is to succumb to the "prudery" of being unwilling to recognize our relationship with nature, which results in being unable to reconcile ourselves with nature as it operates within us and as we operate within a natural system.

Randall Jarrell views Amy's horror at the grave digging (that lifting and plunging) and her fascination with his digging (her creeping down the stairs and back to watch without knowing why) as having a sexual meaning—some combination of resentment at the menace of masculine power and guilt caused both by her child's death and her own sexuality. "She stares with repudiating horror, with accepting fascination, at this obscenely symbolic sight. It is not the child's mound she stares at but the scene of the crime, the site of this terrible symbolic act that links sexuality and death, the marriage bed and the grave."[29] Nothing in the poem forces us to see it this way, and to label the whole problem a sexual one would be to distort it; yet there is no denying that her inability to accept the realities of life and death would probably include her inability to come to terms with the physical aspects of love, to accept the relationship between their sexual union and "what lay in the darkened parlor." Nor can we deny the sexual overtones of his "let me in," her shutting out.

"The Subverted Flower," on the other hand, is explicitly and overtly about the horror, the "meagerness" of heart, with which a girl reacts to her young lover's sexuality.

> She drew back; he was calm:
> "It is this that had the power."
> And he lashed his open palm
> With the tender-headed flower.
> He smiled for her to smile,
> But she was either blind
> Or willfully unkind.
> He eyed her for a while
> For a woman and a puzzle.
> He flicked and flung the flower,
> And another sort of smile
> Caught up like finger tips

The corners of his lips
And cracked his ragged muzzle. (CP 453)

At the beginning the boy was calm, although he "lashed his open palm / with the tender-headed flower" as he acknowledged the power of that flower, a power that, Circe-like, seems to transform his smile to a "ragged muzzle," his choking tenderness to a tiger choking at a bone, his hand to a paw, his voice to a bark. The flower—in every other poem Frost published, an object of fragile beauty, of love, the one object in nature to which Frost assigns no duality, no sinister motive[30] or dangerous invitation— here has such power.

This flower, however, he calls *subverted*—corrupted, destroyed—and the passive voice inherent in the participle leads to our asking: by what or by whom? In "Flower Guidance," a poem Frost never published, he had written:

As I went from flower to flower
(I have told you how)
I have told you what I found
Dead not growing on the ground.
Look upon me now.

If you would not find yourself
In an evil hour
Too far on a fatal track
Clasp your hands behind your back.
Never pick a flower. (EY 584)

As Lawrance Thompson points out, words like "fatal track" and "evil hour" introduce moral overtones to flower picking, suggesting guilt connected with picking flowers or with literal and figurative deflowering.[31] In "The Subverted Flower," however, the flower is not subverted by the male alone. The girl contributes in no small way to the corruption of what has been beautiful, to what she views as the bestialization of the young man and, eventually, of herself. His acknowledgment of the power of the flower awaited her acknowledgment, his discovery awaited her recognition of the same discovery:

> He smiled for her to smile,
> But she was either blind
> Or willfully unkind. (CP 453)

It is only then that he "flicked and flung the flower" (the sounds of that line forcing us almost to spit it explosively out, a spitting out that will find its parallel in the girl's spitting bitter words [CP 455]), and only then that his "bestiality" emerges. The girl's "standing to the waist / In goldenrod and brake, / Her shining hair displaced" shows that she too has participated in the encounter. Yet he reacts by stretching "her either arm / As if she made it ache / To clasp her—not to harm; / As if he could not spare / To touch her neck and hair."

Surely it is in appeal to mutual recognition of their common attraction that he says:

> If this has come to us
> And not to me alone— (CP 453)

But she cannot meet his conditional with any resultant statement or recognition. As in "Home Burial," she replies by stiffening "lest movement should provoke / The demon of pursuit / That slumbers in a brute." Her mother's call makes her afraid, not of being discovered, but of his being provoked by it "to pounce and end it all before her mother came." How distorted her fear is can be seen from his shame—the shame of seeing himself as a beast because that was the way she was seeing him—a beast with a paw and a snout and "an eye become evasive" (454). It seems that even in his own eyes he became what she, according to her "reading" of the scene, was seeing.

Perhaps because of her own immaturity, her fear in the face of something new and potentially overwhelming, and her own part in it, perhaps because of her inability to understand it or reconcile herself to it, the girl "saw the worst" and thus subverted the flower. The narrator makes very explicit his judgment on her failing; in the girl's view the flower had *marred* a man, for she could not see a necessary relationship between the flower and his increasing manhood, only between the flower and his debasement to a beast. Nor could she see her own contribution to the transformation:

> A girl could only see
> That a flower had marred a man,
> But what she could not see
> Was that the flower might be
> Other than base and fetid:
> That the flower had done but part,
> And what the flower began
> Her own too meager heart
> Had terribly completed. (CP 454)

She too undergoes a transformation from the shining-haired girl of the goldenrod to a creature who spits bitter words (words that act like a tenacious bit), who foams at the mouth (455). Her mother not only wipes off the spittle but draws "her backward home," and in that word "backward" we feel her regression as well, not only from girl to beast, but from potential womanhood back to childhood. In the action of being drawn backward we understand, too, that her face is still toward the fleeing boy and the brake of goldenrod.

The woman in "A Servant to Servants," provides still another example of sexuality distorted, here feared, or at the very least associated with madness and ugly bestiality. The woman "has her fancies"; yet these "fancies" and the fears that generate them are grounded in past experience, past history, and present reality. She fears the hired men:

> Coming and going all the time, they are.
> I don't learn what their names are, let alone
> Their characters, or whether they are safe
> To have inside the house with doors unlocked. (CP 84)

And we have no way of knowing whether her fears of them are well founded or of her own making.[32]

She fears for her sanity; she has already "been away," and she finds it an easy out, the Asylum that literally seems an asylum to her from where she stands, too worn out to lift her hand, too behind to try to "catch up in this world." More than this, she fears insanity because "it runs in the family," and the form her uncle's insanity took, the treatment, and her view of the underlying cause are what seem to plague her more than the fact of insanity.

> My father's brother, he went mad quite young.
> Some thought he had been bitten by a dog,
> Because his violence took on the form
> Of carrying his pillow in his teeth;
> But it's more likely he was crossed in love,
> Or so the story goes. It was some girl.
> Anyway all he talked about was love.
> They soon saw he would do someone a mischief
> If he wa'n't kept strict watch of, and it ended
> In father's building him a sort of cage,
> Or room within a room, of hickory poles,
> Like stanchions in the barn, from floor to ceiling,—
> A narrow passage all the way around.
> Anything they put in for furniture
> He'd tear to pieces, even a bed to lie on.
> So they made the place comfortable with straw,
> Like a beast's stall, to ease their consciences.
> Of course they had to feed him without dishes.
> They tried to keep him clothed, but he paraded
> With his clothes on his arm—all of his clothes.
> Cruel—it sounds. I s'pose they did the best
> They knew. And just when he was at the height,
> Father and mother married, and mother came,
> A bride, to help take care of such a creature,
> And accommodate her young life to his.

That was what marrying father meant to her.
She had to lie and hear love things made dreadful
By his shouts in the night. He'd shout and shout
Until the strength was shouted out of him,
And his voice died down slowly from exhaustion.
He'd pull his bars apart like bow and bowstring,
And let them go and make them twang until
His hands had worn them smooth as any oxbow.
And then he'd crow as if he thought that child's play
The only fun he had. I've heard them say, though,·
They found a way to put a stop to it. (CP 85–86)

The caged wild animal her uncle had become, the projected
sexual cause, the implied sexual solution, and the fact that this
had been her mother's introduction into "what marrying father
meant," her mother's having had "love things made dreadful,"
all lie behind this woman's fears and her grim joke that she
would be taking *her* turn in the pen. She may have gotten away
from her parent's house with its frightening associations when
her husband saw the need to move somewhere else, somewhere
with a beautiful view of nature, but she understands:

> . . . there's more to it than just window-views
> And living by a lake. I'm past such help—
>
> . . . .
>
> I s'pose I've got to go the road I'm going:
> Other folks have to, and why shouldn't I? (CP 86)

Her own superior understanding and insight into her own
condition might, if combined with alleviation from overwork,
reverse her direction "on the road" she is going; rest would
certainly be restorative, as the doctor has said. She knows her
uncle's bestiality to have been insane, and aggravated by in-
humane treatment that the family mistakenly thought to be
more human, keeping such people at home rather than send-
ing them away. She also knows enough to understand that her

mother's education into "love things" had been wrong. Still the uncle and his stall and his shouts in the night are part of her "fancies" and part of her weary hopelessness.

Malcolm Cowley found "The Subverted Flower" to be the sole exception (and a late one)[33] in a canon wherein "all the love affairs are etherealized or intellectualized." Cowley is not the only one who finds Frost lacking in sexual explicitness or in willingness to go beyond prudish reticence when it comes to physical passion. Love of the fact in Frost is alleged to be confined to the earth or to the necessity for factual reality in his art. Too seldom until recently was Frost recognized as a great poet of love and marriage,[34] of love *in* marriage, and of sexuality. The insight we have seen on Frost's part into distortions of sexuality, into failure to understand it or come to terms with it as a positive and wholesome aspect of life and love, should dispel the notion that Frost was a "prude."[35]

A case in point is the delightful monologue spoken by "The Pauper Witch of Grafton," which suggests by its close that to be "bewitched" by her was quite all right with her victims and that maybe the real perversion lay in regarding her as a witch.[36] Her husband had been eager to perpetuate the witch myth: "I guess he found he got more out of me / by having me a witch." Underlying this statement, as well as the humor of the poem, is the premise that "witchery" like hers could not have been considered normal and acceptable. It seemed necessary to her Arthur Amy (aimé?) "to let on he was plagued to death with" her, but Arthur Amy was probably the happiest man in town.

> Well, I showed Arthur Amy signs enough
> Off from the house as far as we could keep
> And from barn smells you can't wash out of
>   plowed ground
> With all the rain and snow of seven years;
> And I don't mean just skulls of Rogers' Rangers
> On Moosilauke, but woman signs to man,

Only bewitched so I would last him longer.
Up where the trees grow short, the mosses
     tall,
I made him gather me wet snow berries
On slippery rocks beside a waterfall.
I made him do it for me in the dark.
And he liked everything I made him do. (CP 255)

Randall Jarrell has written of this poem: "When I read the lines that begin *Up where the trees grow short, the mosses tall,* and that end *And he liked everything I made him do* (nobody but a good poet could have written the first line, and nobody but a great poet could have forced the reader to say the last line as he is forced to say it),[37] I sometimes murmur to myself, in a perverse voice, that there is more sexuality there than in several hothouses full of Dylan Thomas; and, of course, there is love there."[38]

The object of a legal battle as to which town's charge she was to be ("Flattered I must be to have two towns fighting / to make a present of me to each other"), she remarks: "I know of some folks that'd be set up / at having in their town a noted witch" (252). She thus turns a case of whose nuisance she must be into a parody of *Oedipus at Colonnus.* Tossed from one town to another, having "come down from everything to nothing," she is at the same time a kind of patron saint or, at least one feels, perhaps she ought to be.[39]

Seeing this side of Frost should also alert us to the possibility that explicitly physical poems may implicitly if not explicitly include the sexual. A good example is "The Strong Are Saying Nothing," which devotes three of its four stanzas to planting. Suddenly the poem ends on the subject of dying and the reservation of hope on the subject of life after death. The language of the poem can surely speak for itself:

The soil now gets a rumpling soft and damp,
And small regard to the future of any weed.

The final flat of the hoe's approval stamp
Is reserved for the bed of a few selected seed.

There is seldom more than a man to a harrowed piece.
Men work alone, their lots plowed far apart,
One stringing a chain of seed in an open crease,
And another stumbling after a halting cart.

To the fresh and black of the squares of early mold
The leafless bloom of a plum is fresh and white;
Though there's more than a doubt if the weather is not
   too cold
For the bees to come and serve its beauty aright.

Wind goes from farm to farm in wave on wave,
But carries no cry of what is hoped to be.
There may be little or much beyond the grave,
But the strong are saying nothing until they see. (CP 391)

Only by refusing explicitness ("I've written a whole book
without the word *sex* in it. That doesn't mean I've left anything
out"),[40] only by not being insistently sexual in the poetry does
Frost leave the door open to such complex multiple meaning,
to the sort of density that we find in "To Earthward," where
love, death, and earth are inextricably fused. It is not that the
love affairs are, as Cowley has stated, "etherealized and intellectualized," but that they deal with the many facets of human
sexuality. T. S. Eliot tells us that humankind cannot bear very
much reality; Frost seems to say that love not only makes it
possible to bear reality but that it forces reality upon us, that
to love is to be engaged—in joy and pain, in life itself, which
is, of course, inseparable from process—and inseparable from
engagement with a human Other and the risks of entanglement
this entails.
   We have seen the devastating effects of the inability to reconcile these seemingly disparate facets of life, the inability to
reconcile one's conception of self with nature—within or with-

out. We have seen the psychic cost of refusing engagement or being, for any reason, deprived of it. It is as if Frost is dramatizing by its absence the importance of love as a potential engaging presence. He also dramatizes in these failures how rare successful engagement can be. In contrast, in some of Frost's poems about love and bringing to life, he demonstrates harmony between man's inner human nature and the forces of nature that are not necessarily human. Bringing to life is, of course, related to love—love of a woman, love of the soil, love of one's artistic creation. In the few poems that approach genuine harmony and reconciliation, all three of these kinds of love are intimately related and in some, inseparably linked.

So united is the couple in "The Telephone" that they seem to be able to communicate across the time and space of a day's walk without, in reality, being able to exchange either word or gesture:

'When I was just as far as I could walk
From here today,
There was an hour
All still
When leaning with my head against a flower
I heard you talk.
Don't say I didn't, for I heard you say—
You spoke from that flower on the window sill—
Do you remember what it was you said?'

'First tell me what it was you thought you heard.'

'Having found the flower and driven a bee away,
I leaned my head,
And holding by the stalk,
I listened and I thought I caught the word—
What was it? Did you call me by my name?
Or did you say—
Someone said "come"—I heard it as I bowed.'

'I may have thought as much, but not aloud.'

'Well so I came.' (CP 147)

She does not deny the reality of the "come" that he heard—she "may have thought as much but not aloud." Her unspoken thought, then, was what he "heard," showing that not only was physical nearness unnecessary to their communication but that words were unnecessary as well. Neither does she deny speaking from "that flower on the window sill."

It is the flower, after all, that he calls "the telephone." It is the flower on the window sill which transmits to the flower in the field a message that could only be transmitted to those who put their faces so close to flowers, who "listen" to them. This couple, then, who can communicate simply by virtue of their shared feelings, their common desire to come near each other (even the rhymes are interrelated: words in the second half of the poem rhyme with words in the first stanza; what he says rhymes with what she says), also communicate by means of flowers. One is reminded of the powerful flower in "The Subverted Flower" or the petal of the rose in "To Earthward," and this flower saying "come" could very well be of the same species.[41] Not only common feelings and common thoughts, but common desire resolves this poem. He feels himself called by what the flower represents, and she does not deny having the same thought, she does not deny the flower on the window sill.

But flower and "come" do not force the sexual connotation. The poem is delightful in its simplicity—the simplicity of its language and the spontaneity of its emotions. It is in that space left between suggestion of sexuality without insistence upon it that Frost is most effective,[42] allowing us insight into the subtler psychological aspects of the sexual. What strikes the reader immediately on even a first reading of the poem is the total communication between the couple (they read each other perfectly), and with sex not made explicit, this exquisite communication is allowed to be at the forefront. We are struck also by another way in which the flowers act as telephone: love of flowers is another common bond between the couple; love of nature somehow harmonizes with love of each other, as if love of nature, nature itself, is a mode of communication between them.[43] This flower is *not* subverted, not denied, but accepted for the lovely thing in nature that it is, and for the bond it creates between the communing lovers, the positive help nature can be to lovers who do not deny her.

Closer still to a genuine reconciliation between humans and nature by means of love is "Putting in the Seed." A remarkable combination of the domestic and the Dionysian, this poem includes not only love—love between humans paralleling love of the earth, love of nature reflecting the nature of love—but it includes and culminates with the creativity of love.

> You come to fetch me from my work tonight
> When supper's on the table, and we'll see
> If I çan leave off burying the white
> Soft petals fallen from the apple tree
> (Soft petals, yes, but not so barren quite
> Mingled with these, smooth bean and wrinkled pea;)
> And go along with you ere you lose sight
> Of what you came for and become like me,
> Slave to a springtime passion for the earth.
> How Love burns through the Putting in the Seed
> On through the watching for that early birth
> When, just as the soil tarnishes with weed,
> The sturdy seedling with arched body comes
> Shouldering its way and shedding the earth crumbs.
>   (CP 155)

No woods here, no wild animals, but a garden close enough to the house for the speaker's wife to come and fetch him "when supper's on the table." In this garden, very much a part of the domestic setting (complete with supper on the table), there is slavery to "a springtime passion for the earth" and burning love.

What makes this poem of "passion for the earth" so much a human love poem as well is the manner in which the speaker assumes that his passion is one shared by his wife. Not only does he need her to fetch him because he fears he will not be able to "leave off" his spring planting, but he recognizes that if he does not go in with her immediately, she too might "lose sight of what [she] came for" and become, like him, slave to the same passion. Potential abandon is shared; it is lavished creatively on the earth, and it is at home.

Love here does not merely burn through putting in the seed.[44] We are not left with merely the passion to plant; it burns *on through* the sprouting of the seedling. The repeated word "through" carries us forward in time, from planting through watching for birth; but it also emphasizes the double meaning of love burning "through the Putting in the Seed" and reminds us that the "seedling with arched body comes" pushing through as well. The selection of the verb "shouldering" reinforces, of course, the different meanings of "seed" with images of different kinds of fruition and birth. Consequently the word "through" is perfect in its uniting planting and sprouting, vegetable and human procreation, and the element of continuation in time.

Originally Frost had written:

> with
> How love burns ~~from~~ the putting in the seed
> On through the watching for that early birth.

Obviously recognizing that "from" makes the putting in of the seed seem like a painful experience already finished, he changed "from" to "with," and he must have decided then that repeating the preposition added emphasis and continuity. The lines became:

> How love burns with the putting in the seed
> And with the watching for that early birth.

In returning to "through" and using it in both lines, he not only hit upon just the right word, but he achieved one of his characteristically well-placed spondees, "burns through" as metrical support to that initial thrust, consistent with the spondee that ends the poem ("earth crumbs") in the image of new growth rending as it comes to life. We are not allowed to forget that new growth breaks up the earth; we are given the image of "arched body," then the "shouldering," and finally the "shedding" so that we cannot fail to connect love and birth, sowing and reaping, creation and destruction. This is one of Frost's rare springtime poems,[45] and while it emphasizes love and creation, and not destruction, as does "Spring Pools," the "springtime passion" is somewhat mitigated by this "shedding [of] earth crumbs" and also by the "tarnishing" of the soil by weeds: a soiling of the soil, somehow, which precedes the birth of the seedling.

Yet in "shedding" there remains something constructive rather than destructive, for shedding is part of development and growth; one layer of skin gives way to the next to allow for growth; one stage in the maturation process is shed for the next. So too the swollen apple ovaries have shed the petals of the apple blossoms as bloom becomes fruit. It is these soft petals that the speaker mingles with his seeds. It is these he buries so lovingly that he is not sure he can leave the task. Beautiful and soft (the twice-repeated "soft" that appeared only once in the original draft further emphasizes the appeal to touch by means of the soft sound of the repeated "s"), they bring to mind the sensual appeal of other flower associations. They certainly fit in with the sexuality implicit in passion and putting in the seed. But, consistent with the poem's insistence on the creativity, indeed the *pro*creativity of love, consistent with love's burning on through the waiting for the birth, is the speaker's recognition that the soft petals would be barren were it not for the seeds mingled with them—"smooth bean and wrinkled pea."

The poem emerges triumphant, like that sturdy seedling, a testimony to creative love, to spring and growth, to man's cooperation with nature. The faint suggestions of crumbling and tarnishing, far from reducing the poem's tribute to life, seem to anchor it to reality, to anchor love to earth as it is anchored to the earth in the literal situation of the poem. Love of the earth, love enriched rather than soiled by its contact with the earth, love bringing to bear in every sense of the word, joy in individual creation for its own sake, and joy in shared creativity, it is the uniting of all these into one experience, one poem, one "springtime passion" which provides that rare near-reconciliation of human and nature, human and another that Frost so often seeks and so seldom finds.

In this poem, rather than a destructive dissolution of boundaries, we see creative union. Unlike the position that "art is nothing but to get ashore out of the stream of animal perpetuations" (LU 204), here we have animal, vegetable, human, and artistic "perpetuations" almost perfectly united—nourishing and expressing one another, figuring in their creative union the creative possibilities of imaginative making. (We have only to remember Frost's sexual metaphors of metaphor to relate sexual love to poetic making.) We notice that in poems such as "The Telephone" shared love is related to shared imagining as well. In "Going for Water" the couple protested that they heard the brook they had gone out to seek, but they more than heard. They refer to "the slender tinkling fall that made / Now drops that floated on the pool / Like pearls, and now a silver blade," a sight they could not have seen but only imagined, even if the "note" they heard was indeed the brook (CP 26). In this poem what they joined to make was not only pleasure, not only a hush, but an imagined vision. The result had been a shared vision, a shared play of imagination. In "The Exposed Nest" the speaker seems to indulge his partner's sense of play, yet it is a kind of play he obviously values. He was even ready to "help pretend." In the same way Joe of "In the Home Stretch" respects his wife's seeing more than she would care to own out the window (CP 140).

This sharing of imagination, or at least valuing what the other imagines, even if it comes from "Ladyland," results, in "West-running Brook," in Fred's theorizing and philosophizing. His intellectual imagining begins with his wife's questions, and is further stimulated by her imaginings. Although he protests that he cannot follow her to Ladyland where a wave is intentionally waving, he takes off from her vision into his Bergsonian lecture. "Speaking of contraries," he begins (CP 328), but no one had been speaking of contraries. No one had mentioned the word, but the couple had been voicing and then creatively joining their very different ways of seeing.[46] What seemed an annunciation to her became a launching of his theory, and so, in a sense, it became an annunciation, a generating of something new. She not only imagines, she names, and he wants to be sure to credit her with that as surely as she wants to credit him with his major assertions (329). She names, and, further, she insists on recon-ciling their very different kinds of contribution. She names, and she brings into relation, be it contraries or their two types of contribution—names and the actual things that they name. We see that the successful "marriages" in the poems bring not only two people into harmony but also words and that which words are attempting to represent.

In this context, we can see "Home Burial" as an illustrative contrast—one most significant to poetic concerns: the manner in which the couple's final failure rests on their different percep-tions of language. How do words function, especially at the end, after her words have finally come out? What are words in this last exchange? To her, words are indelible; they have destroyed a marriage, buried a home. She cannot forgive either his actions in burying the child or his seemingly casual way of speaking about it. In speaking about her resentment, she has recreated the past, recreated by means of words the grief and resentment that are still very real to her. The words have given them new life, have made them almost tangible, certainly "feelable" to one who takes them seriously, one who knows how to listen, to read, or to visualize.

To him, though, they seem only words—out and therefore evaporated. "Oh, you think the talk is all," she cries because he has assumed all is better now that all has been spoken. "The heart's gone out of it: why keep it up?" (734). What words might have made real to him now becomes freed from feeling simply because it has been put into words. In other words, he invalidates the power of language to make real. The words were exhaled; they evaporated. It is all over, but not in the way he thinks. To Amy, the past lived in those words, and those words conveyed past-into-present in feelings that will not go away as easily as the molecules of air in their exhaling. Between them, the words became separated from the chaos and the grief they were expressing. They have become empty, while the grief itself continues to rage or to be formed into words for another who will listen to their content as something memorable, for it was only in words and in memory that the child was alive at all. To him, words stood for grief in the sense of taking the place of real grief; to her, words represented, were emblems of that grief. (For this reason it is especially ironic that she was so incapable of seeing his rotting fence as metaphor. Or maybe not, for the word "fence," to her, had to symbolize a real fence.) In the same way, his words of threat at the end are empty; action and words are separated, or if he makes good his implied threat, we can still say there is a way in which he will never be able to bring her back, not by force, not by words.

We can see the difference between language that "means," that seems to have substance, and language that is empty, merely words. We also see how language, which can create, can just as easily destroy. In "Home Burial" a home was destroyed: first by the husband's words (possibly misunderstood) about rotting birch fences, then by the wife's failure to speak the words that might have allowed healing; finally, by his failure to see that words that are pregnant with meaning and life cannot be treated as if they are empty. Each failed in being able to create a habitable reality for the other by means of words, and thus "Home

Burial" dramatizes not only the failure of a marriage, or even of a couple's ability to communicate, but of language itself.

Language fails in the marriage of "A Servant to Servants" as well. The speaker is clearly depressed, used up, tired, but what is symptomatic of her slipping from sanity is the way words are no longer functioning for her, the way they have become unhinged from reality:

> I can't express my feelings, any more
> Than I can raise my voice or want to lift
> My hand (oh, I can lift it when I have to).
>
> . . . .
>
> There's nothing but a voice-*like*
> That seems to tell me how I ought to feel
>
> . . . .
>
> You take the lake. . . .
> I stand and make myself repeat out loud
> The advantages it has. (CP 82; emphasis mine)

Surely what is exacerbating her depression is her husband's insistence on meaningless platitudes as her solution. "Len says one steady pull more ought to do it" (83), but she knows better. Nor is it medicine or views of the lake that can help, as Len thinks. What she has finally done in this conversation is to name her problems as they really are: "It's rest I want—there, I have said it out" (83); she also tells of her crazy uncle and her fear of going the same way; she speaks of the "doing / things over and over again that just won't stay done." To Len, though, she cannot speak of reality: "I waited til Len said the word. / I didn't want the blame if things went wrong" (86). Nor will she ask him the questions on her mind. What needs saying to her husband she cannot say, what her husband advocates and says has no basis in reality, she speaks to herself in a voice that is no longer a real voice to her because it is trying to tell her things that she knows are just not true, that have no power to help her.

That terrible fear in "Desert Places" of the void that was, to Frost, the greatest terror—"a blanker whiteness . . . with no expression, nothing to express"—has as its corollary a fear of having something to express and no means for doing so. There is also the fear of being misunderstood, expressed in "The Fear of Man." For a poet, especially, undermining the capacity of words to mean strikes at the core of the ordering possibility. Norman Holland sees language as Frost's way of managing what is frightening to him: he speaks of the way Frost uses "words in a magical, evocative way precisely to manage . . . fright,"[47] the way Frost uses the power of words to evoke and then to tame and manage reality. In this context, those for whom language has failed have a tenuous hold on reality and can thus rightly fear for their sanity; the marriages in which language fails cannot hold. In the harmonious marriage dialogues, even those of opposition, words mean, and women and men who communicate create, in large part by means of words. It is in this context that we can, perhaps, best appreciate the way language reflects, evokes, even creates reality in the poems wherein husbands and wives, like words and their meanings, are in concord.

In the beginning of "Paul's Wife," there is the word "wife." Just ask Paul about his wife, we are told, and he disappears (CP 235). The rest is legend, or rather legends. To Paul, the word "wife" and the woman named by the word were inseparable. He wouldn't hear of her spoken in any "way the world knew how to speak" (239), for to speak the word that represented her was to violate her, to profane her. There is indeed a suggestion of sanctity as well as fragility in the way Paul hides that marriage and that wife. Since we are never very certain about how tangible her existence ever was, we carry the concepts of fragility and sanctity beyond Paul to the act of creation, to imagination and its issue. One senses in Paul an almost religious attitude of naming as blasphemy. *Traduttore-traditore:* a translator is a traitor, for language—any language—betrays; no translation of idea, thought, emotion, or beloved other can ever be perfectly captured in words. Hence to name *is* to violate; to put into words, to diminish.

At least so the writer must feel as "what begins as a lump in the throat" becomes limited, reduced to a language that will never make its user feel completely satisfied, that will always leave some part of its wildness, what Iser would call its "virtuality,"[48] uncaptured and elusive. Thus the poem seems to be concerned not only with the fragility and sanctity of Paul's wife, or even of love, but also with the sanctity and fragility of creativity and particularly of the created, creating word. In its impalpability, the issue of the imagination is fragile, and needs to be protected. In its transcendent possibilities of materializing spirit—that "greatest attempt that ever failed" (SP 41; "Kitty Hawk")—it attains a kind of sanctity. Even among the brutish lumberjacks, this couple engendered creativity, for the woodsmen, after all, created and embroidered the legend.

In "The Death of the Hired Man" a couple is reconciled, not only with one another, but with the concerns of language and creating that have been under discussion here. In this poem we find that language not only expresses meaning but creates new meaning. Mary is portrayed as the traditional wife and home-maker, but she is also, literally, a home-maker in that she makes a home for Silas, and, furthermore, makes it with words. She has not simply called an entity by its correct name or even only named what had previously existed namelessly, as did the wife in "West-running Brook." She actually creates Silas's home in the act of saying: "Warren, he has come home to die" (CP 52). Of course, we can see this as a "feminine" nurturing act, but it is also a poetic one; like any poet-maker, she creates with words and is able to win Warren over to the "rightness" of her position, given the validity she feels in her creation. "What else but home?" (53).

When we travel the great psychic distance that separates the couple in "Home Burial" from the one in "The Death of the

Hired Man," from a dominant spirit of failure and emptiness to one of creation and reconciliation, from the failure of language to the creative power of language, we see new ways to understand how Frost needed human relationships, particularly needed love and marriage—in life and in the poetry—to help create. We see that it is when love and need are frustrated and separated, when expression fails, that imagination becomes distorted into neurosis and delusion. Therefore, it is not surprising that Frost saw loving marriage as potentially saving and creative, that he invests it with his greatest poetic concerns. By means of his "marriages" he deals with some of the greatest tensions of his art: how to reconcile fear of the word, with its ephemeral, limiting treasons, and love of it; how to maintain belief in the possibility and validity of such creative union in the face of all that opposes it, all the evidence of its failure, whether in love, marriage, imagination, or language.

Poems are believed into existence, Frost told us, and went on to relate the love belief and the literary belief to one another and to the God belief. "The person who gets close enough to poetry, he is going to know more about the word belief than anybody else knows, even in religion nowadays" (SP 44–45). It seems that to Frost the struggle to maintain belief in the power of the imagination, of words, particularly of his words and their power to mean and create, is also love and is dramatized in the poems of loving marriage. Perhaps this faith is what is most at stake when a poet plays for mortal stakes. Perhaps, too, it is what "is most us" as languaging creatures. Frost is a great poet of love— Poirier calls him our greatest poet of married love since Milton,[49] but in the marriage poems he also shows us that the figure love makes is, in crucial ways, "the same as for" poetry. He shows us what he may have meant when he said: "The figure a poem makes . . . the figure is the same as for love" (SP 18).

7

Felix Culpa: Frost and Eden

Frost makes a grand claim for poetry when he places those who come close to it in the first rank of believers, implying that poetry is a way toward belief, a way of believing; he is more explicit when he says a poem is believed into existence. This latter statement seems to refer to the author's belief in the poem-to-be, but the former, "com[ing] close enough to poetry," could just as easily refer to the reading of it. (We remember he used to mark his literature students for how close they came to poetry.) He seems to tell us that knowing how to read, entering into a creative poet-reader-interpretation contract, also requires belief, and further, teaches and generates belief. Frost insists that both the literary belief and the God belief are related to the love belief as well.

Nowhere do we find so close a fusion of these beliefs as when we read Frost reading that great poem of all three beliefs, the first chapter[s] of Genesis; and nowhere do we so clearly see Frost combining the act of reading with the act of writing. In addition to being reminded how the biblical story combines the God belief, the love belief, and the creative belief (in complex and multiple forms), we are witness to the way Frost reads this monumental text that has never ceased inspiring religious and artistic interpretations, a text that has always evoked exegetic response (very possibly the original reader response activity) and that itself interprets the most fundamental trio of human concern: love, death, and creation rotating in eternal triangulation. We are able to witness what Frost-the-reader made of that powerful and generative text because we read the poems he made out of his reading. "A myth to live by," he called it (I 256), and in reading Frost's oeuvre, as well as reading outside it about what most troubled and frightened him, we can see how it became for him "a gathering metaphor."

In Frost's poetry we see man seeking but only seldom finding harmony between himself and nature, and then it is usually by means of love. We have seen the creativity of love as it manifests itself in harvest, or human birth, or artistic creation. In these ways we can take comfort from our connection with nature and with others in love or communion. But we also share mortality with nature and may never feel reconciled with a reality that has as its inevitable end our own nonbeing—a state we cannot conceive—a return to earth as dust to dust, being "turned under" for future growth.[1] As conscious beings we cannot help resisting the notion of our being simply more organic matter in a nitrogen cycle; yet as humans we cannot help but be aware of this prospect. We have seen elsewhere in Frost that the very awareness of our mortality, our vulnerability, and our isolation is what informs our human vision. At the same time, while forcing us to confront painful reality—future and past, not merely present—this very humanness also seeks perpetually to fashion wholes from fragments, even if only to smash them once more; to make order out of the chaos, even if the order is "momentary"; to see patterns and connections, even if these too turn out to be illusory.

The poet sees connections, sees by means of metaphor what cannot be seen any other way, for there are perceptions and fears and feelings for which there is no logical explanation, no expression or description. With metaphor we are able to take in whole what cannot be made sensible by logical division and reconstruction of its parts; take intuitive, imaginative leaps, and bridge the gap between the known and the unknown by referring to what is known and concrete and within the range of our experience. We can deny, as did Frost, any comfort in death; we can resist, as he did, any reconciliation with it. We can put all the platitudinous statements about life and the continuity of life, love, and creation in any order we choose, and they remain unconvincing and wooden schemata that our feelings balk at and our minds cannot fathom. Yet "the sturdy seedling with arched body comes / shouldering its way and shedding the earth crumbs" says it all and says it in a manner that we can understand and, momentarily at least, accept. This is "the figure a poem makes . . . it assumes direction with the first line laid down, it runs a course of lucky events, and ends in a clarification of life—not necessarily a great clarification . . . but in a momentary stay against confusion" (SP 18).

The poem, however, does not simply clarify; it exists as a work of art whose creator gave it life. "Death is the mother of beauty," [2] Stevens tells us in a line that suggests, among other interpretive possibilities, that death at our back provides a powerful stimulus to create—to leave something, to make what will outlive us. Then, too, death is the subject of our art. When we perceive the paradoxical dualities of life, we have something *from* which to fashion art, about which to write poetry. We also need to create order and harmony to provide for ourselves and our fellows that "momentary stay against confusion," to *create* meaning where we cannot see it. Our being human, then, not only impels awareness of our mortality but drives us to create. Like the rest of nature we die, but unlike the rest of nature we know of death and anticipate it. Limited by our humanity, however, we can neither understand this nor imagine it. Like the rest of nature we mate and reproduce; unlike the rest of nature, we seek to invest such union with communion; we see in procreation some kind of answer, unsatisfactory though it may be, to our individual dissolutions, and of course we see other ways to create, thereby hoping to achieve a measure of immortality. We need only go to Renaissance poetry, Shakespeare's sonnets in particular, to find many examples of the poetic speaker who finds in the poem the way to immortalize his beloved, their love, and not least of all himself and his talent in the monument that the poem will become. He also seeks to "dwell in lovers' eyes"—to put his imprint on future readers as they and his poem interact. Not only will his poem "give life" to the beloved but to the poet and the poem as it is read. Frost, while sharing these concerns, goes further in making us feel that there is an identity between the creative urge and the sexual urge, artistic fulfillment and sexual fulfillment, the work of art and the product of tilling—sexually or agriculturally. We have seen this, for example, in "Putting in the Seed."

It is when we also try to reconcile death with love and creativity that we feel the greatest need for metaphor, in fact for the metaphoric thinking that makes of myth "the explanations a society offers its young of why the world is and why we do what we do, its pedagogic images of the nature and destiny of man," as Austin Warren and René Wellek have put it.[3] They go on to say:

For many writers, myth is the common denominator between . . . poetry and religion. There exists a modern view . . . that poetry will more and more take the place of the supernatural religion in which a more impressive case can probably be made for the view that poetry cannot for long take the place of religion since it can scarcely long survive it. Religion is the greater mystery; poetry, the lesser. Religious myth is the large-scale authorization of poetic metaphor. . . . [Modern literary study] sees the meaning and function of literature as centrally present in metaphor and myth. There are such activities as metaphoric and mythic thinking, a thinking by means of metaphor, or thinking in poetic narrative or vision.[4]

Nowhere is the "image of the nature and destiny of man" captured more resonantly than in the account of Adam and Eve and their loss of Eden, no story more central to the "human condition"—to the relationships between love and death, both of these to acts of creation, and creation to destruction—than is this one. Perhaps it is because it encompasses all of these relationships that Frost found it a congenial metaphor and alluded so often to Eden or the Fall.[5] Obsessed as he was by fear of death, equally obsessed as he was by fears of his own poetic barrenness, and related as the two are to each other and to the need for love, the vision of Eden and the loss of Eden provide for Frost and his readers a metaphoric meeting ground of mutual understanding—a shorthand where little needs to be made explicit once the echo or allusion provides the signal.

The introduction of Eden into the poem "Nothing Gold Can Stay" is such a signal. The changing of seasons and the force of gravity that forces everything in the poem downward would invite our reading the poem to include more than simply the nature of nature; yet the mythic echo makes a larger significance absolutely unmistakable and forces us to see "gold" in the context of "golden age" as well as season.

> Nature's first green is gold,
> Her hardest hue to hold.
> Her early leaf's a flower;
> But only so an hour.
> Then leaf subsides to leaf.
> So Eden sank to grief,
> So dawn goes down to day.
> Nothing gold can stay. (CP 272)

Nothing gold can stay, but then what else stays? Leaves will fall as seasons end; days end; and that "Eden sank to grief" reminds us that among other "griefs" caused by a loss of Eden is the major grief of death and loss which no one can escape. This major inescapable fact of life is told to us in the most matter-of-fact way. The fact that the poem was condensed from three stanzas[6] to one is significant, for there are realities that are pointless to embellish. That autumn will be gold again we need not be told, for what is important is that that gold will not *stay*. That sunsets and sunrises are gold we can supply from our own experience and that these do not stay any more than the leaves—we know this too. The brevity of the poem and of each line, the regularity of its rhythm and its rhyming couplets, the repetitions and the simplicity of its declarative sentences, the fact that the last four lines are one clause per line, emphasizing the increasing weight, the gravitational downward pull of everything in the poem, all of this contributes to a tone that says flatly and simply: This is it. That's life.[7] Every statement and image in the poem is allowed to speak for itself, and what more do we need? There is no sentimentalization, no dramatization. Anything more than the truth would have been too weak.

In earlier versions there are references to the gold of autumn, yet in neither are there references to Eden. In the obviously earlier of the two we find the line "For nothing gold can stay" followed by a playing with the idea of "an end de luxe" and thus:

In autumn she achieves
Another golden flame
And yet it's not the same
It [sic] not as lovely quite
As that first golden light.[8]

The obviously later, typed, three-stanza version, entitled "Nothing Golden Stays," reads as follows:

Nature's first green is gold,
Her hardest hue to hold.
Her early leaves are flowers;
But only so for hours.

Then leaves subside to leaves.
In Autumn she achieves
A still more golden blaze.
But nothing golden stays.

This version goes on to draw the analogy to days and ends by saying in the last stanza:

In gold as it began
The world will end for man.
And some belief avow
The world is ending now:
The final age of gold
In what we now behold.
If so, we'd better gaze,
For nothing golden stays.[9]

We have spelled out for us the various associations with gold: color in early spring, color in fall, material wealth, and even a hint at an apocalyptic conflagration of gold, an idea written into the much later poem "It Is Almost the Year Two Thousand," wherein Frost inserted several of the lines rejected from these earlier versions.[10]

In the version as we have it, Frost has introduced the analogy between changing leaves and passing time ("So dawn goes down to day") and the reference to Eden, which makes us conscious of several kinds of "falling." What Frost has achieved in such concentration is more than simply starkness, matter-of-factness of tone, and superb understatement; there is a compression in the writing which parallels the compression of life and death, spring and fall, dawn and day, and forces us to recognize that fall is implicit in spring; that sunset is implicit in dawn; and that transitoriness is the nature of life since "Eden sank to grief" at the dawn of man's existence.[11]

The poem proceeds downward, like "the universal cataract of death."[12] Here, though, we find no resistance, no hopeful backward motion, no sign of anything being sent up. Even though the time sequences in the poem go backward and forward, reinforcing the cyclical nature of time, every living thing runs a downward linear course. At the same time, forward implies back; earlier implies later. We are told not that the first color is gold but that the first *green* is gold, presumably to be followed by a green that is really green, eventually to be followed by another kind of gold—the gold of autumn. This gold will be gold in color, but it will not be gold in the sense of innocence, purity, genuineness, and the value that attaches to this state. We normally think of flowers following leaves; here we are told that the leaf is flowerlike before it is leaflike—a more beautiful state, as befits goldenness, but also an anticipation of the later state in the earlier one. That leaf *subsides* to leaf is also a curious reversal: leaves developing and opening up increase the leafiness of nature; yet Frost uses a verb that means to sink to a lower level, to become less active, to abate. Likewise dawn is the *rising* of the sun; yet here dawn goes *down* to day, anticipating that days that begin also end. There are no beginnings without endings in this poem. Nothing—not color, not wealth, not innocence, not time, not life itself—nothing can stay.

This becomes clearer in examining the difference between the typed version, whose title and refrain are "nothing golden stays," and the final "nothing gold can stay." There is a difference between golden—*like* gold—and *gold*—the genuine, the original article, the original innocence. In changing the line to "gold," Frost needed another syllable, but the addition of "can" does much more than correct the rhythm. It is not that gold *does* not stay; it is that it *cannot* stay. The more genuine, the more innocent, the more "original," the more impossible it is to "stay." The world in its fallen state can only "go down," "subside." It is a world where purity (as well as time, as well as material possessions) cannot stay, cannot endure.

In addition to implying that nothing can endure, "stay" implies that nothing can remain as it was, that the postlapsarian world cannot be static, for stasis and perfection, while possible in a prelapsarian existence, have no place in our human, mortal world. Process is inevitable, not only to the world as a whole, but to every individual being. In making singulars of the plurals "leaves" and "flowers," Frost shows that each leaf, each flower, each living thing participates separately in this process. In changing "hours" to "an hour" he shows that these singular beings have so little time—another form of compression in this poem. And of course since only humans have this awareness of process, of condensation, of falling and sinking and impending grief, only humans try to "hold," vainly to attempt a "stay."[13]

For attempt something we must, even if what we pull together has no ultimate worth, even if what we make to outwit death leads us only to confront it more directly. In "Gathering Leaves" Frost dramatizes just such an attempt:

> Spades take up leaves
> No better than spoons,
> And bags full of leaves
> Are light as balloons.
>
> I make a great noise
> Of rustling all day
> Like rabbit and deer
> Running away.
>
> But the mountains I raise
> Elude my embrace,
> Flowing over my arms
> And into my face.
>
> I may load and unload
> Again and again
> Till I fill the whole shed,
> And what have I then?
>
> Next to nothing for weight,
> And since they grew duller

From contact with earth,
Next to nothing for color.

Next to nothing for use.
But a crop is a crop,
And who's to say where
The harvest shall stop? (CP 290)

We wonder at the end of this poem whether the speaker has accomplished anything or not. He has gathered, he has "harvested," he has "filled" his shed, but with what? The light anapestic rhythm mocks the endeavor; it reinforces the weightlessness of the harvest, and the quixotic nature of this task, and it fits in well with the notion of weightless mountains. That the harvest is "next to nothing for use" need not trouble the artist, who does not think in terms of use. The creating itself, the creation itself, has value beyond utility. But here the raw material eludes embrace, it eludes form ("Flowing over my arms / And into my face"). Another way of wrestling with Proteus, this activity; still, we have found wrestling with Proteus is a perfect metaphor of an artist wrestling with material that constantly eludes his grasp, trying to impose form on material that resists form, that changes constantly in the working (see chapter 1). In this poem, though, the harvest, the material, is dead, and in its deadness is a reminder of death. "But a crop is a crop," and thus we are made to feel that a harvest, even of dead leaves, is better than no harvest at all; more important, that gathering— even dead leaves—is better than doing nothing; any activity, better than passivity. The question at the end, however, makes such a conclusion uncertain. "And who's to say where / The harvest shall stop?" can imply that this harvest may lead to something after all. Randall Jarrell calls this poem "that saddest most-carefully unspecified symbol for our memories."[14] If so, the past is feeding the future at the same time that we are so conscious of how quickly the future will become the past, emphasizing once more the backward-forward-circular nature of time. Still, even though memories are only the remains of a past reality, out of memories we can create anew. One can just as easily say that these leaves are used-up ideas, calling up the frightened Frost of the "strongbox" ("I keep myself in a strongbox"; see notes to chapter 5), fearing as much as death the withering and drying up of his own creative powers. Here harvesting, gathering what is used up, dried up, no longer fresh and alive, acts as a substitute for failure to do anything, and "creating" out of dead ideas, used words, who knows but something new might grow out of it? [15]

Yet within the framework of this metaphor we can only feel the futility of the question coupled with the glorious heroic response to the futility: to gather, to harvest *nevertheless*. Here we confront the other possibility of the final question: once harvesting mementos of death, who knows where the harvest will lead? Where will it stop? More death and more death, creating, even successfully, out of death, as is implicit in the Stevens quotation, will lead us eventually to confront it even more inexorably; or, at the very least, it can do nothing to prevent that confrontation.

It is in the need to act upon those fallen leaves that the speaker asserts his hold on life; it is in his need to respond creatively that he asserts that human quality of making—trying to impose form and to fill the vacuum of meaninglessness with significance. Seen this way, the poem provides yet another example of a person's working himself through and out of a frightening encounter by creating out of it—the speaker, his pile; the poet, his poem. The Oven Bird may sound what *seems* like a question: "The question that he frames in all but words / Is what to make of a diminished thing" (this world after "that other fall we call the fall"). We take this to mean that he does not quite understand it. We too wonder what to make of this "diminished" world; we too try vainly to understand it. The person also takes the word "make" in its literal sense—what do we *do* about this diminished thing? What shall we *make,* what shall we create out of it? The diminished world inspires us to create, but more than that, in its incompleteness and imperfection it provides material raw enough for us to mold, to create out of. Surely there is a relationship between this concept and Iser's theory that it is the indeterminacies, the gaps in a literary text, that entangle and engage the reader in that other creative process of meaning construction—reading. Any creative activity that attempts unification or making whole has its genesis in imperfection.[16]

That perfection must be essentially static and sterile, that it consequently works against either creativity or viability, is related by Frost to his own artistic development: "In my school days I simply could not go on and do the best I could with a copy book I had once blotted. I began life wanting perfection and determined to have it. I got so I ceased to expect it and could do without it. Now I find I actually crave the flaws of human handwork. I gloat over imperfection. Look out for me. . . . Nevertheless I'm telling you something in a self-conscious moment that may throw light on every page of my writing" (SL 482). He begins this passage by stating that this great change his nature has undergone "is of record in To Earthward," a poem that combines roughness and pain, scarring and tears with love in a gravitational earthward, deathward pull. It is a poem that moves toward, but never arrives (note the "to" plus the "——ward" of the title), a poem about craving that can never be wholly satisfied. To the artist such nonfulfillment and noncompletion are a necessity, and they are surely related to the necessity for imperfection that led Frost to write: "I thank the Lord for crudity which is rawness, which is raw material, which is the part of life not yet worked up into form. . . . A real artist delights in roughness for what he can do with it" (SL 465). And: "You wish the world better than it is, more poetical. . . . I wouldn't give a cent to see the world the United States or even New York made better. I want them left just as they are for me to make poetical on paper. . . . I'm a mere selfish artist most of the time" (SL 369).

Frost's judgment on himself as "selfish" is a recognition that what would make life easier would make art harder-pressed.[17]

But there is more than selfishness involved in the delight in imperfection and in a world where a person needs to create and
feels in imperfection the necessary "rawness" of raw material.
There is implicit in such delight a preference for a "diminished"
world, a fallen world. Such a preference would be diametrically
opposed to an aspect of Puritan doctrine which Frost admired—
that change-for-the-worse is the basic pattern of human response.[18] According to this doctrine, Adam's disobedience began
the downward trend, with change for the better occurring only
in Heavenly Paradise by means of divine grace (YT 601). This
conflict between the perfection man is supposed to want and
the imperfection in which he delights is a conflict that creates
an interesting tension in several poems.

Notwithstanding Frost's admiration for Puritan doctrine, he
may have found a greater kinship with the thinking of the
elder Henry James, who felt that "nothing could be more remote . . . from distinctly human attributes . . . than this sleek
and comely Adamic condition."[19] James felt that Adam had to
fall from innocence in order to enter the ranks of manhood, that
prelapsarian Adam was premoral, "horticultural," "unperturbed
as yet by storms of intellect." The fall into manhood would cause
him to pass beyond childhood in an encounter with evil and
to mature by virtue of the destruction of his own egotism. Life
flowers and fructifies out of tragic depths, and James saw the
development of man's maturity as a drama, a process. The prelapsarian Adam had no ambition to rise from a horticultural
stage to a nobler condition of genuine manhood.[20] The perfection James had in mind is the one "to which no one is born, but
only re-born," but first one had to grow up, and that required
individuating crises like Adam's. The source of James's view
of Adam and Eve was Swedenborg, on whose ideas Frost had
been raised. Swedenborg saw the issue of creation—of Adam as
potentially creative—as the secret of interpreting Adam. Lynen
finds in Frost's poem "The Grindstone" (which Frost himself
had likened to "an image of the naughty world," that grindstone

that stands under "a ruinous live apple tree" and turns on its axis) a recognition that creativity not only means suffering and sacrifice but also involves man in evil, in playing God.[21]

It is one thing to make the most of a diminished thing—to pick up the broken pieces of a fallen world, to create something in the face of mortality—and quite another to *prefer* a diminished thing, to delight in imperfection, to create not just defensively as an act of self-preservation but assertively as an act of self-definition or as a definition of humanness. It is one thing to be created in the image of God and another to create in imitation of God. Still, we do create, taking what we need out of nature, fashioning it, forming it, and then saying, "It is good." This is what the "first singer" seems to be doing in "The Aim Was Song":

Before man came to blow it right
    The wind once blew itself untaught,
And did its loudest day and night
    In any rough place where it caught.

Man came to tell it what was wrong:
    It hadn't found the place to blow;
It blew too hard—the aim was song.
    And listen—how it ought to go!

He took a little in his mouth,
    And held it long enough for north
To be converted into south,
    And then by measure blew it forth.

By measure. It was word and note,
    The wind the wind had meant to be—
A little through the lips and throat.
    The aim was song—the wind could see. (CP 274)

There are no great questions in this poem. The subject is the making of something beautiful out of a natural wild force, making something "right" out of something "untaught." It is about molding, restraining, refining, converting, measuring—in other words about imposing form and structure on something as yet formless and undisciplined, about using nature as raw material, cooperating with nature, so that together man and nature create a *formed* beauty, a work of art.

Here is roughness enough to delight the creator of song: the wind "did its loudest" and did so "In any rough place where it caught"; "It blew too hard." But that was all *before man came,* and man not only knows how to "blow it right" but he teaches. He "came to tell it what was wrong . . . listen—how it ought to go!" Man in exercising his dominion over nature improves nature. In "Pertinax" Frost writes:

> Let chaos storm!
> Let cloud shapes swarm!
> I wait for form. (CP 407)

Here, like the God of Genesis, he does not wait but rather imposes form on chaos. Certain that the wind wanted to become song, he taught the wind "what was wrong" with its blowing. But in creating song, man had to provide the instrument, his lips and throat, and he had to use the wind. To combine wind and instrument, however, he had to exercise control. He not only took wind into his mouth he *held* it, he *converted* it, and then he became the blower, blowing it forth by *measure* in its transformed state. He became instrument as well as artist. We have here in one short stanza a figure for the artistic process as we have seen it according to Frost before: the connection with nature, with reality; the transforming, not merely the reflecting power of art; and very important, the holding power of art, the restraint that molds, that refuses to buckle under pure emotion, pure self-indulgence, pure roughness. He repeats "by measure," for this is important as restraint, as care, and as music. In its repetition he teaches measure, creating a forced stop with a caesura made extra-definite in that "by measure" acts as a full sentence. It is emphasized, and we must stop and consider it, as the wind was supposed to do in the lesson. Likewise the metric roughness of the line "In any rough place where it caught" contrasts sharply with the metrical regularity of the "resolved" last stanza.

The stanza is resolved, of course, on man's terms. If the aim was song, then that was "how it ought to go." And in that case it did indeed become "word and note, / The wind the wind had meant to be." Despite the confident assertion about right and wrong and what it ought to be, despite the triumph of having created a song that the wind could see was what it had really wanted to be, we can ask whose triumph this is, *whose* aim was song, whether the wind had had any intention or any aim at all, and whether it was capable of seeing anything! The triumph remains the man's, as is the delight, as is the aim. We cannot help but share the enthusiasm of that singer who was so pleased with his song that he projected his pleasure onto the wind, for how could the wind help but prefer to be a song? How could anything as vital as wind, as air, the stuff of song and speech[22] alike when "played" through lips and throat, *not* want to be a part of a cooperative artistic endeavor? How could it not want to improve, to become *something?* In suggesting such questions this poem raises the larger issue of ascribing intention not only by a reader to a poet but, once more, by a Frostian speaker within the poem to a natural force he is "reading" *his* way and upon whom he is projecting his own needs and values. We may also ask whether the speaker is "with" us, the readers who resist an intending wind, or "with" the enthusiastic singer. Most likely both. The ironic possibility of difference is left open, surely intentionally, as the published version differs from earlier ones. One previous version flatly states that the wind wondered, was discontented, and that it agreed.[23]

The singer himself, though, is still unselfconsciously alone with the wind, and finds joy in his creating. His solitude does not matter; this is man even before Eve. He seems not to need an audience for his song. It is enough that he is working with the wind. He and the wind and his discovery are company and joy enough in this poem. There is none of the sadness of "Pan With Us," where a deserted, graying Pan stands "in the zephyr, pipes in hand," mourning the passing of an old world, in which his pipes had the "power to stir." Now, because the world had found new terms of worth,

> He laid him down on the sun-burned earth
> And raveled a flower and looked away—
> Play? Play?—What should he play? (CP 33)

In contrast to Pan and his sadness at belonging to an outworn mythology, the man in "The Aim Was Song" stands at the dawn of a world, discovering his ability to use nature, to form out of chaos, to create, and to sing.

We find a more mature protagonist in the earlier "After Apple Picking," one who has already "picked the apple" and has since spent his life in producing and harvesting. Now he is weary of his productive life. It is obvious that we are dealing here with an apple picker who cannot be only an apple picker, with a harvest that cannot be simply apples, with fatigue that cannot be only physical, and with a sleep that is surely ambiguous.

> My long two-pointed ladder's sticking through a tree
> Toward heaven still,
> And there's a barrel that I didn't fill
> Beside it, and there may be two or three
> Apples I didn't pick upon some bough.
> But I am done with apple-picking now.
> Essence of winter sleep is on the night,
> The scent of apples: I am drowsing off.
> I cannot rub the strangeness from my sight
> I got from looking through a pane of glass
> I skimmed this morning from the drinking trough
> And held against the world of hoary grass.
> It melted, and I let it fall and break.

But I was well
Upon my way to sleep before it fell,
And I could tell
What form my dreaming was about to take.
Magnified apples appear and disappear,
Stem end and blossom end,
And every fleck of russet showing clear.
My instep arch not only keeps the ache,
It keeps the pressure of a ladder-round.
I feel the ladder sway as the boughs bend.
And I keep hearing from the cellar bin
The rumbling sound
Of load on load of apples coming in.
For I have had too much
Of apple-picking: I am overtired
Of the great harvest I myself desired.
There were ten thousand thousand fruit to touch,
Cherish in hand, lift down, and not let fall.
For all
That struck the earth,
No matter if not bruised or spiked with stubble,
Went surely to the cider-apple heap
As of no worth.
One can see what will trouble
This sleep of mine, whatever sleep it is.
Were he not gone,
The woodchuck could say whether it's like his
Long sleep, as I describe its coming on,
Or just some human sleep. (CP 88–89)

The poem moves toward a kind of sleep, "whatever sleep it is," first of all by stating directly "I am drowsing off"; "I was well / Upon my way to sleep," and then by referring to dreams. The speaker says that he is overtired, and if he speaks of rubbing strangeness from his sight, we picture a man rubbing his eyes in a gesture either of sleepiness or of attempting to differentiate what he thinks he sees from what is really there. Not only sleepiness but weariness permeates this poem; yet combined with this weariness is the "feel" of a task well done, the "pull and ache of muscle" that attaches to the task while it is being performed and remains afterward both as a painful and a satisfying reminder of the joy of labor as well as its fatigue and drudgery.

The words of the poem tell us of the speaker's weariness, but in addition, the sentences are so constructed as to emphasize the mental and emotional relaxation that accompany physical fatigue. We feel an aged, final exhaustion, not only physical weariness at the end of the day or a harvest season, but a man spent, ready to stop, ready to fade into sleep.

The first six lines combine the feeling of having ended a task with a feeling of incompletion. The speaker does not tell us he has finished his job but that he is "done with" it; recognizing what remains to be done, he has, nevertheless, had enough. That so few apples remain leads us to feel that he has indeed reaped a large harvest. We feel that he is giving it up or, more specifically, giving in. He is drowsing off, but before he tells us that, we feel his keen awareness of what remains to be done—what he felt he should have done. The barrel is not empty, or half empty, or half full; it is a barrel "I didn't fill." The apples that remain are those "I didn't pick." This consciousness of incompletion makes the giving in to fatigue much more compelling, as if the speaker has been overcome. Even the use of "there may be" rather than a definite statement adds to the lethargy of the speaker. He is too tired even to reckon the extent of what remains unfinished.

The following section of the poem intensifies this "drowsing off." In the following lines (7 and 8) the scent of apples becomes the "essence of winter sleep."[24] This is immediately related to "I am drowsing off" but with no logical connection, and thus the sentence suggests either a mind beginning to wander or to engage in fancy. In the "confusion of dreaminess,"[25] past action is indistinguishable from present imagining. In the "drowsing"

process, in the merging of waking and sleeping, memory becomes merged with dream. The poem begins with his drowsing off presumably at night ("Essence of winter sleep is on the
night . . . I am drowsing off"), yet now it flashes back to an
incident of "this morning." It was this morning that the "pane
of glass" broke, but by then he was already well upon his way
to sleep. All of this suggests not only immense fatigue on the
part of the speaker but that this falling asleep is a process: he
was well on his way to sleep in the morning, he is still well
on his way to sleep at night. He is, after all, not dozing off in
line 8 but "drowsing off," and so the lethargy, the tiredness, the
blurring between sleeping and waking is still going on.

The substance of that morning incident fits into this dreaminess well, for he had had a view through "glass" of "hoary grass."
We have here another example of reality being filtered through
a medium—a kind of personal lens; it is a veiled reality, possibly magnified, yet this filtering is made more unreliable by the
fact that the pane was ice not glass. Ice carries further the idea
of "winter sleep," and suggests, therefore, age, death, or at least
a temporary death of nature; it is also more fragile and transi-
tory than glass. The most careful handling cannot prevent its
annihilation in the face of sunlight or contact. After this there
is nothing between the reality and the viewer. Again we have
the feeling of giving up in his passively "letting it fall" once it
began to melt. There was no anger, no rebellion, simply recognition. Even the unspecific reference of "it" and "it" in line 13 adds
to his seeming confusion. Presumably the pronoun reference in
both is the "pane," but this is not immediately clear, nor is that
the only possibility. The world of hoariness could have melted;
so could the vision.

What had he seen? "Grass" that was "hoary," an adjective
usually associated with old age, white hair. It must have been
the frost on the grass that gave him the sudden view of "white
hair"—green grass turned aged—(and a view, perhaps, of Frost
in that frost?) "winter sleep" in the air, on the trough, on the

grass. Or perhaps it was the ice "pane" that made the grass look hoary.

Just as reality and illusion merge in the ice/glass vision, and time loses its boundaries in the telling of it, so too does dream merge with memory, imagination with physical actuality. The magnified apples may be a dream, but even in sleep, the ache in his instep arch is a reality, made even more vivid by the line "It keeps the pressure of a ladder-round." Thus actual physical sensation keeps the poem and the dream from losing touch with reality. "I feel the ladder sway as the boughs bend" works toward the same blurring of dream, memory, and physical sensation in the sense that the swaying he feels is real: we feel the dizziness in his "drowsing off," but his being on the ladder is memory/dream,[26] and as is often true in dreams, the real stimulus or motion gives rise to a dream in which the same sensation appears in an imaginary context. Like the ache, the scent of apples is real, and so is the sound of their rumbling into the cellar bin. These sensory perceptions permeating the dream are what give the dream substance. The rumbling of the apples coming in is part of his sleep, and this auditory sensation of quantities of apples heightens his vision of the imaginary apples and reinforces it in our minds as well. The repetition of the quantitative words "load on load," "thousand thousand," supports the notion of "too much."[27] Previously overwhelmed by fatigue and overcome by it, he is now overwhelmed by the surfeit, the sheer quantity of the labor, the yield, and the desire. He does not say "I have picked too many apples," but: "I have had too much." Whereas the beginning of the poem stresses incompletion through negatives, this section suggests incompletion because of the prodigious quantity—quantity of work completed but outweighed by quantity to be done, to be touched and cherished.

The speaker assumes we can see what will trouble his sleep. The verb is in the future and in the indicative mode; the dream of the magnified apples—their appearing and disappearing "Stem end and blossom end" revolving in his mind even when he needs to rest from, to be done with, apple picking—this activity, this appleness, this dream is not all that worries him.

> There were ten thousand thousand fruit to touch,
> Cherish in hand, lift down, and not let fall.
> For all
> That struck the earth,
> No matter if not bruised or spiked with stubble,
> Went surely to the cider-apple heap
> As of no worth.
> One can see what will trouble
> This sleep of mine

A pressing question that remains to haunt him seems to be what he had done with all those apples. That they were there "to touch" does not make clear whether he actually touched them all or whether they were all there waiting to be touched at some future time, and it does not make clear whether they were there to be touched by anyone, or there for *him* to touch. Thus there is introduced at this point a note of regret and frustration caused by what has not been done, by a realization of what potential will remain unfulfilled, by a recognition that frustration is the inevitable result of too great an aspiration.

The words "touch" and "cherish" convey an importance beyond ordinary apples, and we need not establish their exact nature. The fact that they can represent any man's harvest is more important than pinning apples down to one specific equivalent. The use of "myself" in the line "Of the great harvest which I myself desired" points to the kind of harvest that must be dependent on no one else—the kind of achievement that can never be shared but, like death, must be struggled with alone. This can be artistic creation, it can be what one person brings to his relationship with others, it can represent whatever one desires or struggles to achieve. Related to this is what can only be described as a sense of responsibility he seems to feel toward those apples not to let them fall—a sense expressed with more feeling than is usually applied to apples.[28] Apples that were allowed to hit the earth were not necessarily worthless, merely "As of no worth." Desire, art, human souls, human endeavor must touch the earth. We know how Frost feels about necessity for all human creation, all human feeling to touch the earth, to be in touch with the facts and with reality.

The russet flecks are part of the apple. While they can add to its beauty and variety, they keep it from being perfect. The brownish spots remind us of imperfection, the very imperfection that makes them of this earth, that inspires striving, and reminds us of the fallibility of everyone we cherish. Yet the speaker is haunted by the need to protect these apples from the fall and from the taint of earth. That there is a limit to his power to prevent their touching the earth is emphasized in the rhyming of "fall" with "for all," the only one-foot line in the poem. Still there is a difference between growing out of earth and falling to earth, between being nourished by earth and striking it. There is a difference between letting down carefully and letting fall carelessly. We find a constrast with his letting the pane of "glass" fall and break, and we wonder whether this simply dramatizes the difference between his present weary relaxation, the "letting go" of this morning's "drowsing off," and past ambition that still invades his sleep and reminds him of the conscientiousness under which he labored until now. There could, however, be another difference. The pane of glass is, after all, a filtering medium, merely a *way* of seeing reality. Like Prospero breaking his staff, the speaker lets it fall and break, determined now to let nothing stand between him and the fact of "hoary grass" or green grass, or frost, or whatever it is he saw. But the apples have life; they are not illusions. They are real, and they require labor, nurture, and care. He feels he must handle them gently, to keep in mind what their worth will be to others. There is a sense of commitment to the task. It troubles his sleep.

There is also a need to understand, while it no longer seems pressing or strong, the nature of this oncoming sleep. The final line, "Or just some human sleep," especially when related to "whatever sleep it is," establishes the fact that ordinary sleep is just one of the possibilities he faces. The troubled dreaming, the images of age and finality, of course, suggest death. Therefore the alternative to "human sleep" could be other kinds of sleep: the hibernation of the woodchuck who, after an inhumanly long nap, awakens to the spring; the winter sleep, whose "essence" is on the night. The reductive word "just" used with human may suggest that one of the troubling aspects of the sleep is that he is not as certain about his own "reawakening" as he is about the woodchuck's or the earth's in spring. Still he uses the future indicative, seemingly certain that dreams *will* trouble this sleep when he has shuffled off this mortal coil. The "or" can pose "just sleep" as an alternative to death, but it would still be troubled sleep, a postponement at best, for the strange sight is already indelible in his mind. The undercutting of his species of sleep only heightens ironically the fact that a human being with his fragility and his troubled dreams, his inability to be perennial or to outlast his own "winter sleep," remains superior to the woodchuck, and that of course his very superiority is painful in its human awareness of what awaits him in the future, what *will* trouble his dreams.

He has had too much apple picking, but he is *over*tired from the harvest he *desired*. Unfulfillment is the inevitable result of desiring too much, and it seems that the desire, the aspiration, the striving, or the need to "pick" so much is a greater cause, or perhaps it is the underlying first cause of the weariness we feel in this poem. But is this combination of aspiration, discontent, labor, weariness, and death not the condition of man ever since that first "apple picking"? The ladder, pointed "toward heaven still," remains after the apple picker has retired, and it rises above the tree. It has been seen as pointing toward salvation (the upward motion Fergusen speaks of making more sense here), but for Frost, that "Old Testament Christian," as he called himself, such an answer may not be here-and-now enough. It is not enough to rid the picker of his troubling dreams of apples or the rumbling from the cellar bin. As the poem deepens and widens, from weary harvester to poet—or anyone—contemplating one's aspirations, subtracting one's achievements, facing death and what may or may not follow, we too are forced to contemplate what follows apple picking. Our reading is affected by the fact that we see ourselves after apple picking; that we *come* after that first apple picking; and, not to be forgotten, that we have read about it. Thus we understand that the allusion to Eden encompasses in a nondoctrinary way all of the concerns of the poem, for implicit in the story of the fall of man are such seemingly divergent themes as mortality, carnality, knowledge, labor, discontent. In Eden there was to be fulfillment without desire, plenty without labor; theoretically, then, there was no place for discontent and no cause for weariness. Weariness is the inevitable result of labor and of striving. Desire and ambition motivate the labor, and man is "overtired / of the great harvest" he desired. Necessity, though, can be the motivating force behind the desire, and we have a vicious cycle.

This striving, this need to "pick" and to "harvest," is at once cause and curse: mankind was punished with the need to labor and with its attendant discontent and weariness; yet was aspiration not a great part of the original sin? The Serpent was very clever when he enjoined Eve to eat and be wise—to "be as gods." Adam, made in the image of his Creator, wanted to be a creator, to know and to understand. This seems to me to have been the real temptation, and since it involved conferring upon himself more Godlike powers, it was hubris and no small disobedience. Once Adam ate of that apple, he brought the curse of necessary labor upon himself; lust became a driving force in his life, and death became his inevitable end. Even prelapsarian Adam, then, needed to reach out, and ever since, whether with his hands or into his mind, man has needed to reach and to "pick."

The real question for the man who aspires, creates, makes

love, and lives with unfulfilled desires and ambitions, who "craves imperfection," is whether this "fallen state" is not *worth* it, whether, as James said, "the first and highest service which Eve renders Adam is to throw him out of paradise."[29] Or perhaps whether postlapsarian man, having paid the price for knowledge, for sexual desire, for creativity, paid it in unfulfillment and mortality, cannot any more look back to a perfect world, cannot imagine a world not fraught with dualities, not bound by time. Having been thrown onto his own creative instincts, he cannot see stasis as a desirable goal; he needs to create in a changing world, and he needs the stimulus and raw material of flux and process. Of course to someone like Frost, the needs are contradictory, and as in other dualities, there are opposing pulls: the fear of process, annihilation, age, death, loss of creative powers on the one hand; the need for such "imperfection" and such stimulus on the other.

This pull of opposing feelings becomes apparent when one puts the serious questions implicit in the Edenic allusions, the implications of falling, imperfection, troubled sleep, and aging up against the idyllic quality of the poem—the magnified beauty of the apples, the pleasure in their scent, and the amplitude ("load on load") of the harvest. There is nothing heavy or tragic in the tone of the poem. The ease of rhythm, the lulling repetition of words, the interrhyming, internal rhyming, and assonance that carry us with ease from one line of the poem to the next or across several lines to link words to each other by means of repeated sounds,[30] all this reinforces, it is true, the "drowsing off" of the apple picker; but at the same time it mitigates any harshness one might have felt implied in the subject matter. Occasionally sound reinforces the gravity in the poem: the rhyme of "fall" and "all"; the spondee of "tóo múch" paralleling that of "boúghs bénd"; but most of the poem proceeds euphoneously, rhythmically to its close on the word "sleep"—a word that is used only that once at the end of a line, but a total of six times throughout the poem.[31]

"Never Again Would Birds' Song Be the Same" is a poem unmistakably referring to Eden, explicitly naming Eve. The pull of opposing feelings is accomplished by means of language and rhythm, and it seems to me that in its combination of down-to-earth realism and romantic affection it is a rare poem—one of the finest love poems we have:

> He would declare and could himself believe
> That the birds there in all the garden round
> From having heard the daylong voice of Eve
> Had added to their own an oversound,
> Her tone of meaning but without the words.
> Admittedly an eloquence so soft
> Could only have had an influence on birds
> When call or laughter carried it aloft.
> Be that as may be, she was in their song.
> Moreover her voice upon their voices crossed
> Had now persisted in the woods so long
> That probably it never would be lost.
> Never again would birds' song be the same.
> And to do that to birds was why she came. (CP 452)

It would seem that we have an enchanted Adam, who delights not only in Eve's voice, and by implication her softness, her calls and laughter, her "tones of meaning" that transcend or bypass words, but one who also delights in nature, in the songs of birds. Adam had arrived in the garden before Eve, and thus he was in a position to notice that her arrival had an effect on the birds. It was her soft eloquence, her calls and laughter, her wordless tones of meaning that became part of their song. These soft, perhaps erotic sounds were daylong; they were in concert with the birds' songs, and that is why they became forever a part of them. Since she was in their song, Adam needed only to hear the birds sing, and he would be hearing the voice of Eve as well. This influence carried beyond the particular spot where she stood; it carried to the birds "in all the garden round," a noun adjunct that suggests, in the way "compass round" does in "The Silken

Tent," infinite extension in and around the garden. The sound traveled upward as well: it was carried aloft. But it was not her laughter or her calls that became part of the birds' song. Her calls and laughter were merely the carriers of her wordless "tone of meaning," her "soft eloquence." This intangible essence of Eve, then, is what entered their song.

Not only in space but through time did Eve have this influence, and in manipulation of tenses this poem extends itself almost imperceptibly backward and forward in time, creating (as did Milton) a timelessness within the poem which transcends the time-bound reality that we know Eve also to have introduced. We can assume that the "he" is Adam, since he is listening to Eve in the garden. The first sentence uses "would" as a modal, which hints of futurity even while it is the past of "will." The birds "had added" the oversound "from having heard" Eve's voice—clearly in the past and clearly putting the relationship of Eve's voice and their adding in a sequential relationship. This having been done, "she *was* in their song," still in the past. It is in the lines that follow that time becomes ambiguous: "her voice upon their voices crossed ("crossed" as past participle modifying "voices" or "voice" as it *crossed* with their voices) / Had *now* persisted in the woods so long / That probably it never *would be lost.*" When is "now" we must ask? Did we not know the short term of their stay in the garden, we might be tempted to say this is an older Adam telling us that, after so long, the voices still remained "crossed." But we know how little time was spent in the garden, and we notice that not only has time extended beyond the time of Adam in Eden but so has setting changed from garden to woods. The constant common to all time and all place then is the birds' song, audible in garden and woods, audible then as now, but remarkable in that Eve's voice has remained in their song. "Never again would birds' song be the same" makes it clear that Eve's influence has been a permanent one, perhaps implying that Adam in every man in every time would hear Eve when he heard birds sing.[32]

"Never again" is a very resonant phrase, however. One way to read it is with nostalgia for a past that can never again be re-captured. Eve's influence, as we have been told again and again before ever having read this poem, has not been simply to beau-tify birds' song. Eve's "influence" lost man Eden. Eve's influence introduced mortality, not only erotic pleasure. In fact, with the first couple's new-found knowledge came unsatisfied eroticism. But this poem hints that she came (unmistakably a sexual con-notation) precisely to do that, to introduce this dimension to Adam's life for worse—but also for better.

If we analyze the use of the modal "would" in this poem, we find that it is able to obscure time because it introduces a sub-junctive mode not bound by time precisely because it is not used to report actual fact, past or present, but wish, fantasy, proba-bility, or intent. We see this first of all when we examine the difference between the sentence "Never again *will* birds' song be the same" and "Never again *would* birds' song be the same." In the first we are in a factual present, looking ahead to the future; we would more likely assume from the sentence that now is best, and the future will not be as good. "Would" puts us into a past as it looks ahead into the future. Here, too, time faces in both directions, recalling "Nothing Gold Can Stay," but here there is a difference. In "Nothing Gold" ends are implicit in the begin-nings; here, beginnings are implicit in an end. The hopefulness here and in "West-running Brook" may derive from the same source: the presence of an Eve and whatever meanings—literal or figurative—attach (as we explored in the previous chapter) to marriage.[33] "Would" also implies condition: under given condi-tions there would be a change. If Eve influenced the birds, they would never again be the same. The sentence as it stands in the poem looks both forward and backward, and it can imply either that Eve improved life or that she "diminished" it, for while we are told that she improved birds' song, we bring to the poem our knowledge that she influenced Adam's downfall. Never again would man live in Eden, but something of Eden persists in all time, in all woods. Eve, after all, is with him "wand'ring hand in hand" in a world that lies before them.

This duality of Adam's relation to Eve is reflected in the contrasting tones, the contrasting directions and rhythms of the poem. In fact, the contrasting pulls of tone arise precisely because of these different tones and contrasting voices. There is an uncomplimentary undertone introduced into this lovely lyric of bird song. There are men who would consider the "daylong voice" of a woman to be nagging and unpleasant. Here Eve's voice "crossed" that of the birds; it persisted. There is also the aggressive quality of the expression "to do that to," and when one comes to do something to birds, it could mean that one comes with a purpose, an intent. This too is woman; but combined as it is with beauty and song, softness and sexuality, combined with nature as we see it here in garden, woods, birds, these more aggressive qualities seem to mitigate what would otherwise be sentimental. The combination seems to tie even Eve, even the Eve principle, to reality—daylong, persistent, day-to-day, long-term, but still loving reality. (One is reminded that in "My Mistress' Eyes Are Nothing Like the Sun" what begins as less than complimentary emerges, just for that reason, as a far more sincere declaration of love than we find in many more effusive love sonnets.)

Contrasting with birds and garden and the softness not only named but implemented by means of sound—the predominance of unvoiced consonants, especially "s" and "f"; the predominance of liquids such as "r" and "l" and the semivowel "w," contrasting with the lyric, idyllic qualities of the sonnet—we find the language of argument. What room is there in such an atmosphere for words like "admittedly," "moreover," and "be that as may be," which carries with it echoes of the more usual "be that as it may" as well as the doubting, noncommittal "maybe." It takes a poet confident and sure of what he is doing to throw words like this into such an atmosphere; and it takes a good poet to *succeed* in that these words sound right. They sound right because they carry forward the undertone that maintains the duality of the poem, of man's position in love and in the world we inherited from our first parents. They also inject the everydayness that makes the celebration of love so real—the everydayness of Eve, the Eve-ness of everyday—and they allow us to see the humor and the self-irony of a man who persists in defending what, in actual fact, is totally indefensible.

The poem tells us what he "would declare," which expresses, as we have already noted, both a hypothetical situation and an intention. It also expresses what was habitual. What he would declare is that the birds have added an oversound to their song— Eve's tone of meaning. But he soon sees that there is something illogical in this; "admittedly" such a soft eloquence would not be heard by the birds. Well, it would be when call or laughter carried it up; that is, the more seductive, appealing sounds will act as transmitters to the birds, and it is of course that note which will remain of Eve in all future birds. "Be that as may be, she was in their song." The speaker concedes that his claim is only within the realm of possibility, even of make believe; but we also "hear" the oversound of "be that as it may," which we use when we mean: well, it's like that *anyway*. In either case, it is as if he says: I know it doesn't make sense, I know your argument is sounder, but even so, this is the way I see it. *She was in their song.*

There are only two indicative sentences in the poem, only two sentences that state fact as we are to believe it really was: (1) "she was in their song" and (2) "to do that to birds was why she came." Ironically, these two "givens" are, in light of provable fact and reason, the most difficult to believe. We can have no evidence for either; yet these are the declarations of the poem. Everything else is expressed with "would" and "could": he would declare, he could believe, only in a particular way could her voice have influenced their song, probably it would not be lost, never again would it be the same. After all, doing this to birds was her intention; it was her reason for coming. He would declare it, and he could believe it.

What everything must finally depend on, of course, is his *belief* that this is so. Again it is ironic that "he would declare" precedes "and could himself believe." The order of the verbs is ironic, but so is the modal "could" and so too is the emphatic "himself." (Emphasis is also added by a reading of "would" that can lend a tone of stubborn insistence to his declaration, as in "he would do it despite our warning.") He plans to declare this strange phenomenon almost as if he must do so to make *himself* believe it, as if he talks himself into it with his argumentative line of reasoning that finally breaks down to be rescued by belief. He has not only convinced himself, but he has given in to what his perceptions and his feelings tell him, contrary to all logic and reason. These self-deceptions are not only declared as fact but are declared in metrical regularity as opposed to the jagged rhythm of the voice of logic: "Be that as may be, she was in their song." The self-deceiving first line is also completely regular. The spondaic "birds there" and "birds' song" are picked up in the last line, which ends, nevertheless, as if in answer, in regularity as well as statement of fact: "And to do that to birds is why she came."

So we are expected to believe that Eve came to do something to the birds. In one way, it seems absurd; in another we say, of course, she did something to the way birds *sounded,* to the way birds were to sound to Adam and all his descendants. She did something to affect, if not the birds themselves, then at least man's perception of birds. From the perspective of the perceiver it is all the same. Looking at the poem in this way, we see that it is no longer simply about human love and the garden of Eden but also about the way man *perceives*—reads— the world around him. It is also about the way Frost reads the Edenic story. It is about the power of imagination as well as the power of love. The humor in the poem comes from the gentle self-irony of the man who would declare and defend. The pull is between two voices, but it is also between two modes of hearing. We hear two kinds of voices in the poem: the idyllic and the argumentative; but the speaker also hears two voices: the voice of reason and the song of birds.

This Adam is not stupid; any deception is self-deception with his conscious collaboration. There is surely something mysterious about soft tones being transmitted to birds who "admittedly" cannot hear them all and something mysterious about such "learned" song when it is transmitted to an indeterminate future. So be it, because it is being declared by someone who knows it is in his imagination, but who believes in the truth of his imagination. Therefore this poem is about art as surely as it is about love.[34] All tradition would be behind our agreement that no man could have taught the birds how to sing as Eve did. The upward lilt of the phrases ("elóquĕncĕ sŏ sóft," "ínflŭĕncĕ ŏn bírds," "cárrĭĕd ĭt ălóft") reinforces the lilt and softness of a lyrical female voice, the beauty and softness of an Eve. But at the same time it took an engaged listener—an Adam—to perceive it and to appreciate it, and this required two things: the capacity to love, and the capacity to imagine, to look at nature and create with her, whether a human relationship or a work of art.

There is no other paradise, and man must therefore create his "paradise within." Frost has evoked the powerful story of Eden, but he will not accept, it seems, the traditional Christian view of the Fall (again, the Old Testament Christian) or of Eve's role. Yes, Eve can be a problem, but listen to what she did to bird song. Listen to her eloquent softness, her call, her laughter. See what it all did for our powers of perception, our creative imagination. To do all *that* is why she came.

This poem, in showing an Adam who loves and who has the capacity to imagine, who not only makes the best of his lot but positively enjoys it, presents us with a positive and hopeful view of Adam—for all Adams. When one thinks of the conventional view of Eden—the view even in Frost's "Nothing Gold Can

Stay"—one welcomes hope in the face of the "natural" forces that threaten to erode or destroy us, but, paradoxically, without which there would be no life and no creativity.

When man fell "earth felt the wound." Man, who had once been in harmony with nature even while he had dominion over it, now could no longer be secure in his dominion, a dominion that was no longer in harmony within itself. Weather and wildness threatened even as they still exerted the pull of attraction— the attraction of elements that had once been together. Death and decay became the ultimate threat. Because man would need shelter, he had to become a builder; because he had to wrestle with earth, he had to learn to cooperate with it and to sweat. No longer provided with a perfect environment, and goaded at the same time with lust and fear, he had to build not only a house but a loving human relationship within that house. Because he felt pain and fear, he had to cry out; because he feared extinction, he was driven to create, not only shelter and human relationships, but bids for eternity. No longer the image of God as perfection, man had become an image of God as creator, and as creator, he not only made the best of imperfection, but, as we have already observed, he *needed* it. No longer in harmony with nature, he needed to explore ways of creating harmonies, limited and temporary as they might be.

That Frost professed a belief in Genesis (YT 629–30) is not as important to us as the fact that he found in the story of Eden "a myth to live by" (I 256; see also note 5 above), a perfect metaphor for his deepest concerns. It provides no answers to the problems of death and the questions of how we fit into nature. Unlike Milton, Frost never tries to justify the ways of God to man. They won't bear too close examination, he tells us in "The Fear of God" and implies in *The Masque of Reason*. But like Milton, Frost invites the reader to look forward and outward to the possibilities of paradise within individual human beings and between them. Frost's versions of Eden do not explain, they assume a world after Eden. Even Milton points us outward to that fallen world, "all before them where to choose / Their place of rest." His enjambed line carries the reader outward, forward to the next line just as Adam and Eve were forced outward and forward. Milton's syntactic strategy of suspending closure of the sentence by delaying the verb, his open-vowel line endings ("slow," "way") coming at the end of so long and powerful an epic, also suggest opening out, suggest the impossibility of closure, suggest that the story is really just beginning even as he brings his epic to a close with the closing of Eden to the couple. We are also reminded that as Eden closed, a world opened; so did choice. And Adam and Eve approached that world of difficulty and choice hand in hand.

In "A Question" "men of earth" are asked "if all the soul-and-body scars / Were not too much to pay for birth." Frost's poetry shows us that the price *is* enormously high; yet there is much in the poetry that replies: it is nevertheless a price we are willing to pay. It buys, after all, something of great value.[35] Frost's Old Testament view of the Fall, it seems, does not interpret *felix culpa* in traditional Christian terms, with hope and joy in future salvation; man is only *felix* in what he, his mates, and his fellows create on earth or labor along with nature to produce—here and now. He does not bring divine redemption into his poems or into his Eden. The search for the Grail will be through New England desolation; here, too, salvation can only come through human questing and imagination. In this quest, as in the quests for meaning necessitated by that very lack of resolution and closure, whether in life or in poetry, Frost holds out an invitation to the reader.

8

Epilogue: The Height of the Adventure

A voice is speaking to me in "Directive"—*out* of it. "You," it keeps saying and keeps itself modestly in the background. "If you'll let a guide direct you" gives me a graceful out, for I have no way of knowing as yet that I am being addressed by the guide himself. It *is,* of course, an invitation, but in the form of a test, for if its indirectness gives me an easy out, I pass the test of motivation and curiosity by not refusing and, even before that, by realizing that this time I *have* been invited.[1]

This is no easy step over into a pasture, though. And I'm not being asked just to watch some "I." I am *being* watched, spoken to. The focus is on a "you"—*me.* I am being asked to do something active and strenuous. It is a long hard walk, desolate, and sometimes chilly. The air is full of noises. I am going uphill. Beginning the journey is one test, continuing it is another. I learn by going how I have to go, and in going, I realize that the one who addressed me is also in fact the guide. I listen as he talks about the sights, gives me tips, explains, as good guides do, the history and geology of the terrain we are passing. It is only at the destination, though, that he commits himself to saying "I" and thereby opens the possibility of engaging himself in a real face-to-face I-thou conversation. As if I have entered his home, I am welcomed: he says make yourself at home; he gives me a drink. I had to be willing to come with him, I had to withstand the journey to deserve that treatment. I had to be willing to get lost and more: to pull up the ladder road I climbed, making it even more difficult ever to return to the lower land and the populated towns I came from.

Who is this guide and why has he chosen me? Does he stand around as so many guides do, offering himself to the tourists, hoping that he will get a day's work out of it? Is he one of those self-styled guides who so loves this land and its history that guiding is his avocation and his reward is sharing the place and the story, taking that walk and talking to a willing listener? Does he choose select people to address? Have I been singled out, or does he let the test itself weed out those who are either not fit enough or interested enough to take the journey?

Like all directives, this one speaks in the imperative, but never down to me. It is gentle, seems to give directions to get to someplace I want to go, even if I hadn't realized it.

I *feel* singled out. I feel adventurous and brave, alone, and yet not alone. Who is this stranger walking beside me through the desert? If he is leading me to the Grail, perhaps he is an apparition, and I must find it myself; perhaps I am really talking to myself, making myself up a cheering companion as well as a cheering song. Like Percival, I am treated to an illusory feast when I reach my destination. If he is Virgil, then I am touring a sort of hell as part of my trial and my education. I am also being cast in the role of a poet. Perhaps this journey will make me some kind of poet; perhaps I have to be one to be invited— or maybe only "poets" accept.

The voice seems to be saying: "For once, let *me* be the guide. Stop being the critic. Just come." All right, I will.

Like the stream in "West-running Brook," this road goes down and up, and because I cannot refuse adventurous invitations, because I am not put off by a guide who has only at heart my getting lost, I go uphill, I take the road of greatest resistance, up, up. I may be going toward the source of the west running brook—it goes the wrong way, like Donne on Good Friday, but by going up to it I am going eastward.

On this incline, as we have seen on others, time goes both ways and does so with the cooperation of space: the man who may be ahead of me is long gone; the road I travel may be the one he took home from work. The wheel tracks tell the story or, rather, suggest it for me to fill in. I am asked to imagine a past, to put people and houses and creaking wagons where there is now only desolation. I am asked to interpret the rustle of trees as the excitement of their brash youthfulness against pecker-fretted older trees. Fretted, galled. It's part of the pain I will be asked to imagine as well.

For once I get there, I am told not only to put up a CLOSED sign, pull up the ladder road, and drink, but I am instructed to weep—for the little things that make children glad, and for the grown-up hurts, the hurts in earnest, for a house-in-earnest, for cultures gone, fields so painfully shrunk they are likened to a gall. I am reminded that travelweariness is not the only pain I am to suffer: I am to weep for others. I need to keep up my morale by making up a cheering song, but in what sense can it be cheering—only in the making of it, surely, and in the singing.

I have been invited to join in play with the children's toys; the playhouse has survived while the house-in-earnest has not, but that may be because the playhouse is really a tree. I do not really need a goblet to drink if I am willing to go to the true source, put my hands and face in the cold, cold spring.

Who says the water is saving, that it will make me whole and beyond confusion? My guide, who has made all this up, who is himself playing a game and allowing me to share it only if I am willing to play too. The water is only saving if I think it is, but of course, that's how the whole adventure has been. There has been no real climb, no real voice. Even the poet is not really climbing or really speaking. It is words on a page, and when

I look up, or somehow get outside them, say "It's just words," then I am back here at my word processor. But if, for a moment, I can truly imagine myself on the road as I read, then the two "cultures" dissolve, fade into one another. It is the height of the adventure. The reader has become the book; the poet, his poems *and* his admirers. I have accepted the invitation he so seldom gives. This poetic voice, unlike so many others in this volume, does not withdraw his invitation, he just makes it difficult to accept. It requires braving, this journey. If I do follow him, though, he gives me the water, offers me the goblet that he keeps hidden from most others.

It occurs to me that this directive may not be to me at all. It may be to himself, and it is to himself he whistles a happy tune to keep up his courage, tells himself to make up a cheering song as he traverses New England desolation. Does that mean, then, that he is making me up too? It seems that either he is teaching me to read poetry or teaching himself to read the landscape, instructing me or himself to cope with it by singing. But is there a difference that matters? Virgil and his poet-pupil occupy the same book. If this guide is a Virgil, he has made me a poet for the duration of the journey—not for my talent, but for my willingness to take it.

It has required a paradox of me: active submission. Willingness to lose myself, but not passively. I chose to come. I climbed hard. I have journeyed into the book, into the poem, by means of the poem. The poem has been my guide.

One question, though, remains. What does he want from me? Why has he invited me? Is it possible that he offers me the journey and the drink not just because it's good for me but because he needs me to come along as much as I need to go? If so, he has had to imagine me, just as I have had to imagine him. The difference no longer matters. But, of course, that is the point.

Notes

Preface

1. Cook, "The Serious Play of Interpretation."
2. Cook, "Dilemmas of Interpretation."
3. Lentricchia, *Robert Frost,* 3.
4. Brower, *The Poetry of Robert Frost;* Poirier, *Robert Frost.*
5. Lynen, *The Pastoral Art of Robert Frost.*
6. Perkins, "Robert Frost and Romantic Irony."
7. Fish, *Is There a Text in This Class?* 171.
8. And here is Robert Frost on dating poems, as reported by Burnshaw: "Why should anyone think it important for any reader to know the date of a poem's composition? And what was the meaning of 'date'?—when the writing had first begun—In the mind? On paper? Or the time of completion, if it had not been done at a stroke? It was wrong to try to trace any 'upward Darwinian line' in a writer's attitude or faith or thought" (*Robert Frost Himself,* 169).

Chapter 1. Braving Alien Entanglements

1. The comparison of the noun "poem" to an aggressive action suggests that the poem, rather than being a static object, has been, and we could say continues to be, active. Certainly Louise Rosenblatt (*The Reader, the Text, the Poem*) and Stanley Fish (*Is There a Text in This Class?* 25), though they come from different poles, would agree. They both call a poem an event.

2. Frost once said: "If people are looking for something to be brave about, there's their chance in poetry. . . . It's one of the ways of being brave" (cited by Rood, "Robert Frost's 'Sentence Sounds,'" 206). His use of the verb "brave" also recalls his early love of hero stories. See too: "the utmost reward / of daring should be still to dare" (CP 28). These examples remind us of Frost's desperate need always to be the

winner, which Lawrance Thompson makes much of in his biography. There Thompson relates it to his mother's influence; in LT he relates it as well to Karen Horney's theories on the neurotic's search for glory in *Neurosis and Human Growth*. (More will be said on Horney's influence.) Frost himself said: "Your pride is in what you dare to take liberties with, be it word, friend or institution" (SP 78). And then there are the words Frost wrote to Lesley on his deathbed: "I'd rather be taken for brave than anything else" (SL 595).

3. Frank Lentricchia sees egotism and incipient paranoia in the phrase "alien entanglement" (*Robert Frost,* 177). In seeing even the potential pathology of such an attitude, he is not so far off from Thompson—and Horney.

4. Thompson quoting Frost, Notebook, England, 1957.

5. On Tate's definition of poetry as communion, Frost (in 1961) said: "It's better than most, but still not right. Poetry is correspondence: Its images bring forth a response from the feelings and thoughts of the reader because the reader has similar feelings and thoughts. It goes back to the reader's performing his part in a serious engagement" (Burnshaw, *Robert Frost Himself,* 172).

6. Bartlett, "Notes on Conversations with Robert Frost"; Cook, "The Critics and Robert Frost," 27. Other conflicting statements are: "Readers' rights are very extensive. One doesn't always see the ulterior. It annoys me" (Frost lecture at University of Maryland, 28 March 1941). He wrote of giving in to outsiders' views of one's writing (SP 24); and that "The heart sinks when robbed of the chance to see for itself what a poem is all about" (SP 96).

7. Morrison, "The Agitated Heart." The quotation from Mark is: "Unto you it is given to know the mystery of the kingdom of God: but unto them that are without, all these things are done in parables: That seeing they may see, and not perceive; and hearing they may hear, and not understand; lest at any time they should be converted, and their sins should be forgiven them" (Mark 4:11–12).

8. "Language exists only when it is listened to as well as spoken. The hearer is an indispensable partner. The work of art is complete only as it works in the experience of others than the one who created it. . . . even when the artist works in solitude all three terms [of the triad] are present" (Dewey, *Art as Experience,* 106).

9. Eco's term, *The Role of the Reader.*

10. Dewey, in *Art as Experience,* says: "For to perceive a beholder must *create* his own experience. And his creation must include relations comparable to those which the original producer underwent. . . . The beholder must go through these operations [organizing, selecting, condensing] according to his point of view and interest (54). I am grateful to Iser, *The Act of Reading,* Rosenblatt, *The Reader, the Text, the Poem,* and Lentricchia, *Robert Frost,* for pointing me toward Dewey and/or E. H. Gombrich, *Art and Illusion.*

11. "Any authentic artist will avoid material that has previously been esthetically exploited to the full and will seek out material in which his capacity for individual vision and rendering can have free play" (Dewey, *Art as Experience,* 88–89). E. H. Gombrich writes of an emerging function of art in which "the artist gives the beholder increasingly 'more to do,' he draws him into the magic circle of creation and allows him to experience something of the thrill of 'making' which had once been the privilege of the artist" (*Art and Illusion,* 202); also cited by Miller, "Dominion of the Eye in Frost," 147. And here is James, *Principles of Psychology,* 1:259, on the "gap we cannot yet fill with a definite picture, word, or phrase, but which . . . influences us in an intensely active and determinate psychic way. Whatever be the images and phrases that pass before us, we feel their relation to this aching gap. To fill it up is our thought's destiny." Unless otherwise noted, all subsequent references to James will be to *Psychology,* volume 1.

12. Iser, *The Act of Reading.* Dewey makes a similar point (*Art as Experience,* 282): "the self is created in the creation of objects, a creation that demands active adaptation to external materials, including a modification of the self so as to utilize and thereby overcome external necessities by incorporating them in an individual vision and expression."

13. John Ciardi, in saying Frost was always playing the role he had learned to perform, points out that Frost never quoted Latin poetry, that he could quote Chaucer, but never did because he was not supposed to know that in his country-boy role (Cifelli, "Ciardi on Frost," 477).

14. Spacks, *Imagining a Self,* 21. In this context too see Dewey on creating a self in creating objects (note 10 above); also his saying that communication is the process of creating participation, that in being communicated, the conveyance of meaning gives body and definite-

ness to the experience of the one who utters as well as to that of those who listen (244).

15. Salomon, *Desperate Storytelling,* 18–19.

16. EY, Introduction. See also Sutton, "Problems of Biography."

17. In an excellent article relating subjectiveness of view and in-determinacy in Frost to the theories of Heisenberg and Bohr in physics, Guy Rotella finds that the several voices of poems such as "Mending Wall," "Home Burial," "The Death of the Hired Man," and "The Hill Wife" multiply points of view, in order to show that any point of view is indeterminate and to leave all points of view as unresolved as their complements in action ("Comparing Conceptions," 188).

18. "As long as it is animated by this vital inbreathing inspired by the act of reading, a work of literature becomes at the expense of the reader whose own life it suspends a sort of human being, that it is a mind conscious of itself and constituting itself in me as the subject of its own objects" (Poulet, "Criticism and the Experience of Interiority," 47).

19. "In an experience, things and events belonging to the world, physical and social, are transformed through the human context they enter, while the live creature is changed and developed through intercourse with things previously external to it" (Dewey, *Art as Experience,* 246). This can also be related to Norman N. Holland's theory of feedback loops. See, for example, *The Brain of Robert Frost,* chapter 5.

20. "The reader is absorbed into what he himself has been made to produce through the image; he cannot help but be affected by his own production" (Iser, *The Act of Reading,* 140). "Text and reader are linked together, the one permeating the other. . . . Thus the meaning of the literary text . . . does not exist independently of him; just as important, though, is that the reader himself, in constituting the meaning, is also constituted" (150).

21. See Beach, *The Concept of Nature in Nineteenth-Century English Poetry,* and Brower, *Robert Frost,* chapter 3.

22. Such expression will transfigure emotions and natural objects, according to Dewey, and the resulting art object will in turn produce esthetic emotion "and because it is evoked by and attached to this material it consists of natural emotions that have been transformed. Natural objects . . . induce it. But they do so only because when they are matter of an experience they, too, have undergone a change similar

to that which the painter or poet effects in converting the immediate scene into the matter of an act that expresses the value of what is seen" (77).

23. Von Frank, " 'Nothing That Is,' " 129–30.

24. Gombrich would say he will be more able to see because of that making (*Art and Illusion,* 11 and 295).

25. See Lentricchia's chapter "The Redemptive Imagination," in *Robert Frost,* and Holland, *The Brain of Frost,* especially 23.

26. We remember that the metaphor, "whose manage we are best taught in poetry" is all there is of thinking, too (SP 43); that the lost soul is the one with no gathering metaphor to throw the material into shape and order (41). And then, Frost's saying of Thoreau and his *Walden:* "a real gatherer, to which everything in him comes tumbling. . . . Think of the success of a man's pulling himself together all under one one-word title. Enviable!" (I 143). Once more, see Holland, *The Brain of Frost,* 23.

27. Wimmers, *Poetics of Reading,* 154.

28. On the artificiality of separating aesthetic reception from production, see Dewey: "We have no word . . . that includes what is signified by the two words "artistic" and "esthetic." Since "artistic" refers primarily to the act of production and "esthetic" to that of perception and enjoyment, the absence of [such a] . . . term is unfortunate" (*Art as Experience,* 46). In her discussion, Wimmers quotes other theorists. In making the distinction between finding meaning in a text and finding significance, she cites Ricoeur on appropriation: "The appropriation of a text is completed in the self-interpretation of a subject who henceforth understands himself better, who understands himself differently, or who even begins to understand himself." And it is this kind of reading, he claims, that gives texts their *signification* (*Poetics of Reading,* 8). Proust is cited as saying that "the recognition by the reader in his own self of what the book says is the proof of its veracity" (11).

29. Wimmers, "Approaches to the Novel," and *Poetics of Reading,* 67.

30. Lentricchia has also cited James's sculptor metaphor (*Robert Frost,* 9), and goes on to say: "James suggests that . . . the unique subjective character of a personal consciousness . . . can only be known as it expresses itself, as it is impelled outward to interact with objective conditions. . . . the significant measurement of Frost's participation in and dissent from major modern theories of imagination is his Jamesian

commitment to the powers and limits of human consciousness to re-create its world in accordance with the needs and desires of the self" (17–18).

31. Edie, *William James and Phenomenology.*

32. On knowledge as construction, see Frost: "Facts come to mind as stars come out in the sky in the evening, scattered broadcast, thin at first and then thick enough to suggest constellation. The lines between them that bring out the figures are ours, the final and only conscious part of our world building. A world you didn't make? Yes you did too. There is proof that there were countless offerings to the senses that you kept out unconsciously" (*Prose Jottings of Robert Frost,* 73).

33. See John Keats, Letter to Benjamin Bailey, in *Complete Poems and Selected Letters,* 526; Keats's marginal notation on *Paradise Lost,* cited by Bate in *John Keats,* 254; see also Letter to Richard Woodhouse ("A Poet is the most unpoetical of any thing in existence, because he has no Identity") in *Complete Poems and Selected Letters,* 576. A. Bartlett Giamatti, speaks of Proteus as the type of the poet in *Play of Double Senses,* chapter 11.

34. Patricia Meyer Spacks writes: "the gossip I call serious . . . exists only as a function of intimacy, . . . a crucial means of self-expression, a crucial form of solidarity" (*Gossip,* 5). See also Cohen, "Metaphor and the Cultivation of Intimacy." Frost also said that he did not much like novels, but did like diaries (Bartlett, "Notes on Conversations with Robert Frost").

35. Frost asked Louis Untermeyer not to publish his letters while he was alive: "I like to be read as a poet but I guess I really hate the literary life and hate to be gossiped about for my part in it" (LU 382). Frost also said: "Gossip exalts poetry. Poetry is the top of our guessing at each other" (Burnshaw, *Robert Frost Himself,* 253).

36. Ibid., 6 and 202.

37. On the similarities but still the ultimate differences between fiction and biography, see Siebenschuh, *Fictional Techniques and Factual Works.*

38. Morse, "'The Subverted Flower,'" 172.

39. Thompson, Notebooks, 19 January 1957.

40. Sutton, "Problems of Biography." Another important insight into the process, its decisions and conflicts comes from Thompson himself

in two speeches: "The Robert Frost Controversy" and "Robert Frost and the Biographer as Critic."

41. Ample evidence in *Newdick's Season of Frost* edited and discussed by Sutton. On conflicting accounts of Frost as person, teacher, parent: the differences in versions of what Lesley told of their childhood, which Thompson cites in his notes and which Elizabeth Sergeant cites, are as amusing as they are disturbing—the parents were "always mild" with the children (Sergeant, *Robert Frost,* 81); Irma, a "chronic invalid" (374).

42. Spacks writes that Boswell was always feeling Johnson his superior, characteristically subordinating his immediate desires to his mentor's; "Boswell reasserts himself by collecting and setting down stories: an activity comparable to gossip . . . but most of all as controller of their significance, Boswell raises questions about what personal narrative means to the narrator and to the subject of narration. . . . At the narrative's heart lies Boswell's discovery of his own power in an asymmetrical relationship with an overwhelmingly powerful man" (*Gossip,* 103). And this, written by Frost to introduce Cox's book about him: "The author probably knew me better than he knew himself and contrariwise he very likely portrayed himself in it more than me" (Introduction to Cox, *A Swinger of Birches,* vii).

43. Sheehy, "The Poet as Neurotic," 406.

44. "You know, one of the worst things in the world is people who belittle glory" (V 188).

45. Thompson, Notebooks, 20 January, 1957.

46. "You have to be attractive enough to get people within striking distance" (*Prose Jottings of Robert Frost,* 81).

47. Cifelli, "Ciardi on Frost," 484. Compare Roy Cowden, who saw Frost's presence at Michigan as a highlight in the lives of the students. He quotes Frost's saying of living next door to a fraternity house: "How can I write poetry beside a fraternity house? I like all those boys and they come over. I can't find myself!" (Sergeant, *Robert Frost,* 246).

48. Reginald Cook says of this same question: it is one "every critic has to face . . . if he is worth his critical salt" ("The Critics and Robert Frost," 16).

49. *Prose Jottings of Robert Frost,* 13, for example, a concept Brower discusses in his *Robert Frost.*

50. Frost, Lecture at University of Maryland, 1941.

51. Thompson, Notebooks, 24 February, 1940.

52. And, as Richard Poirier says, "Criticism works best on him when it gets close, and stays close" (*Robert Frost,* 10).

53. Lentricchia, *Robert Frost,* 123–24.

Chapter 2. Au Lecteur

1. Iser's term, *The Act of Reading.*

2. It may be useful at this point to see these terms, and this chapter's title, in their original context. "Au Lecteur," the first poem in Charles Baudelaire's *Les Fleurs du Mal,* ends as follows: "Tu le connais, ce monstre délicat, / —Hypocrite lecteur,—mon semblable,— mon frère!"

3. How to have his students—and his readers—read is a recurring motif in his wonderful pronouncements on teaching throughout his letters, talks, interviews, in LT, *Prose Jottings of Robert Frost,* and Notebooks.

4. *Complete Poems of Robert Frost.* Unless otherwise noted, all Frost poems will be quoted from the 1949 edition. There are occasional variations between this one and the 1969 edition edited by Edward C. Lathem, and I have chosen to rely on the edition that Frost himself had supervised.

5. Paul Fussell, Jr. uses this poem as an example of Frost's metrical skill. He shows how Frost manages the transition between two atmospheres—reasonable detachment to physical, muscular commitment—by means of meter, which changes at the "turn" in line 10 (*Poetic Meter and Poetic Form,* 107–8).

6. "Why look upward in prayer when upward is only outward as now we know?" (Memorandum Book, England, 1912–15).

7. That "range-finding" has larger philosophical application is apparent from Frost's dedication to Elinor of his book *A Further Range:* "for what it may mean to her that beyond the White Mountains were the Green; beyond both were the Rockies, the Sierras, and, in thought, the Andes and Himalayas—range beyond range even into the realm of government and religion."

8. This view differs somewhat from Lynen's in *The Pastoral Art*

of Robert Frost, 155–57. Lynen says that nature is mechanical; that man thinks, feels, suffers, while nature only exists. He is, of course, quite right and this quotation corresponds with what I have said of the poet-narrator and reader. Lynen, however, does not make a distinction between these and the soldier. In this poem, however, I find them to be separated, and this separation to be an important factor in the fragmentation that is so much a part of the poem.

9. Frost wrote to Amy Lowell: "Would it amuse you to learn that Range Finding belongs to a set of war poems I wrote in time of profound peace (circa 1902)? Most of them have gone the way of waste paper. Range Finding was only saved from going the same way by Edward Thomas who liked it . . . he thought it so good a description of No Man's Land" (SL 220).

10. Black, "Metaphor," 38.

11. Frost, in one of his Harvard lectures, spoke of "the evil search for synonyms." Thompson explains that he "was expressing his prejudice in favor of using images which imply (rather than state) analogies, images, and actions which merely hint metaphoric and symbolic extensions of meaning" (YT 647).

12. Black, "Metaphor," 41. Turbayne, in *The Myth of Metaphor,* 214, makes the point that "a new metaphor changes our attitude to the facts. Once we see the world from the point of view of one metaphor, the face of it is changed . . . a good metaphor, like a good portrait, does not hold a mirror up to the face of nature but vividly illustrates some features of it and neglects others."

13. Black, "Metaphor," 40–42.

14. Harries, "Metaphor as Transcendence."

15. Stevens, "The Poem that Took the Place of a Mountain," *Collected Poems of Wallace Stevens,* 512.

16. Yet Frost shied away from the terms "symbolism" and "symbolical poet." "I can't hold with those who think of me as a symbolical poet, especially one who is symbolical pretense. Symbolism is all too likely to clog up and kill a poem—symbolism can be as bad as embolism. If my poetry has to have a name, I'd prefer to call it Emblemism—it's the visible emblem of things I'm after" (LU 376).

17. Sergeant, *Robert Frost,* 325.

18. Sergeant, "Good Greek Out of New England," 149.

19. Thompson, "Cryptic" Lecture.

20. Holland, *The Brain of Robert Frost,* 23.

21. This puts me into dispute with Reginald Cook (V 264), John C. Kemp (*Robert Frost and New England*), and others, as George Monteiro points out in "The Facts on Frost." As Monteiro also points out in the same article, the poem does not square with entomological facts. David Perkins sees it as a parody, an example of Frost's "romantic irony" ("Robert Frost and Romantic Irony"). Also of interest is that Frost saw poetry as a web (*Prose Jottings of Robert Frost,* 14).

22. A question also raised by Bagby in "Frost's Synecdochism."

23. On this subject, see SL 462.

24. Levin, *Metaphoric Worlds.*

25. Bagby, "Frost's Synecdochism," 379.

26. Dewey, *Art as Experience,* 87.

27. Black, "Metaphor," 41.

28. Saha, "Metaphorical Style as Message," 42.

29. The latter two are, respectively, from Memorandum Book, England, and *Prose Jottings of Robert Frost,* 44. Frost also wrote: "the only thing that can disappoint me in the head is my own failure to make metaphor. My ambition has been to have it said of me: He made a few connections" (LU 189).

30. I am indebted to Kelly Searsmith for *this* metaphor.

31. Coale, "The Emblematic Encounter of Robert Frost."

32. "Subsidiary" is Black's term; the X and Y of metaphor, in Nowottney's *The Language Poets Use,* 175. Perrine's fourth class is described in his "Four Forms of Metaphor," 325–27.

Poirier, in *Robert Frost,* discusses the ladder in "After Apple Picking" as a metaphor of metaphor (we remember, as does he, that Frost had used the ladder metaphor in his metaphor-lesson speech, "Education by Poetry"); the two-pointed stick, as the terms "head in a parallel and mutually supporting direction. Ultimately, however, the relationship comes to an end or leaves off; the metaphor necessarily breaks down. The progress or movement of analogy brings us to something beyond it, like faith or a belief" (295). We might add that it leaves "heaven" or anything up there, out there, open, the way to it still sticking up. The feet can only go so far, but the hands more so, the eyes, to the limits of horizon or vision, the imagination, infinite. As Frost once told a graduate student about to do a Frost dissertation: "Take it all the way to please me." The other side of this, the other way of seeing the terms—vertically, rather than horizontally—is that the ladder is still firmly on the ground. And of course, as Poirier also says, it is a literal ladder, another characteristic of Frost's metaphors.

33. Lodge, *The Modes of Modern Writing.* I find it uncanny how Jakobsonian Frost was in saying, "The couplet is my game just as the metaphor is my game. The couplet is the symbol of the metaphor" (V 135). On the connection, see Jakobson, "Closing Statement."

34. Emerson describes the poet as one who "stands among partial men for the complete man" (*Complete Works,* 3:5). It would seem that he too, at least in his role as poet, is a synecdoche.

35. On this point, see Poirier, *Robert Frost,* 278: "Frost's poetry is quite directly about the correlative work of writing and of reading it." See also Dewey in *Art as Experience,* 106: "What is true of the producer is true of the perceiver. . . . If he perceives esthetically, he will create an experience of which the intrinsic subject matter, the substance, is new. . . . A new poem is created by everyone who reads poetically."

36. "A poem would be no good that hadn't doors. I wouldn't leave them open though" (from Frost's journal kept in England in a pocket notebook; quoted in EY 397).

37. After line 22—between "with all her matter-of-fact about ice-storms" and "I should prefer to have some boy bend them"—there had originally been a line in parentheses: "(Now am I free to be poetical?)"—a coy line that Frost quite correctly realized he did not need ("Birches," MS in Dartmouth College Library).

In the earlier version of this, Frost had written "with all her matter of fact." The change to "matter-of-fact" is one of emphasis from fact to tone, from the matter of fact to the manner of asserting it. Edward Connery Lathem, in his edition of *The Poetry of Robert Frost,* returns to the original version and removes these hyphens. Again, the punctuation that Frost supervised may be preferable. Hyphens made an important difference to Frost, as is evidenced by the following: "There's another thing about little noticings—what you call scholarly noticing. . . . It says in Keats, 'Thy hair soft-lifted by the winnowing wind'; I happened to think when I was reading it one day . . . there ought to be a hyphen there. If you say 'winnowing wind' it means it's winnowing her hair, and if you say 'winnowing-wind' it's the regular wind that winnows the grain. The hyphen makes all the difference. . . . The same kind of thing happened to me in one of my poems [e.g., "Mending Wall," cf. "old-stone savage," a Paleolithic savage]. You've got to notice" (V 51).

38. "Many sensitive natures have plainly shown by their style that they took themselves lightly in self-defense. They are the ironists" (SL 299).

39. Reflecting the fact that he does not focus directly on the birches is the change in the first draft, which focused directly on the birches at the outset, followed by "I think." Then, too, in changing "I think" to "I like to think," Frost has put more weight onto imagination, and more distance between the reality of ice storms and the wistfulness about boys swinging birches. One can also see that he must have debated with himself on the subject of addressing a second person "listener." The MS in the Jones Library, Amherst, reads as follows:

When I see
  ~~Seeing~~
~~The way the~~ birches droop to the left and right
Across the lines of straighter, darker trees
  ~~I like~~ I'm [?]
Sometimes I think some boy's been swinging them.
But swinging doesn't bend them down to stay
              ~~How~~ often I
Ice storms do that. ~~Often~~ you must of have seen them.

40. I am indebted to Roger Salomon for this insight.

41. On control as force, see Frost: "Your fist in your hand. A great force strongly held. Poetry is neither the force nor the check. It is the tremor of the deadlock" (*Prose Jottings of Robert Frost,* 12). One could also find a parallel between these birches bending left to right "across the line of straighter, darker trees" and "the possibility for tune from the dramatic tones of meaning struck across the rigidity of a limited meter" (SP 18).

42. While in earlier poems such as "Birches," "Mowing," or even "The Death of the Hired Man" perfect artistic fusions seem just to "happen," such issues as metaphor and figuring, the creating word or vision, artistic process and transformation surface more overtly and

self-consciously as subjects in the poems published in 1923 and 1928 ("Maple," "Paul's Wife," "A Boundless Moment," "A Hillside Thaw," "Gathering Leaves," "The Aim Was Song," "For Once Then Something" in 1923; "The Rose Family," "The Freedom of the Moon," "Fireflies in the Garden," in 1928. "Time Out," with its focus not on nature but on how we read it, was published later still, in 1942).

43. This expression is the title of an article by Robert S. Newdick, "Robert Frost and the Sound of Sense." The following are examples taken from letters written around 1913, 1914: "To be perfectly frank with you I am one of the most notable craftsmen of my time. . . . I alone of English writers have consciously set myself to make music out of what I call the sound of sense. . . . The best place to get the abstract sound of sense is from voices behind a door that cuts off the words. . . . It is the abstract vitality of our speech. . . . One who concerns himself with it more than the subject is an artist. . . . An ear and an appetite for those sounds of sense is the first qualification of a writer, be it of prose or verse. But if one is to be a poet he must learn to get cadences by skillfully breaking the sounds of sense with all their irregularity of accent across the regular beat of the meter (SL 79–81).

"The living part of a poem is the intonation entangled somehow in the syntax idiom and meaning of a sentence. It is only there for those who have heard it previously in conversation. . . . Vowels have length there is no use denying. But the accent of sense supersedes all other accent overrides and sweeps it away. . . . [A word] is as long as the sense makes it. . . . Words exist in the mouth and not in books" (SL 107–8).

"A sentence is a sound in itself on which other sounds called words may be strung. You may string words together without a sentence-sound to string them on just as you may tie clothes together by the sleeves and stretch them without a clothes line between the trees, but—it is bad for the clothes. . . . The ear is the only true writer and the only true reader" (SL 110–12).

44. See Poirier, "Robert Frost: The Sound of Love and the Love of Sound," 54.

45. Borroff points out that in "Mowing" one of the meanings of "fact" is the Latinate one—something done or made, from *factus* (*Language and the Poet,* 31). I was also struck by Frost's wordplay in his Memo-

randum *Book from England:* "You must feel that the thing happened that way not for the purpose of the author. Why should it happen so? you don't know, but it did. It is the didness of it that makes it taste strong."

46. In Philip N. Youtz's copy of *A Boy's Will* (p. 56), Frost had written of the two lines "Anything more than the truth would have seemed too weak" and "The fact is the sweetest dream that labor knows": "These two sentences are the key to all my work. I wrote them unconsciously, but they best express what I have tried to do." (This comment was written in 1918.)

47. In addition to tradition as opposed to new styles in poetry (e.g., Gertrude Stein), a new use of metaphor is also an issue here. Of course, the Rose was traditionally used in comparisons with ladies; in *The Romance of the Rose* the Rose was the love object spoken about as if it were a lady. In "Maple" the girl ponders: "What was it about the name? Its strangeness lay / In having too much meaning. Other names, / As Lesley, Carol, Irma, Marjorie, / Signified nothing. Rose could have a meaning, (But hadn't as it went. / She knew a Rose)" (CP 222). The point that relates to use of metaphor is the point of metaphor as fresh, as that which makes us see something in a new way. "Every poem is a new metaphor inside or it is nothing," writes Frost in "The Constant Symbol" (SP 24). Stale metaphors have lost the function to do that. Thus Rose, by now a common name, had lost its quality of metaphor, whereas Maple—or pear or plum or apple—is new. In the case of the fruits, the connection is meaningless, for there is no shared presupposition. In the case of Maple, the metaphor, as we saw, was capable of generating multiple meanings.

48. As Sydney Lea has pointed out, there's a double meaning in "A Missive Missile": "The metaphor, the symbol lies" ("From Sublime to Rigamarole," 942).

49. Aristotle, *The Poetics,* 21.4.

50. Interestingly enough, with no reference to intentional veiling as motive, or to Frost, Riffaterre, in *Semiotics of Poetry,* says the same thing, naming this quality, in fact, as the one constant factor differentiating the language of poetry from common linguistic usage: "Poetry expresses concepts by indirection. To put it simply, a poem says one thing and means another" (1). He goes on to describe the structure of meaning in a poem, not in terms of tropes, but of dialectic between

text and reader that is set in motion when the literary representation, or mimesis, is threatened, and the result is levels of reading that
begin with the mimetic, proceeding to retroactive reading, triggered by
something disruptive or ungrammatical in what would be a referential
text, to significance (2, 5) that he defines as "what the poem is really
about: it arises through retroactive reading when the discovery is made
that representation (or mimesis) actually points to a content that would
demand a different representation in nonliterary language" (167). Admittedly, such significance will vary from one reader to another, or
one reading to another. In Frost, we keep returning, though, to those
poems in which the disruption is not obvious, nor is it obvious if there
has been one. Here we have another example of the ways in which
a seemingly simple Frost can present greater difficulties than a seemingly opaque Mallarmé. Deciding where or if the literal "points to that
'something else'" is an attempt to bridge a gap that may or may not be
there. The need to decide that is itself evidence of a gap.

51. Quoted by Morrison in "The Agitated Heart."

Chapter 3. "Me, Myself . . . Godlike"

1. See Hollander, *The Figure of Echo.*
2. Ovid, *Metamorphoses,* Book 3, lines 409–12. All citations from
Ovid in this chapter will be made parenthetically in the text to lines in
this book.
3. See also James, *Psychology,* 1:288–89 on the "me" and the "not-
me."
4. Ragland-Sullivan, *Jacques Lacan,* 49.
5. Felman, *Jacques Lacan,* 67. Frost too prefers an oval, that is a
figure with two centers—good and evil—to Emerson's monism (SP
118), not only because he found it more realistic, but because he felt
that same dialogic need: "It is from having stood contrasted / That
good and bad so long has lasted" (V 215). And he said in many places
how they need one another, to hold one another off, as he has said
of other oppositions: like struts, kept together *and* apart (Thompson,
"Some Subtleties in Robert Frost's Art"). See also *Prose Jottings of Robert
Frost,* 99.
6. Frost wrote to Untermeyer: "Don't look into books to see your-

self reflected" (LU 191–92). We remember Wimmers's discussion (see my chapter 1) of the dangers of narcissism in reading. Ragussis extends the warning to writers: "Echo comes as a warning to all writers; she knows full well the dangers of narcissism" (*The Subterfuge of Art,* 232).

7. Ragland-Sullivan, *Jacques Lacan,* 24.

8. For an excellent discussion of Echo as ironic muse, see Ragussis, *The Subterfuge of Art,* 230–33. Surely one of the most frightening and frustrating aspects of a hall of mirrors or an echo chamber is the combination of illusion of others and exits where in fact there are no others and no visible exits. The very appearances and sounds of those illusions mock as they frighten, mocking the very desire for escape.

9. Emerson writes, on the subject of miracles having ceased: "Have they indeed. . . . Pick up that pebble at your feet, look at its gray sides, its sharp crystal & tell me what fiery inundation of the world melted the minerals like wax & as if the globe were one glowing crucible gave this stone its shape. There is the truth[-]speaking pebble itself to affirm to endless ages the thing was so (J 5:423). As Emerson speaks of the pebble, the thing exists in affirmation of the process in its making. The process was the miracle; its being, the assertion. Emerson seems to see being as language. At least it is the language pebbles speak. But of course it speaks of miracles ages ago and does not testify to miracles now.

10. The poem stands witness to the possibility of echo or reflection, or pebble, as creative when something else is brought to it or built out of it. This relates to Ragussis's discussion of Echo as Muse, *The Subterfuge of Art,* 230.

11. Or *behind* it, as one variant in Frost's own hand indicates: "behind the surface" is the way he wrote it by way of inscription to George Whicher on the fly leaf of his book, a second edition of *North of Boston.*

12. Frost told Thompson about his hearing voices as a child that repeated everything he said but with a different inflection, as if mocking his thoughts (LT 108). One can see an ironic posture here even at a young age.

13. *OED,* for uses of "most." One is interesting and close: the quasi-substantive "the most I can concede," but note that this is followed by a relative clause, not by "of it." The term with "of it" is used with the least, not "the most." I do not find it used quite in Frost's way anywhere in the *OED.* One possibility is the phrase "to make the most

of" something. Another is the obsolete or dialect meaning of "almost." This poem was originally called "Making the Most of It." In leaving off "Making," Frost seems to be refusing to restrict the meaning only to that one.

14. Brower finds this a pure symbol according to Jung's definition: "The best possible expression of a relatively *unknown* fact" (*The Poetry of Robert Frost,* 135).

15. Frost, "The Most of It," MS in Amherst College Library. Other changes seem worth noting:

Line 2 originally read: "For all the voice in answer he could wake." Frost had crossed out "for" and replaced it with "since," a conjunction of cause, but at the same time a conjunction of time sequence. It would be very likely that in blurring specific time in favor of a repeated psychological state, or a cosmic timelessness, Frost chose to reinstate "for" and remove the conjunction that might have introduced a temporal sequence.

Line 8 was changed from "But signs of counter love—response" to "But counter-love—original response." There is a greater immediacy, a greater demand for the thing itself in the second version—not *signs* of love, but love itself, and that has something to do with originality of response. A similar gaining of immediacy seems to occur in line 18. Frost had begun to write "landed like" before he crossed out "like," shifting the simile from the noun to the action: "landed pouring like a waterfall."

16. During his depressed state in the forties, Frost said: "What life craves most is signs of life. A cat can entertain itself only briefly with a block of wood. It can deceive itself longer with a spool or ball. But give it a mouse for consummation. Response response. The certainty of a source outside of self—original response whether love or hate or fear" (Dorothy Judd Hall, *Robert Frost,* 39–40).

17. Knowing how Frost loved playing with words, one could ask whether there is some joke in reversing the expression "keeping someone company" with "keeping the universe alone." The loneliness here and in "Old Man's Winter Night," where we are told "one man alone can't keep a house, a countryside," is what distinguishes these uses of "keep" from that of "The Vantage Point," where the cattle kept the lawn, more in the sense of being in possession.

18. For the discussion following, I am indebted to P. K. Saha for

sharing with me an insight into the workings of this poem as demonstrated by Roman Jakobson in a lecture based upon an approach developed by himself and his students. His assumption is that, once past line 10, the poem raises the possibility that there is some response—perhaps superhuman; then the last line ends weakly, which seems to indicate that Frost wants both possibilities—some kind of cosmic response or nothing at all—kept open. Jakobson substantiated his theory by analyzing the relation of stress to pause in the poem. He found the poem to be very regular in its meter. Nevertheless, there is a marked difference between the beginning of the poem and the end with regard to prepausal stress. In the first seven lines there are twenty-five terminal junctures following strong stresses (that is, twenty-five such prepausal stresses out of a total of thirty-five feet). The last seven lines, by contrast, contain only sixteen such prepausal stresses, with four of those sixteen occurring in the last line. Since the absence of prepausal stress is what speeds up a line of poetry, we find that, with the nearing of the "embodiment" in the form of the buck, we have greatly increased the speed of the lines by virtue of the scarcity of prepausal stresses. The last line, intended as a pulling back from the great sense of power to the possibilities left open by "and that was all," slows its pace, with four prepausal stresses in a five-foot line.

19. Lentricchia quotes Walter J. Ong's *The Barbarian Within:* "Is it not in the last analysis cruel to face a human being with merely an object as such, a being which is less than a person? As soon as contemplation enters beyond a certain state of awareness, is not the human being going to be unsatisfied if he cannot find another, a person, a YOU, in whatever he is concerned with?"—a question clearly applicable to "The Most of It" (*Robert Frost,* 123).

20. While I agree with Poirier (*Robert Frost,* 162) that "The Most of It" is too powerful a poem to be simply a reply to Van Dore or anyone else, there is an element of potential irony in the difference between the man on the beach and the poet or narrator telling us of him that "He thought he kept the universe alone."

21. Surely this poem refers to a time during the courtship of Robert Frost and Elinor—probably the crucial summer before she went to college.

Frost wrote to Louis Untermeyer that in 1894 he began as a re-

porter on the Lawrence *American,* where he wrote "paragraphs," some
of which, though in prose, were really eclogues. Out of these came
"Mending Wall," "The Woodpile," and "Two Look at Two." Robert and
Elinor were married in 1895. (LU 355)

22. Contrast "An Old Man's Winter Night." Poirier says that a major
question in Frost's poetry is: how close can anyone who is alone, who
does not have a human partner, get to "nature"? (*Robert Frost,* 37).

23. Frost, "Two Look at Two," TS in Dartmouth College Library.
Another difference is: "She saw them in their pasture; they saw her/In
hers" rather than "in their field." The use of "field" instead of "pasture"
and the omission of "saw" allows us to think not only of the spot of
ground nor only of a doe-mind, but it encompasses fields of vision, and
it makes more prominent the reflective aspect of the mutual seeing.

24. For this reason alone, it is better that Frost chose to end the
poem where he does rather than publishing it with these additional
lines that were originally there:

"It is not hot pursuit. And yet he seeks her.
That is the meaning of the way they walk—
Together on, on, over everything,
Always so far apart, in single file,
Against the wind, that always in their breath
Pervades their minds with fancies."
                              "When the wind
Blows in a new direction do they turn?"
"They turn and face it."
                    "Do they keep their order?
If the west wind should suddenly be east,
Behind her mate. Would she be seeking him then?"
The way they walked would have another meaning.
He would be *seeking* her when she walked first.
He would be *leading* her when he walked first.

See "Escapist—Never!" where some of this turns up.

25. Frost has written about his feelings when he is writing—that
most lonely of activities: "I always notice I am most cowardly when
writing or just after writing. I mind the cellar at night worst then"
(SL 406).

26. Compare "A Hillside Thaw," where "holding" is creative. Here it is sterile and clutching at nothing.

27. Ragussis quotes Nietzsche: "Those who live alone do not speak too loud or write too loud, for they fear the hollow echo—the critique of the nymph Echo" (*The Subterfuge of Art,* 232).

28. The use of the indefinite article—"An old man," not "The old man"—universalizes this man, as does the omission of the definite article before "Woods" in "Stopping by Woods."

29. Hollander, *The Figure of Echo,* 35–36.

30. This seems to be an example of form influencing content: in order to end his canto with a rhyming word, Dante rhymed the last line of the canto with the "b" line of the previous tercet. To do this, of course, is to have a "remainder" of "1," that is, one line more than any number divisible by three. In Frost's poem, to do as Dante did would have been to have, as Dante had, one line more than this last tercet, yielding thirteen lines. This would not have been a sonnet, and Frost was combining the sonnet form with the terza rima. Shelley had done the same thing in "Ode to the West Wind," and had also ended with a rhymed couplet. Frost, however, made his final couplet repeat the rhyme scheme of lines 1 and 3, thus permitting the repetition of the first line, which, on the one hand, resolves his problem of how to end the sonnet and, on the other, emphasizes the circularity of the predicament.

31. For the relationship between this poem and Frost's actual habits of going off into the woods, see EY, 309.

32. Frost said: "There are no two things as important to us in life and art as being threatened and being saved. What are ideals of form for if we aren't going to be made to fear for them? All ingenuity is lavished on getting into danger legitimately so that we may be genuinely rescued" (Barry, *Robert Frost on Writing,* 76).

33. The same phenomenon is apparent—and evidently for the same reasons—in an unusually self-revealing letter: "And I try not to think of it as often as I can. . . . I hold them easily . . . too easily for assurance that they will go with a rush when I let them go" (SL 221). A similar confusion can be found in the letter quoted in the text of this chapter: "govern my loneliness without making me feel less alone" (SL 470).

34. Craig, "Robert Frost at Amherst," TS, 7.

35. "Most of the iceberg is under the water. Most of oneself should

be within oneself. A man must do that in order to be somebody when he comes out to market with other folks. He should be a large-proportioned individual before he becomes social. If a man is wastefully alone, he should be better company when he comes out" (I 77–78).

"Talking is a hydrant in the yard and writing is a faucet upstairs in the house. Opening the first takes all the pressure off the second. My mouth is sealed for the duration of my stay here" (quoted by Sergeant, *Robert Frost,* 351). See also Frost's advice to Bartlett on not doing too much letter writing (Anderson, *Robert Frost and John Bartlett,* 121).

36. Frost to Sidney Cox, 17 July 1920, unpublished, Dartmouth College Library. See the strange letter Frost wrote in 1912 about seeing his "double" (SL 45).

37. "Meet the Press," 25 December 1955, TS, 12.

Chapter 4. Reading from Emerson to Frost

1. Brower, *Robert Frost,* 89.

2. Thompson reports Frost's saying that more important was to remember that our primary concern is with those attributes that the poet brought to what he found (Thompson, Notebook, 78).

3. See Dewey, *Art as Experience,* 53: "There is, therefore, no such thing in perception as seeing *plus* emotion. The perceived object or scene is emotionally pervaded throughout . . . the esthetic or under-going phase of experience is receptive. . . . It involves surrender, but adequate yielding of the self is possible only through a controlled activity that may well be intense."

4. Frost's debts to Emerson and Thoreau have been amply noted: Monteiro, in *Robert Frost and the New England Renaissance,* provides the most exhaustive and detailed parallels between lines, images, and concepts in Frost and those in Emerson and Thoreau. Also obviously helpful to me have been: Brower, *Robert Frost;* Poirier, *Robert Frost;* Cook, "Emerson and Frost"; Parini, "Emerson and Frost"; Waggoner, *American Poets from the Puritans to the Present.* My approach, however, will be to concentrate on the ways Emerson and Thoreau are helpful to Frost as a poet and "reader" of the natural world; how they helped Frost to read emblematically, to see correspondence, but how they did

not go far enough in seeing the "texts" as provisional, and themselves as capable of being constructed into them.

5. Thompson, "cryptic" lecture and YT, 693–95.

6. Burnshaw, *Robert Frost Himself,* 172.

7. "Frost . . . was not a white-haired old saint. He could in season be a mean old son-of-a-bitch. That's part of the man's energy. The best way I've found to say it (and I mean it as an admiration): he had a magmatic mass at his core. He burned at a higher heat than is commonly known. When this man erupted, it produced glories. It was Mount Frost the volcano. But volcanoes have their sulfurous sidestinks." And both, Ciardi pointed out, are products of that enormous energy (Cifelli, "Ciardi on Frost," 475).

8. McIntosh, *Thoreau as Romantic Naturalist,* 49.

9. Frost spoke of his "ulteriority complex." YT, 314; I 188.

10. Frost said: "What is man but all his connections? He's just a tiny invisible knot so that he can't discern it himself: the knot where all his connections meet" (I 119).

11. Rotella writes that neither Frost nor Bohr, no more than James, is incapacitated by his awareness that meaning may be a human imposition or construct, in contrast to Emerson: "Any distrust of the permanence of laws, would paralyze the faculties of man" ("Comparing Conceptions," 184).

12. Emerson also wrote: "I can find my biography in every fable I read" and "A good scholar will find Aristophanes and Hafiz and Rabelais full of American history" (*The Heart of Emerson's Journals,* 318 and 222). Another example: "The reading of books is, as I daily say, according to the sensibility of the scholar, and the profoundest thought or passion sleeps as in a mine, until an equal mind or heart finds it and publishes it" (J 16:79).

13. See Frost: "Draw a string of words through anyone's mind and you find registered emotion" (Sergeant, *Robert Frost,* 325).

14. Holland, "The Reader in the Brain."

15. See McCormick, *Thoreau,* 243–44.

16. Compare Frost: "Why will we be looking for the bottom of things that haven't got a bottom?" (Memorandum Book, England).

17. Whicher, "Emerson's Tragic Sense." Frost felt Whicher failed in his attempt to see Emerson as dualist (LT 665).

18. See Emerson's writing: "Let us treat the men and women well; treat them as if they were real; perhaps they are" (W 4:303).

19. In light of what we have been saying throughout on the subject of reading, interpretations, and the relativism of texts, it is instructive to compare Emerson's reading of Montaigne with the words of Montaigne on the pain of his stones in "On Experience" (*Essays*): "The fear and the pity that people feel at the sight of this malady serve you as occasions for vainglory. . . . It is gratifying to hear people say of you: There is strength now! There's patience!" (376). He goes on to discuss the ways illness helps one to prepare for death. Another value: "Is there any delight comparable to that sudden change when by the passing of a stone, I come at a flash from extreme pain into the fair light of health" (378). He cites Socrates' taking pleasure in reflecting how closely pleasure and pain are allied (379). Closest to Emerson is Montaigne's saying that his malady "rouses rather than stupefies one," as he compares it to maladies such as fever or headache that affect the mind (380).

20. Carpenter, in "William James and Emerson," 54, writes of James's marginal comments on Emerson (in "The Method of Nature"). Emerson wrote: "What is genius but a finer love, a love impersonal, and a love of the flower and perfection of things." And James writes: "But there is no such flower, and love and genius both cleave to the particular objects which are precious because at the moment they seem unique" (54).

21. Montaigne, *Essays*, 343–44.

22. Emerson writes of the differences, much as Coleridge did, calling imagination central, fancy superficial, and comparing them in terms of amusement vs. expansion and exaltations; accidental vs. spontaneous; painting vs. sculpture (W, 8:28–29).

23. In speaking of Shakespeare, Frost noted that "none" in "They that have the power to hurt and do none" rhymes with "stone." He had been contrasting this to villainy in Shakespeare. I find a recognition here of the problem in not being passionate, hence less than alive, and therefore certainly not tragic (V 169).

24. Memorandum Book, England. This is one of those rare reminders that Frost was not really a New Englander, that until the age of eleven he was raised in California.

25. Sergeant, *Robert Frost,* 191. See also SL 182.

26. It is interesting that the Thoreau passage influenced a letter, not a poem, although the idea is in poems. Does this mean it was unconscious, or that he was more consciously literary in letters than we have previously believed?

27. Quoted by McIntosh, *Thoreau,* 89: from a letter to Lucy Brown, 1841.

28. McIntosh, *Thoreau,* 287–88.

29. Ibid., 72. See also Brower, *Robert Frost,* 128: "But beside Frost, Thoreau seems inexperienced and virginal, less thoroughly acquainted with 'the undeveloped,' less willing to face the ever present terrors in both literature and life. In literary terms this means that irony is sporadic in Thoreau, continuous in Frost." We see even in "Ktaadn," where nature is wild and inhospitable to man, Thoreau voices no anxiety: this was a portion of the Earth "savage and awful, though beautiful . . . [but] not his Mother Earth. . . . Man was not to be associated with it. . . . There was clearly felt the presence of a force not bound to be kind to man." And so man can, maybe should, steer clear of such regions, or travel them in awe, at his own risk. Still, in the grip of that awe-filled experience, one in which he felt himself excluded from nature, Thoreau seems to have come closer than he does anywhere else to admitting his difficulty in assimilating body to spirit, for he stands in awe of his body as well: he fears bodies, and he stands in questioning wonder at "the *solid* earth! the *actual* world! *Contact! Contact!* (TS 524–25).

30. To put it another way, Frost wrote in his England Memorandum Book: "reproductiveness is not a part of us: we are part of it."

31. Contrast Emerson: "We believe in ourselves as we do not believe in others. . . . Every man thinks a latitude safe for himself, which is nowise to be indulged to another. . . . No man believes he can be lost" (W 3:78).

32. Parini, "Emerson and Frost," 221, also acknowledges that the dissolution Emerson claims to be good was terrifying to Frost.

33. McIntosh, *Thoreau,* 33.

34. Waggoner, *American Poets,* 294–302.

35. See Perkins, "Robert Frost and Romantic Irony."

36. Nell, *Lost in a Book.*

Chapter 5. Nature and Poetry

1. Emerson's "Snow-Storm" (*Complete Works* 9:41–42) provides a telling contrast with its radiant fire and cozy privacy; but Emerson may have been in the city, which allows a more "social" storm. Besides, his storm is an artist, not a beast; and we are, for the most part, given the point of view of the storm, not of the sighing farmer. The only reference to people is "come see." They are not facing it, really; rather they are observing it, and not feeling themselves in the presence of a dangerous adversary as in Frost's poem. Written during the Derry years when such storms must have seemed more immediately threatening, "Storm Fear" contrasts as well with Frost's later poems wherein a more philosophical speaker faces nature, for example, "Spring Pools," a discussion of which follows.

2. Poirier points out that while both flowers and pools may shiver, only pools have the power to chill. "This yoking of a transitive and a normally intransitive verb is a grammatical indication of the forced effort to make things identical when they are only . . . similar." He sees this as an illustration of "the way the voice can be said to be victimized by its own energies . . . betrayed by grammar as much as by the logical implications of the metaphors" (*Robert Frost,* 17).

3. The first version read "may well think." Frost changed it to the imperative form and in so doing, strengthened this note of warning (variant shown in *The Poetry of Robert Frost,* ed. Lathem, 552).

4. In a television interview Frost said of nature: "I know it isn't kind . . . nature is more or less cruel. . . . The woods are all killing each other anyway. That's where the expression came from, 'a place in the sun.' A tree wanting a place in the sun it can't get. The other trees won't give it to it" ("At Home with Robert Frost," 6). In 1947 Frost said that he was not a nature poet. He wrote one nature poem, however, when he lived in Ann Arbor. The reference was to "Spring Pools" (I 114).

5. While this poem appears in *West-running Brook* (1928), it was written in 1893 when Elinor and her mother left their summer home, and Elinor went back to college (EY 153).

6. Griffiths has called the Frostian man a "cosmic paranoid" in imagining nature's slights, assuming nature's indifference to be antagonism. Griffiths then uses "Bereft" by contrast as a poetic example of a nature *who* knows (italics mine) ("Frost and the American View of

Nature"). Griffiths, in using "who" as well as in ascribing knowledge to nature, or the speaker's view of nature, is too prone to take the poem straight. I feel that the wind and the leaves know nothing, that the speaker *is* being a trifle paranoid—not in any cosmic way—and Frost knows it.

7. In this connection it seems pertinent that Frost once planned his fourth book to be entitled *Pitchblende* (SL 202). Another title he had thought of using was "Melanism," which indicates the darkness of color resulting from an abnormal development of black pigment in the epidermis of animals. Thompson finds that this blackness could well be used as a metaphor, since another title Frost contemplated was "The Sense of Wrong" and since the word is not unrelated to "melancholy" (EY 402). A similar metaphoric extension of darkness seems to under-lie these remarks of Frost in speaking about "Stopping by Woods": "I've had people say—someone who ought to know better—quote me as saying [in] that poem, 'the coldest evening of the year.' Now that's getting a thermometer into it. And 'The darkest evening of the year' 's better—more poetical some way. Never mind why. I don't know. More foolish. . . . Got to be a little foolish. . . . But then it goes on and says 'The woods are lovely, dark and deep,' and then if I were reading it for somebody else, I'd begin to wonder what he's up to" (V 81).

Also pertinent is the following notebook entry labeled "Dark Darker Darkest": "Here where we are life wells up as a strong spring perpetu-ally piling water on water with dancing highlights fresh upon it. But it flows away on all sides as into a marsh of its own making. It flows away into poverty, into insanity into crime. . . . There is a residue of extreme sorrow that nothing can be done about and over it poetry lin-gers to brood with sympathy I have heard poetry charged with having a vested interest in sorrow. Dark darker darkest. Dark as it is that there are these sorrows and darker still that we can do so little to get rid of them the darkest is still to come. The darkest is that perhaps we ought not to want to get rid of them. They may be the fulfillment of exertion" (absence of punctuation in the original) (Hall, *Robert Frost,* 39).

8. For representative examples of Frost's own terror of night and of a tree at his window which gave him nightmares, see EY, 279 and 309. The following entry appears in Lesley Frost's journal: "Papa once made up a story about being seronded by birch trees and that makes

us imagine that the birch trees were after us sometimes. Yesterday we
really thought a birch tree was after us, any way Irma and Carol did,
so *I* pretended I thought it, but really it wasn't. . . . The wind blew
it back and forth and made it look as if it was walking but of course
I knew it wasn't. I showed it to the children and they said 'let's run
home,' so we went. . . . After that we went in the house but we didn't
tell mama. We kept it a secret till now (*New Hampshire's Child,* 82–83).
In the biography, we see also his fear of tramps, another link between
himself and the hill wife. See also his poem "The Night Light."

9. And also fear of assault (thus tying in with her fear of the
stranger and his smile and his watching them in "Her Word"). The hill
wife would then be very like Frost's sister Jeannie and his daughter
Irma. Lentricchia, *Robert Frost,* 71, sees the dark pine as "decidedly
phallic" and the house as representative of female genitals. He refers
to an earlier version of the poem in which the pronouns referring to
"tree" were masculine and third-person singular. One need not be quite
so graphic in exact metaphoric correspondence, but her fear as sexual
could also be supported by the ambiguity of the reference to "two"—
whether the "other" one, the one unafraid, is the husband or the tree.

10. Edwards sees this poem not as a representation of nature as
sinister, but as a portrait of human misrepresentation ("Pan's Song,
Revised," 110).

11. In "Now Close the Windows" similar sounds are less welcome.
The speaker consciously shuts out the sounds that the wind causes the
fields and trees to make. It seems significant that whereas the poem
reads "Now close the windows and hush all the fields: / If the trees
must let them slightly toss," the original draft, entitled "In November,"
had "winds" for "trees." Whatever part "trees" play in Frost's poetic
imagination and in the expression of his moods, he saw fit to add it
to this poem, introducing tossing trees, and the need to silence these
trees, in a poem that would have had no trees in it at all.

12. Perhaps apropos here is Frost's writing: "One sickness and another in the family kept us till I could have cried out with the romantics
that no artist should have a family" (LU 204).

13. What Dewey says of response to art can here be said of nature,
and its becoming "expressive": "Expression is the clarification of tur-
bid emotion; our appetites know themselves when they are reflected in

the mirror of art, and as they know themselves are transfigured. Emotion that is distinctively esthetic then occurs . . . an emotion that is induced by material that is expressive, and because it is evoked by and attached to this material it consists of natural emotions that have been transformed. Natural objects . . . induce it. But they do so only because when they are matter of an experience they, too, have undergone a change similar to that which the painter or poet effects in converting the immediate scene into the matter of an act that expresses the value of what is seen" (*Art as Experience,* 77).

14. Contrast Emerson: "In the woods, we return to reason and faith. There I feel nothing can befall me . . . which nature cannot repair" (*Complete Works,* 1:10).

15. As might be expected, there has been much written on the subject of woods imagery in the poetry of Robert Frost. Lentricchia finds "the image of the 'dark trees' . . . obsessive. . . . Ultimately the journey into the immense dark wood becomes a metaphor for a journey into the dark immensity of the self's wildness which will finally stimulate, once again, the need for community" (*Robert Frost,* 26). He finds it to be a metaphor of the irrational, and goes on to say: "In his dark wood the self is damned, not redeemed, because what may be unveiled and unloosed there is everything in us which must be kept under tighter control" (88).

The "irrational appeal" of the dark woods is also discussed by Dendinger, "The Irrational Appeal of Frost's Dark Deep Woods," as it relates to other major American literature (e.g., *Huck Finn, The Scarlet Letter, The Bear*) in which the wilderness exerts similar fascination and brings with it the temptation to escape the human condition, an escape that is morally wrong as well as being impractical. Yet he points out that "the dark unfathomable core of human nature relates man most surely to his swirling, unmeasurable universe, to all its inhabitants, and to their common . . . environment, the lovely wood dark and deep."

In this sense of a greater tie with all humanity and with nature, the journey into the woods is not all "damned" and unredeemed, as Lentricchia has it. Some nod to wildness, some "retreat" into the dark self and into the freedom of woods is necessary for one's keeping in touch with oneself and one's humanity, necessary to creativity. This must be what Frost meant, when he defined poetry as being "like a wild-game preserve. . . . It's where wild things live. This is the ultimate in poetry, and it has to be there" (I 137).

As Rechnitz writes in "The Tragic Vision of Robert Frost," 140: "Keep the wildness down we have to; but if we keep it too completely down we shall discover it breaking out in us, ourselves."

Frost himself recognized our ambivalence toward keeping ourselves "under tightest control." In defining puritanism he said: "It is that in you that fears your own pleasure, that distrusts your own pleasure . . . there ought to be in you something that forbids yourself. . . . There ought to be something in you that hates to be checked . . . that you better not need to be checked—that ought to be self-checked. That's Puritanism, too" (V 90–91).

John T. Oglivie, who also sees dark woods as a place where one can lose the self as well as find it, states that in the later poems Frost cannot be enticed into the woods at all; he projects himself outward and, to do so, shifts his imagery from woods to stars. Oglivie finds the whole pattern demonstrated in "Come In" ("From Woods to Stars"). There is some risk in basing assertions on the order of the appearance in print of Frost's poetry, as he saved up poems to be used much later. There is a "star" poem in A Boy's Will, and a few "woods" poems are in In the Clearing.

Woods can lure us to our destruction, but as Poirier points out, "home" can destroy by stifling and smothering (*Robert Frost*, 89, 96, 125).

16. Thoreau speaks of a poet's "having" a landscape: "The crusty farmer supposed [the poet] had got a few apples only, Why, the owner does not know it for many years when a poet has put his farm in rhyme . . . has fairly impounded it, milked it . . . got all the cream, and left the farmer only the skimmed milk" (*Walden*, 82–83). Emerson also speaks of such "ownership" (*Complete Works*, 3:42).

17. This distinction, as well as the one below about man's capacity to dream, is made by Warren, in "The Themes of Robert Frost," 218–33. Warren finds as a recurrent theme in Frost man's need to accommodate his capacity to contemplate and dream with action.

18. Coale, in "Emblematic Encounter," 103, sees it differently: "'And miles to go before I sleep' in their repetition are a sleepy final attempt to deny what in fact is already happening. The speaker is stopping,

coming to an hypnotic halt; the repetition of the final lines suggests that the poem has come to a full spellbound stop." (A similar view is expressed in the same volume by Carmichael, "Robert Frost as Romantic," 162.) Coale also feels that Frost has slipped into a sort of "self-hypnosis. Always before, he has resisted the spellbinding, seductive quality of the encounter with nature" (102). Coale seems, however, to be confusing the speaker with Frost (as he also does in his discussion of "After Apple Picking"). Frost may be showing such seduction and, in the process, seducing the reader. The poem is not written at the moment of seduction. That is not to say, though, that the act of writing cannot cause seduction. This may very well be a poem about the hypnotic qualities of poetry—its writing and its reading.

19. Thompson's remarks on Ciardi are contained in the notes to EY, 595–97. The article in question is Ciardi, "The Way to the Poem," 147–57. The article first appeared in *The Saturday Review,* 12 April 1958.

20. Ciardi, however, must have felt himself chastised, for when he reprinted the essay in his poetry text, he omitted the paragraph in question (*How Does a Poem Mean?* 670–77). He later refers to a passage he had cut from that article: an analogy to scuba divers so caught by the "rapture of the deep" that they go further and further until they do not have enough air to come up, so hypnotized by beauty, they are drawn into oblivion. He cut this to the parenthetical death wish. He recanted on the death wish but still believed in the oblivion part of his discussion. So do I (Cifelli, "Ciardi on Frost," 483).

21. An interesting earlier use of the word "sensibilist" occurred when he was writing about his sister Jeannie's insanity: "She has always been anti-physical and a sensibilist. I must say she was pretty well broken by the coarseness and brutality of the world before the war was even thought of. This was partly because she thought she ought to be on principle" (LU 247).

22. MS of "New Hampshire."

23. Letter to Sidney Cox, 18 May 1939. Part of this is quoted in LY 377.

24. A valuable insight into the creative process is comparing the quiet loveliness of the poem with the actual incident that Thompson had from Frost: "A bleak wind began to blow fine flakes of the year's first snowfall and Rob could feel the chill penetrating to his bones so ominously. . . . As the darkness settled in the wind-blown snow felt like

fine sand against his face. Snow began to pile and drift in the road just enough to hinder the tired horse and threaten serious difficulties. Rob lost his way in the dark, had to stop at a farmhouse to ask for directions, grew more and more miserable as he got closer to home, and finally drove into his barn near midnight sick with rage and disgust" (EY 266).

Bleau's account refers to the time Frost related to him that the incident took place on "the darkest evening of the year"—22 December; it was before Christmas, and there was no gift money. "I just sat there and bawled like a baby." Lesley confirms it was what he had told them ("Robert Frost's Favorite Poem," 175–77).

25. For discussions of the way this ending came about, might have come about, and how it works, see YT, 596, quoting R. C. Townsend. See also Cooper and Holmes, *Preface to Poetry*, 604–7, which draws on a discussion with the poet and prints a facsimile of the original draft. Interesting as conjecture and insight into the poetic process is Ciardi's article, cited above.

26. "At Home with Robert Frost."

27. Ciardi, as the article appears in *How Does a Poem Mean?*

28. EY, 267.

I am like a dead diver after all's
Done, still held fast in the weeds' snare below,
Where in the gloom his limbs begin to glow
Swaying at his moorings as the roiled bottom falls.
There was a moment when with vainest calls
He drank the water, saying 'Oh let me go—
God let me go!'—for then he could not know
As in the sun's warm light on earth and walls.

I am like a dead diver in this place.
I was alive here too one desperate space,
And near prayer in the one whom I invoked.
I tore the muscles from my limbs and choked.
My sudden struggle may have dragged down some
White lily from the air—and now the fishes come.

29. The letters to Louis Untermeyer can be found in SL, 270–71 and 497, respectively. The final version of the poem is in the latter:

To prayer I think I go,
I go to prayer—
Along a darkened corridor of woe
And down a stair
In every step of which I am abased.
I wear a halter-rope about the waist.
I bear a candle end put out with haste.
For such as I there is reserved a crypt
That from its stony arches having dripped
Has stony pavement in a slime of mould.
There I will throw me down an unconsoled
And utter loss,
And spread out in the figure of a cross.
Oh, if religion's not to be my fate
I must be spoken to and told
Before too late!

30. At this point some of Frost's other remarks on this poem seem in order:

On the question of its being a suicide poem: "I never intended that, but I did have the feeling it was loaded with ulteriority" (I 188).

"That one I've been more bothered with than anybody ever has been with any poem in just the pressing it for more than it should be pressed for. It means enough without its being pressed. . . . I don't say that somebody shouldn't press it, but I don't want to be there" (V 52).

Frost once called this poem "my best bid for remembrance" (LU 163). But most significant of all is Frost's remark that "Stopping by Woods . . . contains all I ever knew" (quoted by Cook, "Robert Frost's Asides on His Poetry," 357).

31. Frost, in one of his Harvard lectures, spoke of "the evil search for synonyms." Thompson explains: "Robert Frost, in referring to 'the evil search for synonyms,' was expressing his prejudice in favor of using images which imply (rather than state) analogies, images and actions which merely hint metaphoric and symbolic extensions of meaning. A convenient example is the familiar poem " 'Stopping by Woods' " (YT 647).

32. Langbaum, in "The New Nature Poetry," 329, says that Frost turns into a kind of consolation "that perception of an internal void

which would be for another poet the most terrifying perception of all." Obviously I do not agree; for Frost too it is "the most terrifying perception of all."

Poirier, in *The Renewal of Literature,* 52, finds "carried into the poetry of Robert Frost" the "terror of blankness and lassitude" that Emerson and James expressed in their obsession with action (this despite Emerson's "admit[ting] that he is a cold fish"). In Frost, Poirier locates the fear in "Stopping by Woods." True, action is the antidote to lassitude in "Stopping," but the "terror of blankness" seems much more the subject in "Desert Places," and Frost's "action," the making of it into art.

33. In a letter to Untermeyer about his sister Jeannie's insanity, Frost expresses his grief and his feelings of guilt. Then he adds: "And I suppose I am a brute in that my nature refuses to carry sympathy to the point of going crazy just because someone else goes crazy, or of dying because someone else dies. As I get older I find it easier to lie awake nights over other people's troubles. But that's as far as I go to date. In good time I will join them in death to show our common humanity" (SL 247–48).

34. In the first printing of the poem, the line read "Up, my knee, to keep on top." In the *Complete Poems* it read "Up my knee to keep on top." Lathem, in his editing of the latest complete edition—*The Poetry of Robert Frost*—restores the commas, presumably "for achieving greater textual clarity" (256), but I find the ambiguity preferable.

35. See also "In the Home Stretch" for another poem wherein trees stand for passing time; there too they are threatening even as the couple is drawn to them.

36. We have spoken before (and cited Holland) on the importance for Frost of the gathering metaphor and its relation to the task of gathering leaves. But there is a subtle irony in that here Frost has the speaker crushing metaphors that the poet created. He could be crushing what those metaphors, or romantic conventions, express or represent—the act, too, of metaphor-making and its frustrating limits of control.

37. The comparison between fireflies and stars shows up in 1906 in Lesley's journal (written at about age seven), which may be the result of Frost's having pointed the difference out to her, or it may simply be her own very fertile imagination:

in the damp medows the fireflys
go in and out and in the
sky the stars look down at
the fireflys that look up
at them that never go in
and out like the fireflys in the
damp medows fly. (*New Hampshire's Child,* IV, 10)

38. This is not the case in an unpublished version at the Dartmouth College Library, wherein there is a colon at the end of line 11.

39. Originally the poem had been entitled "March Moment." This poem, in its conscious extending of bounds by means of imagination, seems to illustrate what Frost meant when he said "imagination . . . must be requisitioned" (I 21). The following excerpt from Lesley's journal shows this kind of "requisitioning" in action as Frost practices it and teaches his daughter to do so: "Papa and I make beleave we can see people on mars, and children and houses and everything ells on the earth. We say these things when we go after the cow at night, we say we will no more than the astronomers do with telliscopes. We say o what are those things climing those trees they look like snakes but they must be children. o there comes a man to tell them to come down because their mama said they might tear their stokings and when we go in we are interested in taulking about mars and teliscops and things" (*New Hampshire's Child,* 82–83).

40. Emerson, *Complete Works,* 3:34.

41. "Poetry is a measured extravagance of the spirit, but on a measure of beat, you know, *held*" (italics mine) ("Meet the Press," 4).

42. Thompson reports conversations with Frost wherein they tossed sexual metaphors of metaphor back and forth: Frost liked Thompson's "engendering," noting that some metaphors seemed sexual—a bringing together of a male and a female element to create propagation of thought (LT 544–45). He went on to call the process "pollenating" (550). My favorite, though, is: "There was something wrong with a writer who couldn't get into his subject and screw it to a climax: if you were going to find metaphors for the artistic process in the functions of the body, that was the way you ought to do it" (659).

43. "The most exquisite line in the poem," according to Brower, *Robert Frost,* 82.

44. This is also a good example of Black's "interaction" principle (see chapter 2 above).

45. Frost, "Hyla Brook," MS.

Chapter 6. Bond and Free: The Human Encounter

1. Cifelli, "Ciardi on Frost," 495.

2. *Prose Jottings of Robert Frost,* 144. Thompson was much more judgmental: "Where does Frost draw the line? That would be hard to say. . . . I think he has been about as guilty of violating the ten commandments as anyone could be, although in a far more subtle way than most people violate them. He says he doesn't know where to draw the line. If you don't know you don't draw it. You pose as drawing it. . . . He seems to me to have been willing to withdraw secretly into the remotest areas from the battle line, in so far as moral and ethical questions are concerned" (LT 277).

3. There are examples in the letters of Frost's punning on his name. For example:

"[I'm] not the same frost as I was when winter came on last year" (SL 481–82).

"In this case it is the frosts we are running away from and Frosts can hardly help going with us since Frost we are ourselves. If you ever talk of me in print you may notice that it is my frostiness that is more and more played up. I am cold, snow-dusted and all that" (Letter to Sidney Cox, 17 July 1920).

Particularly relevant to this poem is this in a letter to Lesley: "It is material that has come to the surface of my mind in reading just as frost brings stones to the surface of the ground" (Grade, *Family Letters,* 49).

4. Of interest here is the known fact of Frost's own conservatism, and in connection with what is said below, it might be useful to examine the letter that relates "orthodoxy" in politics, religion, and love to the gloom and the fears from which he suffers (SL 221).

5. The real-life neighbor on the other side of the wall, Napoleon Guay (the same neighbor who figures in "The Ax-Helve"), was in reality a very good neighbor indeed. He helped Frost by taking over some of the farm responsibilities. Frost had been in Guay's house but never invited *him* to visit. It seems that, in real life, he kept the wall between them! (EY 313).

The fact that the poem can be taken in different ways seems supported by some of the things Frost has said about it. When he chose to read it in Moscow, while the Berlin wall was such a sensitive subject, there were those who felt it was "too political" for him to have read. Frost denied any political motive: "I've had lots of adventures with that poem, he said after reciting it. People are frequently misunderstanding it or misinterpreting it. The secret of what it means I keep" (LY 316). This might leave room for the possibility that the poem is not "political" because it is not a wholesale condemnation of walls, but an ambivalence toward them, a realistic, if sad, view of walls. In a letter replying to the question of whether Frost's intention had been fulfilled with the character and atmosphere of "Mending Wall," he said: "I should be sorry if a single one of my poems stopped with either of those things—stopped anywhere in fact. My poems—I should suppose everybody's poems—are all set to trip the reader head foremost into the boundless. Ever since infancy I have had the habit of leaving my blocks carts chairs and such like ordinaries where people would be pretty sure to fall forward over them in the dark. Forward, you understand, *and* in the dark. I may leave my toys in the wrong place and so in vain. It is my intentions we are speaking of—my innate mischievousness" (SL 344).

On another occasion he said of this poem: "I played exactly fair in it. Twice I say 'Good fences' and twice 'something there is—.'" Cook, "Robert Frost's Asides on His Poetry," 355.

6. Montgomery writes of the different categories of barriers in Frost's poetry. He feels that Frost insists on recognizing, not tearing down, barriers between man and man ("Robert Frost and His Use of Barriers," 57, 339–53).

Frost wrote to Louis Untermeyer: "I happened to notice when I was reading from your Modern American Poetry that you had left a line out of Mending Wall. 'There where it is we do not need the wall.' It just barely hurts the sense" (LU 149). Frost politely acknowledges that the poem *can* make sense without this line, but it is not the whole sense, the maximum sense.

7. There have been several psychoanalytical readings of "Mending Wall," for example, Holland's on the oral implications in "Unity Identity Text Self," and Marcus's on the latent homosexual ones in "Psycho-

analytical Approaches to 'Mending Wall.'" Both of these articles cite others.

8. Fromm, *The Art of Loving*.

James was also a help in this respect.

And this is what Frost had to say: "It is our virtue to be half unselfish and equally our virtue to be half selfish. Out of the one comes the insistence on our consideration of the rights of others; out of our selfishness comes our insistence on our consideration of the rights of ourselves. All art flourishes in that second insistence. Without it there could be no art, and art is the highest expression of humanity as a whole. Banish selfishness, and with the evil of selfishness goes the good of it" (LT 167).

9. On this issue Robert Frost was taken to task by such critics as Cowley, "The Case Against Mr. Frost" and Winters, "Robert Frost." In this connection it is also relevant to see again the letter Frost wrote about the insanity of his sister Jeannie in which he claims that one cannot go crazy because someone else does (SL 247–48). See above, chapter 3.

While both "Two Tramps" and "Mending Wall" probe social relationships, "Two Tramps," written in the thirties, is more closely related to economic issues and the attendant ethical questions. The earlier "Mending Wall" raises questions that are more apt to invite psychological probing, exploring as it does ambivalence about personal relationship, not the more abstract, distant issue of relationship with "society." In its being more concerned with psychology, with walling in or out and thereby suggesting anxiety over what may enter or erupt, it is closer to a poem like "A Servant to Servants," in the same volume (*North of Boston*, 1914). "Two Tramps," in its raising artistic questions on love and need, spending and keeping, and the selfishness art requires, can be related to "A Drumlin Woodchuck," in *that* same volume (*A Further Range*, 1936).

10. Lawrence Perrine finds it erroneous to assume that Frost kept the task for himself ("Two Tramps in Mud Time and the Critics"). De Selincourt makes the same point in "Poet of Sanity," 253.

11. Craig spoke of "play" in Frost's work. Speaking of dialectic in which questions are held open, he said that each poem is an act that makes room for both the speaker and his question to live in the same

world. He makes room to look at questions. The first type of play Craig speaks of is the play between the question and the asker. Then he speaks of play in the way that the guy ropes have play ("The Silken Tent"); play as the room beyond the poem to fling ahead the unused phrases (see "The Figure a Poem Makes," "The Constant Symbol," and "Unharvested"); rough play, as in play for mortal stakes; and play in the sense of drama, make-believe ("Robert Frost as Teacher"). See also the articles in the section entitled "Play" in Tharpe's *Centennial Essays II*, and Cook's "The Serious Play of Interpretation."

12. A naughty poem, a wicked one, Frost called it (LT 83).

13. Brower makes a similar point (*Robert Frost,* 185).

14. "Guys" is derived from the French "guier," which means "to guide," another aspect of the relationship. In a poem to Louis Untermeyer, he writes of "good guys" as keeping something upright—"Well I have had Kay Lesley you and Larry" (LU 337).

15. Contrast this with "The Impulse" portion of "The Hill Wife," in whose marriage "Sudden and swift and light as that / the ties gave." We are told:

> It was too lonely for her there,
>   And too wild,
> And since there were but two of them,
>   And no child,
>
> And work was little in the house,
>   She was free,
> And followed where he furrowed field,
>   Or felled tree.
>
> She rested on a log and tossed
>   The fresh chips,
> With a song only to herself
>   On her lips.

Frost intensifies her feeling of, or perhaps her insistence on, solitude in the stanza that follows. The manuscript in the Dartmouth College Library shows the manner in which he did this:

>   went to break a bough
> And once she ~~begged the knife to cut~~

Of

~~The~~ black alder.

The poem stands as revised.

16. In "The Constant Symbol" Frost writes: "Form in language is such a disjected lot of old broken pieces it seems almost as non-existent as the spirit till the two embrace in the sky. They are not to be thought of as encountering in rivalry but in creation. No judgement on either alone counts" (SP 28).

17. Compare another Frost image: "feeling easy in your harness" (I 135). Poirier makes a similar point in *Robert Frost,* xiv.

18. For example, in the sentence "A group of boys played," "group" is the grammatical subject, but "boys" is the logical one.

19. This also solves the problem of excessive embedding; the sentence now branches right. It also relieves the strangeness of what could be a stative/non-stative combination, were "is made aware" to be considered the verb governed by "tent": she *is* as a silken tent *is made aware.*

20. The only use of "as" as a preposition is in the sense of in the role of, in the function or capacity of. An example would be: "He acted as umpire." In this case we do not create an analogy, the second NP (noun phrase) being a specific, not a generic noun. He did not act the way an umpire acts; he played the part of umpire.

21. In a handwritten copy of the poem (Dartmouth College Library), line 5 reads: "And its supporting central pole." The line was thus short two syllables, and adding "cedar" provided that. It also added still more "s" alliteration. It may, however, be possible that the addition of "cedar" alludes to the most famous uses of cedars in the Bible, both of which are appropriate here: the description of Solomon's Temple, and the various references to cedars in his *Song of Songs.* Cedar was a favored material for the temple because of its strength, its height, and its hardness. Presumably it was prized for its majestic beauty as well (*1 Kings,* 5 and 6).

In its being the primary building material for an edifice of magnificence dedicated to God, in its being tall and strong, it shares qualities with the supporting cedar pole "that is its pinnacle to heavenward/ and signifies the sureness of the soul." To these qualities are added a woman's love and the building of a haven of love in *The Song of Songs,* as one can see from the following verses:

> Behold, thou art fair, my beloved, yea, pleasant;
> Also our couch is leafy.
> The beams of our houses are cedars,
> And our panels are cypresses (1:16–17)

> His legs are as pillars of marble
> Set upon sockets of fine gold;
> His aspect is like Lebanon,
> Excellent as the cedars. (5:14)

22. The use of "round" raises still other possibilities: the roundness of the circle that a compass creates can be seen as the roundness of infinity. Then there is the suggestion that it is not only that which the circle (or the area of the tent) covers which is affected by "her ties"; rather they affect an infinite area surrounding the tent, encompassing it, but also radiating outward. This tribute to a woman becomes a tribute as well to the reach of her influence, suggesting the worlds upon worlds, the globes, the completion possible in infinite love—perhaps echoing Donne, and suggesting, as Donne did, the interconnectedness of these worlds to each other, not only as lovers, but human beings concerned, bound up with each other, and bound to the promontory, the mainland, the earth. One suspects echoes of Donne: "Valediction Forbidding Mourning," "Valediction: Of Weeping," and "Meditation XVII."

23. Cf. these lines from "Kitty Hawk":

> Spirit enters flesh
> And for all it's worth
> Charges into earth
> In birth after birth
> Ever fresh and fresh.
> We may take the view
> That its derring-do
> Thought of in the large
> Was one mighty charge
> On our human part
> Of the soul's ethereal
> Into the material. (*The Poetry,* 435–36)

Also, from "Education by Poetry": "Greatest of all attempts to say one thing in terms of another is the philosophical attempt to say matter in terms of spirit, or spirit in terms of matter, to make the final unity. That is the greatest attempt that ever failed. We stop just short there. But it is the height of poetry, the height of all thinking, the height of all poetic thinking, that attempt to say matter in terms of spirit and spirit in terms of matter. It is wrong to call anybody a materialist simply because he tries to say spirit in terms of matter, as if that were a sin" (SP 41).

Matter and spirit are expressed in an image of sexuality and birth in the first quotation, in terms of poetry in the second. The relationship of all these at once is something we have noted before and will note again below. Frost felt that earth and spirit have to be united in poetry *and* in love.

Originally entitled "In Praise of Your Poise," this poem was written to Kathleen Morrison, whose devotion, attention, and efficiency literally saved Frost after the death of Elinor. She became his personal secretary and manager, a position she kept until his death. He used to say of her that Kay took him in hand and managed him when he was not able to manage himself. She and her husband, Theodore Morrison, were the loving, caring friends he needed. His feelings for Kay were a complex mixture of gratitude, respect, obedience, dependency, and love (LY 4–24). See also Morrison's *Robert Frost: A Pictorial Chronicle,* which is impressive for its reticence, discretion, and tact. There are many allusions to their relationship in LT.

24. In this connection, on the subject of manliness, Frost wrote to his son Carol: "Your . . . poem is powerful and splendid. You have hammered it close and hard and you have rammed it full of all sorts of things, observations both of nature and human nature—and humor and picturesqueness too. And best of all . . . it is no sissy poem such as I get from Poetic boys generally. It is written with a man's vigor and goes down in to a man's depth. You perhaps don't realize what that means to me" (SL 390). Of Frost, William Dean Howells wrote: "His manly power is manliest in penetrating to the heart of womanhood" ("Editor's Easy Chair," 45).

25. While the raw material of this poem was the marital estrangement of Nathaniel and Leona Harvey after the death of their first-born child in 1895, Thompson feels that the writing of it cannot be sepa-

rated from the grief that Robert Frost and Elinor shared after the death of their first-born, Elliott. Elinor said repeatedly, at that time, "The world's evil." Frost also told Lawrance Thompson that he never read "Home Burial" aloud because it was "too sad" for him to do so (EY 597–98). According to Youtz in "Robert Frost's Comments on His Poetry," the poet says of this poem: "This is my most dramatic poem. I couldn't read this to anyone I knew."

26. Frost mentions this line as well as the one that says "Don't, don't, don't don't" in a letter on the way his poems talk. He liked these lines particularly and says: "It is that particular kind of imagination that I cultivate rather than the kind that merely sees things, the hearing imagination rather than the seeing imagination, though I should not want to be without the latter" (SL 129–30).

27. Still a third reading of this line is Poirier's: "It is as if 'home' were a burial plot for all of them" (*Robert Frost,* 124). This ties in with his theory that "Home exerts such a simultaneous restraint on and incentive to expressed need for ventilation" (145). As I see it, home is only suffocating when the marriage within it is unhappy. Poems like "In the Home Stretch" and "Putting in the Seed" certainly do not make one feel the "need for ventilation." Consistent with his relating restraint and "extra-vagance" to matters of form and "imaginative license," Poirier relates "Home Burial" to questions of poetics: "It could be said that the central subject of this poem is poetic form seen in the metaphor of domestic form" (135). While this too could be a subject of the poem, I find "Home Burial" too dramatic, too tragic, too realistically tied to failure in human love to have poetic form as its principal subject. A poem like "West-running Brook" is far more likely to be a metaphor of two positions expressed in "domestic form."

28. Lynen, *The Pastoral Art of Robert Frost,* 145.

29. Jarrell, "Robert Frost's 'Home Burial,'" 219–22.

Thompson reports that Elinor "hated the indignity of having a doctor explore her before childbirth; she thought it robbed life of its grace and charm" (LT 149)—a fascinating combination of romance and revulsion.

30. One exception could be the white flower in "Design," but there he has asked, "What had that flower to do with being white?" The fault lying not in the flower but in the designer/painter of the scenic trap.

31. EY 584–85. Lawrance Thompson also refers to the line in "Despair" in which Frost had written: "My sudden struggle may have dragged down some / White lily from the air."

32. Both Frost's sister Jeannie and his daughter Irma, in their insanity, entertained irrational fears of men and assault.

33. Cowley, "The Case Against Mr. Frost."

"The Subverted Flower" first appeared in *A Witness Tree* in 1942; however, an earlier version of this poem (for which no draft is known to exist) was written early enough for inclusion in *A Boy's Will*. Thompson reports in EY, chapter 13, the biographical incident behind the poem and assumes that, since the poem was so daring and also autobiographical, Elinor would not have permitted him to publish it; therefore it was never published during her lifetime.

It seems appropriate, not only in connection with this poem but as background for all the discussion in this chapter on sexuality, to bring to bear some of the biographical information on Frost's awareness of his own sexuality, his guilt because of it, and possibly Elinor's limitations in this respect. Lawrance Thompson speaks of Frost as "intermittently guilt-ridden by his own sexual drives" (EY 552). This is especially interesting in light of poems such as "The Subverted Flower," which dramatize inability to come to terms with one's sexual nature, and in contrast with the poems in which we shall find a redemptive harmony, not only between the partners, but with the sexuality in their love.

Hall, in *Remembering Poets* and in "Vanity, Fame, Love, and Robert Frost," discusses Frost's constant feelings of guilt. That Elinor died without asking to see him was a crushing blow to him, and consonant with her tendency to "punish" him with "eloquent silences" (YT 494). His guilt was intensified by his feeling that his passionate demands had brought six children upon a woman whose heart was weak, and therefore that he had, in a sense, killed her (YT 494). He wrote a letter to Sidney Cox apologizing for not being able to come as planned: "things that follow in the train of marriage keep me—babies and the fear of babies . . . we haven't known just what we were in for. We don't know now. It seemed like a last putting forth. At times we have been afraid it was something more solemn. At any rate I don't think I ought to be away from Elinor as she is" (SL 218).

In an obviously bitter moment, the man who wrote of his wife as "the unspoken half of everything he ever wrote" gave vent to the following: "That's an unpardonable attempt to do her as the conventional helpmeet of genius. Elinor has never been of any earthly use to me . . . catch her getting any satisfaction out of what her housekeeping may have done to feed a poet! Rats! She hates housekeeping . . . prefers high living" (LU 224).

The fact is that Elinor did prod him on in his writing, and she did, obviously, understand his poetry (YT 246); she objected to his dissipating his time and energy lecturing and teaching rather than writing, even though the lecture platform was far more lucrative. In this respect the letter seems grossly unfair. Yet put together with knowledge of her nature, her silences, her reticence, one can see in this letter an underlying dissatisfaction in his marriage. "Of no earthly use" and "feeding a poet" could conceivably, even if not consciously, refer to the ways in which her affection was inadequate for him. We can never know, and even if such a conjecture were correct, we could not know whether such inadequacy would have been owing to "meagerness of heart" or fear of the consequences.

One feels Elinor's reticence even in a famous letter Frost wrote acknowledging her importance to his life and to his poetry: "Pretty nearly every one of my poems will be found to be about her if rightly read. But I must try to remember they were as much about her as she liked and *permitted them to be. Without ever saying a word she set limits* I must continue to observe. One remark like this and then no more forever" (emphasis mine; SL 471–72).

34. Poirier writes: "By placing 'Never Again Would Birds' Song Be the Same' between 'The Most of It' and 'The Subverted Flower,' Frost once again reveals his deep commitment to married love as a precondition for discovering human 'embodiments' in nature, for discovering Adam and Eve" (*Robert Frost,* 169).

35. In the letters to Louis Untermeyer, and in a file named Revealing Notes in Thompson's papers (University of Virginia Library) there is much evidence of Frost's "bawdy," his willingness and ability to create double entendres. Here is one version of a poem he titled sym-ball-ism:

The symbol of the number ten—
the naught for girls, the one for men—
defines how many times does one

in mathematics or in fun

go as you might say into zero.

You ask the heroine or the hero (LT Notes, 1687iiii).

One can analyze Frost's word play here: note the I(1) *in* heroine! Also the word play on hero-IN; there could also be a suggestion of being invited IN, in "ask the hero IN."

36. It is telling that Frost's discussion of "pukes" and "prudes" (see also my chapter 5) appears in the same volume (*New Hampshire*, 1923).

37. This seems a perfect example of what Frost was talking about when he wrote of speech tones, tones of voice "that mean more than words." "Sentences must be so shaped as definitely to indicate these tones. Only when we are making sentences so shaped are we really writing. . . . A sentence *must* convey a meaning by tone of voice and it must be the particular meaning the writer intended. The reader must have no choice in the matter. The tone of voice and its meaning must be in black and white on the page" (SL 204).

38. Jarrell, "To the Laodiceans," 64.

39. Frost insisted there are no abnormal people in his poetry (LT 42). This would bear out the notion that it is not the "witch" who is abnormal. The poem, incidentally, is based on a true story (YT 141–42).

40. Quoted by Hall, *Robert Frost*, 7.

41. See below, discussion of "Never Again Would Birds' Song Be the Same," whose last line is "And to do that to birds was why she came."

Appropriate to the sense of resolution with which the poem ends is the structure of the sentence "I came"—a simple declarative that resolves not only by statement but rhythmically in a perfect iambic foot that ends the line and ends it with a consonant that closes our lips.

42. Related to the question of implicit meaning as opposed to explicit realism, Frost has said: "There are two types of realist—the one who offers a good deal of dirt with his potato to show that it is a real one; and the one who is satisfied with the potato brushed clean. I'm inclined to be the second kind" (quoted by Untermeyer, "Man and Poet," 176).

43. See "Flower-Gathering" and the many other flower/love poems in *A Boy's Will*.

44. Frost had not capitalized "Love," "Putting," or "Seed," in the

manuscript in The Jones Library, Amherst. Further references to revisions are to this same manuscript.

Cox points out that this poem is a "wedding" of Shakespearean sonnet and dramatic monologue and to see this is to comprehend how
the poem is a complete fusion of form and action. The power of the
poem lies in the way the colloquial idiom, working through two traditional structures to seize on the most primal passion, recapitulates
the action of converting flower petals to a nourishing substance. He
goes on to praise the masterful control that carries the poem from the
colloquial idiom and action of lines 1 and 2 to line 10, where action becomes a pure figure (introduction to *Critical Essays,* pp. 12–13). This
heightening of style at line 10 may have prompted that capital "L" so
reminiscent of Renaissance profusions on Love.

45. See recognition of this rarity in "A Cloud Shadow."
46. See Hall, "An Old Testament Christian."
47. Holland, *The Brain of Robert Frost,* cited in chapter 1.
48. Iser, *The Implied Reader,* 42.
49. Poirier, *Robert Frost,* 22.

Chapter 7. Felix Culpa: Frost and Eden

1. See "Build Soil" (CP 428).
2. Stevens, "Sunday Morning."
3. Warren and Wellek, "Image, Metaphor, Symbol, Myth," 196.
4. Ibid., 196, 214–17, 197–98. See also Turbayne, *The Myth of
Metaphor,* 59–61, 214–17.
5. Related to all of this, of course, is the pursuit of "knowledge"
and the attendant loss of innocence. In this connection Frost says:
"And then the story of the Garden of Eden and the fruit of the Tree of
Knowledge, you see—that's some mythology, isn't it, from our point
of view? But it's about all the boys I've ever taught. At the age I get
them they just come out of the Garden of Eden. They're having a go
at the apple, you know. *And it's a thing I have had to deal with all the
time*—they've had to deal with all the time, and we have to deal with it
decently without talking too much about psychology or psychiatry or
going to anybody at all about it—but it's the whole thing, you see. All
the books we're reading, all the things we're thinking, have to do with

that knowledge" (V, 177, emphasis mine). His referring to Eden and the "apple" as "a thing I have had to deal with all the time" is another way of acknowledging this story as "a myth to live by." This is further borne out by the fact that poems related to the subject span most of his career—1914 to 1942 in this chapter alone.

6. As Frost once wrote to Louis Untermeyer: "I would only gain in compression. No poem I give up but appears later as one line or one epithet" (LU 268).

7. Smith in *Poetic Closure,* 135, uses this poem to illustrate "how subtle the relation between logical sequence and other elements of a lyric may be, and how powerful, also, the forces for closure that may result from that relation."

8. Frost, MS of "Nothing Gold Can Stay" and "It Is Almost the Year Two Thousand."

9. Frost, "Nothing Golden Stays," TS.

10. We see an example of the way lines appear in other poems much later by comparing both of the earlier versions (MS, The Jones Library) and then the published "It Is Almost the Year Two Thousand." Note how prophetic this last seems in light of the dropping of the atom bomb. (See also the various plays on the word "gold" in "The Lost Follower" and "The Vindictives.")

We well may raise our heads
From weeding garden beds
And sewing in our laps
And annotating books
To look at what perhaps
     (gaze)
     surer
~~Is better while it's there~~
~~Rebelion and reform~~
~~To feed and keep us warm~~
~~But soon must fade away~~
~~For nothing gold can stay.~~
And   looks
             books
At such an end deluxe
May be an end de luxe

In autumn she achieves
    Another golden flame
    ~~Though~~
  And yet
But still it's not the
    same lovely ~~liquid~~
    It not as ~~limpid~~ [?] quite
As that first golden light
And yet will have to do
Say I and what say you?

Stanzas 1 and 3 of the typescript are quoted in the text (stanza two has no real basis of comparison with either published poem).

It Is Almost the Year Two Thousand

To start the world of old
We had one age of gold
Not labored out of mines,
And some say there are signs
The second such has come,
The true Millennium,
The final golden glow
To end it. And if so
(And science ought to know)
We well may raise our heads
From weeding garden beds
And annotating books
To watch this end de luxe (Lathem, ed., *The Poetry of Robert Frost,* 361).

11. Fergusen uses the same evidence to draw a far more optimistic conclusion. He sees rise implicit in the falling. I find his *felix culpa* view applicable in other poems, but not in this one ("Frost and the Paradox of the Fortunate Fall," 438–39).

12. For the suggestion to include in this chapter a discussion of retrograde motion, especially as we see it in "West-running Brook," I am grateful to Jarold Ramsey.

13. See "A Hillside Thaw," which shows an artistic "holding" and "staying" (CP 293–94). In this life and death context, we are also reminded of the term "stay of execution."

14. Jarrell, "To the Laodiceans," 67.

15. On the subject of the death of the poet in the poet, Frost wrote: "It is interesting to see the things poets find to die away into. They die into self-imitators, into virtuosos, and they die into philosophers. The last is the best death." He goes on to say that philosophers stay with one simile all their lives, while poets toss them off one a day (YT 604).

16. Compare J. Hillis Miller, *The Form of Victorian Fiction: Thackeray, Dickens, Trollope, George Eliot, Meredith, and Hardy,* 32–33. Miller speaks of the Godless man. He sees him characterized by "a lack, a hun-

ger for fulfillment . . . a spontaneous energy of volition which reaches out in longing to substantiate itself by the assimilation of something outside itself."

17. Compare the following lines from "New Hampshire":

The glorious bards of Massachusetts seem
To want to make New Hampshire people over.
They taunt the lofty land with little men.
I don't know what to say about the people.
For art's sake one could almost wish them worse
Rather than better. How are we to write
The Russian novel in America
As long as life goes so unterribly?
There is the pinch from which our only outcry
In literature to date is heard to come.
We get what little misery we can
Out of not having cause for misery.
It makes the guild of novel writers sick
To be expected to be Dostoievskis
On nothing worse than too much luck and comfort (CP 207).

Asked whether the world is better off now than it was, Frost replied: "If it is, I'm afraid that it won't have enough adversity in it for the good of the arts" ("At Home with Robert Frost," 9).

18. Frost wrote of talking with some priests: "the idea [he was concerned with] in the two-word phrase *felix culpa*. It could be turned against me personally and I am willing it should be: I am less and less on the defensive" (LU 327).

19. Lewis, *The American Adam,* 6.

20. Ibid., 55–59, 6. I question this last statement; see below, discussion of "After Apple Picking."

21. Lynen, *The Pastoral Art of Robert Frost,* 91–93.

22. See Frost: "Make no mistake about the tones of speech I mean. They are the same yesterday, today, and forever. They were before words were—if anything was before anything else. They have merely entrenched themselves in words. No one invents new tones of voice. So many and no more belong to the human throat. . . . The imagination is no more than their summoner" (*Prose Jottings of Robert Frost,* 118).

"A sentence carries a certain number of words and those have their sound, but the sentence has a sound apart from the words which is the sentence sound proper. It was before the words were. It still has existence without the embodiment of words in the cries of our nature. The mind or spirit is not really active unless it is finding constantly new tones of voice" (Memorandum Book, England).

23. Included in a letter to Lesley, 5 November 1918.

24. Poirier, in discussing "Unharvested," points out that "the scent is the best part of the apples; it is the soul which is 'unharvested,' an idea beautifully developed in 'After Apple Picking'" (*Robert Frost*, 262).

25. Brower, *Robert Frost*, 25.

26. On Poirier's discussion of the ladder as metaphor of metaphor, see my chapter 2.

27. I am grateful to Maureen Morley for pointing out to me that not pluralizing "thousand" or "fruit" implies an "infinity of fruit," impossible to number logically. This seems to me to emphasize the nonliteral quality of "fruit." The phrase is also irregular grammatically, and if we go on to analyze the nature of the irregularity of "ten thousand thousand fruit," we find that "fruit," as an uncountable category noun subsuming "apples," should, in fact, be singular (e.g., there was so much fruit to touch). What makes us look again, and look nonliterally, is the fact that "fruit" is modified by a number, as if it were a countable noun (e.g., ten thousand thousand apples). Frost thus has it several ways at once: an infinite number of *individual* items; a great, unmeasurable spiritual responsibility; a grammatical signal that there is something going on here whose irregularity merits our close attention; and our conflating of categories.

28. Brooks and Warren make the point that the details of "After Apple Picking" do not all remain within a literal possibility; they constantly imply a kind of fantasy (*Understanding Poetry*, 365).

29. Lewis, *The American Adam*, 58.

30. For a superb analysis of the relationship between syntax and rhyme, see Brower, *Robert Frost*, 24–25.

31. A much more extreme example of Frost's unwillingness to allow serious matters to sound too serious—of his insistence that "if it is with inner seriousness it must be with outer humor" (SP 65)—is "The Cow in Apple Time." What begins as a celebration of the forces of life,

sounding at the outset like a companion piece to "Mending Wall," ends in shriveling and drying up. The poem has been read as a moral treatise on irresponsible motherhood (EY 605), and it certainly carries echoes of Eden in the cow's new found "knowledge" that leads her to scorn the pasture and ultimately to "go dry." Yet the view of that intoxicated flying cow is surely meant to be funny. These "sweetening" apples are also "spiked" with stubble and "worm-eaten"; they send the cow "flying" and they render her unproductive as well as ridiculous. Her bellow is probably some combination of uncontrollable intoxicated ecstasy and pain—she *has to* fly for both reasons simultaneously. And thus the poem is simultaneously comic and serious. That drooling cow, flying, bellowing on a knoll, is a grotesque but comic cow.

At a poetry reading Frost used this poem to point a barb at Amy Lowell, whom he could never quite forgive for having written that he had no sense of humor (YT 4). Referring to this accusation of hers that he had no sense of humor, he read "The Cow in Apple Time" and pointed out that Amy Lowell seemed to think his cow must be a tragic cow and the jump a tragic jump (212). Not tragic (perhaps mock-tragic), certainly not lacking humor, but containing "inner serious" elements nevertheless.

32. This extension of the "Eve principle" beyond defined time or space seems borne out by the fact that Frost read this poem at his eighty-eighth birthday celebration in praise of Kay Morrison. At the end of a twenty-five-minute speech, he closed by praising the woman who had been his "devoted secretary" for more than twenty years. He then recited "Never Again Would Birds' Song Be the Same," which, according to LY, he had written for her. We know that Frost had had romantic feelings for her (see above, notes to chapter 6 on "The Silken Tent"); yet one feels that, in addition to the feelings he had for Kay, his long experience as passionate lover and husband of Elinor surely also informs this poem (and, I suspect, "The Silken Tent"). In Grade, *Family Letters,* the chapter that follows Elinor's death is entitled "Never Again Would Birds' Song Be the Same." I find this to be similar to the confusion that attended "The Silken Tent." Thompson's notes tell of Lesley's wanting to inscribe its first line on Elinor's tombstone until Thompson told her it had been written for Kay (LT 963).

33. See also the discussion of ends, beginnings, and middles in "In

the Home Stretch," where the couple are "dumped down in paradise and . . . happy" (CP 144).

34. All of this is consistent with Frost's contention that not only do we believe in love and art, but we believe them in—into existence. The best-known expression of this is included in "Education by Poetry." He speaks of four beliefs—self-belief, love-belief, art-belief, and God-belief: "There is . . . the belief in someone else, a relationship of two that is going to be believed into fulfillment. . . . Then there is the literary belief . . . the literary one in every work of art, not of cunning and craft, mind you, but of real art; that believing the thing into existence . . . and then finally the relationship we enter into with God to believe the future in—to believe the hereafter in" (SP 44–46).

35. See SL 470–71, for how the "bad" world is qualified by "mitigating things."

We must not forget, of course, the value in the creative process itself. On the subject of the joy in it, the following remarks by John Ciardi are pertinent: "What do we mean by a dark poem? . . . Is there any such thing as an unhappy or a pessimistic poem? I think it could be argued that the act of writing a poem well has to be a joyous act, no matter what your subject matter. The subject matter can be tragic, but the act of finding what strikes you as a true equivalence has to be joyous" (Cifelli, "Ciardi on Frost," 492).

Chapter 8. Epilogue: The Height of the Adventure

1. I would like to acknowledge the influence of Lentricchia's chapter, "The Redemptive Imagination," in *Robert Frost,* 112–19. The reader will also have noticed echoes of Auden, Donne, Shakespeare, Stevens, and Dylan Thomas.

Works Cited

Works by Robert Frost

"The Aim Was Song." MS included in a letter to Lesley. 5 November 1918. Robert Frost Collection (#'s 6261-y, 6261-aq, and 6261-a). Clifton Waller Barrett Library, Manuscripts Division, Special Collections Department, University of Virginia Library, Charlottesville.

"Birches." MS, Robert Frost Collection. Dartmouth College Library, Hanover, New Hampshire.

"Birches." MS, Robert Frost Collection. Jones Library, Amherst, Massachusetts.

A Boy's Will. Copy owned by Philip N. Youtz. Contains Frost's handwritten annotations of poems, 1918. Robert Frost Collection. Amherst College Library, Amherst, Massachusetts.

Complete Poems of Robert Frost. New York: Holt, Rinehart and Winston, 1949.

"Hyla Brook." MS, in Copybook 5. Robert Frost Collection. Jones Library, Amherst, Massachusetts.

"The Impulse." MS, Robert Frost Collection. Dartmouth College Library, Hanover, New Hampshire.

Lecture at University of Maryland, 1941. 1938–48 Robert Frost—Lectures and Interviews. Robert Frost Collection (#'s 6261-y, 6261-aq, and 6261-a). Clifton Waller Barrett Library, Manuscripts Division, Special Collections Department, University of Virginia Library, Charlottesville.

The Letters of Robert Frost to Louis Untermeyer. New York: Holt, Rinehart and Winston, 1963.

Letter to Sidney Cox, 17 July 1920. Robert Frost Collection. Dartmouth College Library, Hanover, New Hampshire.

Letter to Sidney Cox, 18 May 1939. Robert Frost Collection. Dartmouth College Library, Hanover, New Hampshire.

Memorandum Book, England, 1912–15. Robert Frost Collection (#'s 6261-y, 6261-aq, 6261-a). Clifton Waller Barrett Library, Manuscripts Division, Special Collections Department, University of Virginia Library, Charlottesville.

"The Most of It." MS, Robert Frost Collection. Amherst College Library, Amherst, Massachusetts.

"New Hampshire." MS, Robert Frost Collection. Jones Library, Amherst, Massachusetts.

North of Boston. Inscription to George Whicher on the flyleaf. Robert Frost Collection. Amherst College Library, Amherst, Massachusetts.

"Nothing Gold Can Stay" and "It Is Almost the Year 2000." Draft, in Copybook 5. Robert Frost Collection. Jones Library, Amherst, Massachusetts.

"Nothing Golden Stays." TS, Robert Frost Collection. Amherst College Library, Amherst, Massachusetts.

"Now Close the Windows." MS, Robert Frost Collection. Jones Library, Amherst, Massachusetts.

Poetry and Prose. Edited by Edward Connery Lathem and Lawrance Thompson. New York: Henry Holt and Co., 1972.

The Poetry of Robert Frost. Edited by Edward Connery Lathem. New York: Holt, Rinehart and Winston, 1969.

Prose Jottings of Robert Frost: Selections from His Notebooks and Miscellaneous Manuscripts. Edited by Edward Connery Lathem and Hyde Cox. Lunenberg, Vermont: Northeast-Kingdom Publishers, 1982.

"Putting in the Seed." MS, Robert Frost Collection. Jones Library, Amherst, Massachusetts.

Selected Letters of Robert Frost. Edited by Lawrance Thompson. New York: Holt, Rinehart and Winston, 1964.

Selected Prose of Robert Frost. Edited by Hyde Cox and Edward Connery Lathem. New York: Collier Books, 1966.

"The Silken Tent." MS, Robert Frost Collection. Dartmouth College Library, Hanover, New Hampshire.

"Two Look at Two." TS, Robert Frost Collection. Dartmouth College Library, Hanover, New Hampshire.

Related References

Anderson, Margaret Bartlett. *Robert Frost and John Bartlett: The Record of a Friendship.* New York: Holt, Rinehart and Winston, 1963.

Aristotle. *The Poetics.* In *Aristotle's Poetics.* Translated by S. H. Butcher. Introduction by Francis Fergussen. New York: Hill and Wang, 1961.

"At Home with Robert Frost." NBC, 23 November 1952. TS of videotape, Robert Frost Collection. Amherst College Library, Amherst, Massachusetts.

Bagby, George F. "Frost's Synecdochism." *American Literature* 58 (1986): 379–92.

Barry, Elaine. *Robert Frost on Writing.* New Brunswick, N.J.: Rutgers University Press, 1973.

Bartlett, John. "Notes on Conversations with Robert Frost." Robert Frost Collection (#'s 6261-y, 6261-aq, 6261-a). Clifton Waller Barrett Library, Manuscripts Division, Special Collections Department, University of Virginia Library, Charlottesville.

Bate, Walter Jackson. *John Keats.* Cambridge: Belknap Press of Harvard University Press, 1963.

Beach, Joseph Warren. *The Concept of Nature in Nineteenth-Century English Poetry.* New York: Pageant Book Co., 1956.

Black, Max. "Metaphor." In *Models and Metaphors.* Ithaca: Cornell University Press, 1962.

Bleau, N. Arthur. "Robert Frost's Favorite Poem." In *Centennial Essays III.* Edited by Jac Tharpe. Jackson: University Press of Mississippi, 1978.

Borroff, Marie. *Language and the Poet: Verbal Artistry in Frost, Stevens, and Moore.* Chicago: University of Chicago Press, 1979.

Brooks, Cleanth, and Robert Penn Warren. *Understanding Poetry,* 3rd ed. New York: Holt, Rinehart and Winston, 1938, 1950, 1960.

Brower, Reuben. *The Poetry of Robert Frost: Constellations of Intention.* New York: Oxford University Press, 1963.

Burnshaw, Stanley. *Robert Frost Himself.* New York: George Braziller, 1986.

Carmichael, Charles. "Robert Frost as Romantic" In *Frost: Centennial Essays.* Edited by Jac Tharpe. Jackson: University Press of Mississippi, 1974.

Carpenter, Frederic I. "William James and Emerson." *American Literature* 11 (1939): 39–57.

Ciardi, John. *How Does a Poem Mean?* Boston: Houghton Mifflin Co., 1959.

————. "The Way to the Poem." In *Dialogue with an Audience*. Philadelphia: J. B. Lippincott Co., 1963.

Cifelli, Edward. "Ciardi on Frost: An Interview." In *Centennial Essays*. Edited by Jac Tharpe. Jackson: University Press of Mississippi, 1974.

Coale, Samuel. "The Emblematic Encounter of Robert Frost." In *Frost: Centennial Essays*. Edited by Jac Tharpe. Jackson: University Press of Mississippi, 1974.

Cohen, Ted. "Metaphor and the Cultivation of Intimacy." In *On Metaphor*. Edited by Sheldon Sacks. Chicago: University of Chicago Press, 1978.

Cook, Marjorie E. "Dilemmas of Interpretation: Ambiguities and Practicalities." In *Robert Frost: The Man and Poet*. Edited by Earl J. Wilcox. Winthrop Studies 3. Rock Hill: Department of English, Winthrop College, 1981.

————. "The Serious Play of Interpretation." *South Carolina Review* 15 (Spring 1983): 77–87.

Cook, Reginald. "The Critics and Robert Frost." In *Centennial Essays*. Edited by Jac Tharpe. Jackson: University Press of Mississippi, 1974.

————. "Emerson and Frost: A Parallel of Seers." *New England Quarterly* 31 (1958): 200–217.

————. *Robert Frost: A Living Voice*. Amherst: University of Massachusetts Press, 1974.

————. "Robert Frost's Asides on His Poetry." *American Literature* 19 (1948): 351–59.

Cooper, Charles W., and John Holmes. *Preface to Poetry*. New York: Harcourt, Brace and Co., 1946.

Cowley, Malcolm. "The Case Against Mr. Frost." *New Republic* (11 September 1944): 312–13; (18 September 1944): 345–47. Reprinted in *Robert Frost: A Collection of Critical Essays*. Edited by James M. Cox. Englewood Cliffs, N.J.: Prentice-Hall, 1962.

Cox, James M. Introduction to *Robert Frost: A Collection of Critical Essays*. Englewood Cliffs, N.J.: Prentice-Hall, 1962.

————, ed. *Robert Frost: A Collection of Critical Essays*. Englewood Cliffs, N.J.: Prentice-Hall, 1962.

Cox, Sidney. *A Swinger of Birches.* New York: New York University Press, 1958.

Craig, G. A. "Robert Frost as Teacher." An address on the seventy-fifth birthday of Robert Frost (26 March 1950) at the Jones Library in Amherst. TS, Robert Frost Collection. Amherst College Library, Amherst, Massachusetts.

————. "Robert Frost at Amherst." Chapel Talk, 15 June 1965. Robert Frost Collection. TS, Amherst College Library, Amherst, Massachusetts.

Dendinger, Lloyd N. "The Irrational Appeal of Frost's Dark Deep Woods." *Southern Review* 2 (1966): 822–29.

de Selincourt, Basil. "Poet of Sanity." In *Recognition of Robert Frost: Twenty-fifth Anniversary.* Edited by Richard Thornton. New York: Henry Holt and Co., 1937.

Dewey, John. *Art as Experience.* 1934. Reprint. New York: Perigee Books, G. P. Putnam's Sons, 1980.

Eco, Umberto. *The Role of the Reader: Explorations in the Semiotics of Texts.* Bloomington: Indiana University Press, 1979. First Midland Book Edition, 1984.

Edie, James M. *William James and Phenomenology.* Bloomington: Indiana University Press, 1987.

Edwards, Margaret. "Pan's Song, Revised." In *Frost: Centennial Essays.* Edited by Jac Tharpe. Jackson: University Press of Mississippi, 1974.

Emerson, Ralph Waldo. *The Complete Works of Ralph Waldo Emerson.* Biographical introduction and notes by Edward Waldo Emerson. Centenary Edition. 12 vols. Boston: Houghton Mifflin Co., 1903.

————. *The Heart of Emerson's Journals.* Edited by Bliss Perry. Boston: Houghton Mifflin Co., 1926.

————. *The Journal and Miscellaneous Notebooks of Ralph Waldo Emerson.* Edited by William H. Gilman, Alfred R. Fergusen, Merrell R. Davis, Merton M. Sealts, Jr., Harrison Hagford. 16 vols. Cambridge: Belknap Press of Harvard University Press, 1960–1983.

Felman, Shoshana. *Jacques Lacan and the Adventure of Insight: Psychoanalysis in Contemporary Culture.* Cambridge: Harvard University Press, 1987.

Fergusen, Alfred R. "Frost and the Paradox of the Fortunate Fall." In *Frost: Centennial Essays.* Edited by Jac Tharpe. Jackson: University Press of Mississippi, 1974.

Fish, Stanley. *Is There a Text in This Class? The Authority of Interpretive Communities.* Cambridge: Harvard University Press, 1980.

Fromm, Erich. *The Art of Loving: An Inquiry into the Nature of Love.* New York: Harper and Row, 1956.

Frost, Lesley. *New Hampshire's Child: The Derry Journals of Lesley Frost.* With notes and index by Lawrance Thompson and Arnold Grade. Albany: State University of New York Press, 1969.

Fussell, Paul, Jr. *Poetic Meter and Poetic Form.* New York: Random House, 1965.

Giamatti, A. Bartlett. *Play of Double Senses: Spenser's Faerie Queene.* Englewood Cliffs, N.J.: Prentice-Hall, 1975.

Gombrich, E. H. *Art and Illusion: A Study in the Psychology of Pictorial Representation.* Bolingen Series 35:5. Princeton: Princeton University Press, 1960, 1961, 1969.

Grade, Arnold, ed. *Family Letters of Robert and Elinor Frost.* Albany: State University of New York Press, 1972.

Griffiths, Clark. "Frost and the American View of Nature." *American Quarterly* 20 (1968): 21–37.

Hall, Donald. *Remembering Poets.* New York: Harper and Row, 1978.

———. "Vanity, Fame, Love, and Robert Frost." *Commentary* 64 (December 1977): 51–61.

Hall, Dorothy Judd. "An Old Testament Christian." In *Frost: Centennial Essays III.* Edited by Jac Tharpe. Jackson: University Press of Mississippi, 1978.

———. *Robert Frost: Contours of Belief.* Athens, Ohio: Ohio University Press, 1984.

Harries, Karsten. "Metaphor as Transcendence." In *On Metaphor.* Edited by Sheldon Sacks. Chicago: University of Chicago Press, 1978.

Holland, Norman N. *The Brain of Robert Frost: A Cognitive Approach to Literature.* New York: Routledge, 1988.

———. "The Reader in the Brain." Paper presented at the annual convention of the Modern Language Association, 28 December 1988.

———. "Unity Identity Text Self." In *Reader-Response Criticism: From Formalism to Post-Structuralism.* Edited by Jane Tompkins. Baltimore: Johns Hopkins University Press, 1980.

Hollander, John. *The Figure of Echo: A Mode of Allusion in Milton and After.* Berkeley: University of California Press, 1981.

Horney, Karen. *Neurosis and Human Growth: The Struggle Toward Self-Realization.* New York: W. W. Norton & Co., 1950.

Howells, William Dean. "Editor's Easy Chair." Reprinted in *Recognition of Robert Frost: Twenty-fifth Anniversary.* Edited by Richard Thornton. New York: Henry Holt and Co., 1937.

Iser, Wolfgang. *The Act of Reading: A Theory of Aesthetic Response.* Baltimore: Johns Hopkins University Press, 1978.

———. *The Implied Reader: Patterns of Communication in Prose Fiction from Bunyan to Beckett.* Baltimore: Johns Hopkins University Press, 1974.

Jakobson, Roman. "Closing Statement: Linguistics and Poetics." In *Style in Language.* Edited by Thomas A. Sebeok. Cambridge: MIT Press, 1960.

James, William. *The Principles of Psychology.* 2 vols. New York: Henry Holt and Co., 1890.

Jarrell, Randall. "To the Laodicians." In *Poetry and the Age.* London: Faber and Faber, n.d.

———. "Robert Frost's 'Home Burial.'" In *The Third Book of Criticism.* New York: Farrar, Straus and Giroux, 1969.

Keats, John. *Complete Poems and Selected Letters.* Edited by Clarence DeWitt Thorpe. Indianapolis: Bobbs-Merrill, 1935.

Langbaum, Robert. "The New Nature Poetry." *American Scholar* 28 (Summer 1959): 323–40.

Lathem, Edward Connery, ed. *Interviews with Robert Frost.* New York: Holt, Rinehart and Winston, 1966.

Lea, Sydney. "From Sublime to Rigamarole: Relations of Frost to Wordsworth." *Studies in Romanticism* 19 (Spring 1980): 83–108.

Lentricchia, Frank. *Robert Frost: Modern Poetics and the Landscapes of the Self.* Durham: Duke University Press, 1975.

Levin, Samuel. *Metaphoric Worlds: Conceptions of a Romantic Nature.* New Haven: Yale University Press, 1988.

Lewis, R. W. B. *The American Adam.* Chicago: University of Chicago Press, 1955.

Lodge, David. *The Modes of Modern Writing: Metaphor, Metonymy, and the Typology of Modern Literature.* London: Edward Arnold, 1977. Reprint. Chicago: University of Chicago Press, 1988.

Lynen, John. *The Pastoral Art of Robert Frost.* New Haven: Yale University Press, 1960.

McIntosh, James. *Thoreau as Romantic Naturalist: His Shifting Stance toward Nature.* Ithaca: Cornell University Press, 1974.

Marcus, Mordecai. "Psychoanalytic Approaches to 'Mending Wall.'" In *Robert Frost: Studies in the Poetry.* Edited by Kathryn Gibbs Harris. Boston: G. K. Hall & Co., 1979.

"Meet the Press." 25 December 1955. TS, Robert Frost Collection. Amherst College Library, Amherst, Massachusetts.

Miller, David L. "Dominion of the Eye in Frost." In *Centennial Essays.* Edited by Jac Tharpe. Jackson: University Press of Mississippi, 1974.

Miller, J. Hillis. *The Form of Victorian Fiction: Thackeray, Dickens, Trollope, George Eliot, Meredith, and Hardy.* Notre Dame: University of Notre Dame Press, 1968.

Montaigne, Michel de. *Essays.* Translated and with an introduction by J. M. Cohen. Bungan, Suffolk: Penguin Classics, 1983.

Monteiro, George. "The Facts on Frost." *South Carolina Review* 22 (Fall 1989): 87–108.

———. *Robert Frost and the New England Renaissance.* Lexington: University Press of Kentucky, 1988.

Montgomery, Marion. "Robert Frost and His Use of Barriers: Man Against Nature Toward God." *South Atlantic Quarterly* 57 (1958): 339–53. Reprinted in *Robert Frost: A Collection of Critical Essays.* Edited by James M. Cox. Englewood Cliffs, N.J.: Prentice-Hall, 1962.

Morrison, Kathleen. *Robert Frost: A Pictorial Chronicle.* New York: Holt, Rinehart and Winston, 1974.

Morrison, Theodore. "The Agitated Heart." *Atlantic* 220, no. 1 (1967): 72–79.

Morse, Stearnes. "'The Subverted Flower': An Exercise in Triangulation." In *Centennial Essays III.* Edited by Jac Tharpe. Jackson: University Press of Mississippi, 1976.

Nell, Victor. *Lost in a Book: The Psychology of Reading for Pleasure.* New Haven: Yale University Press, 1988.

Newdick, Robert S. "Robert Frost and the Sound of Sense." *American Literature* 9 (1937): 289–300.

Nowottney, Winifred. *The Language Poets Use.* London: The Athlone Press, University of London, 1965.

Oglivie, John T. "From Woods to Stars: A Pattern of Imagery in Robert Frost's Poetry." *South Atlantic Quarterly* 58 (1959): 64–76.

Ovid. *Metamorphoses.* Translated by Rolfe Humphries. Bloomington: Indiana University Press, 1955.

Parini, Jay. "Emerson and Frost: The Present Act of Vision." *Sewanee Review* 89 (1981): 206–27.

Perkins, David. "Robert Frost and Romantic Irony." *South Carolina Review* 22, no. 1 (1989): 33–37.

Perrine, Lawrence. "Four Forms of Metaphor." In *Contemporary Rhetoric: A Conceptual Background with Readings*. Edited by W. Ross Winterowd. New York: Harcourt, Brace, Jovanovich, 1975.

———. "Two Tramps in Mud Time and the Critics." *American Literature* 44 (1973): 671–76.

Poirier, Richard. *The Renewal of Literature: Emersonian Reflections*. New Haven: Yale University Press, 1987.

———. *Robert Frost: The Work of Knowing*. New York: Oxford University Press, 1977.

———. "Robert Frost: The Sound of Love and the Love of Sound." *Atlantic* 223, no. 4 (1974): 50–55.

Poulet, Georges. "Criticism and the Experience of Interiority." In *Reader-Response Criticism: From Formalism to Post-Structuralism*. Edited by Jane Tompkins. Baltimore: Johns Hopkins University Press, 1980.

Pritchard, William H. *Frost: A Literary Life Reconsidered*. New York: Oxford University Press, 1984.

Ragland-Sullivan, Ellie. *Jacques Lacan and the Philosophy of Psychoanalysis*. Urbana: University of Illinois Press, 1986.

Ragussis, Michael. *The Subterfuge of Art: Language and the Romantic Tradition*. Baltimore: Johns Hopkins University Press, 1978.

Rechnitz, Robert. "The Tragic Vision of Robert Frost." In *Centennial Essays*. Edited by Jac Tharpe. Jackson: University Press of Mississippi, 1974.

Riffaterre, Michael. *Semiotics of Poetry*. Bloomington: Indiana University Press, 1978.

Rood, Karen Lane. "Robert Frost's 'Sentence Sounds': Wildness Opposing the Sonnet Form." In *Frost: Centennial Essays II*. Edited by Jac Tharpe. Jackson: University Press of Mississippi, 1976.

Rosenblatt, Louise M. *The Reader, the Text, the Poem: The Transactional Theory of the Literary Work*. Carbondale: Southern Illinois University Press, 1978.

Rottela, Guy. "Comparing Conceptions: Frost and Eddington, Heisenberg, and Bohr." *American Literature* 59 (1987): 167–89.

Sacks, Sheldon, ed. *On Metaphor.* Chicago: University of Chicago Press, 1978.

Saha, P. K., "Metaphorical Style as Message." In *Analogical Reasoning: Perspectives of Artificial Intelligence, Cognitive Science, and Philosophy.* Edited by D. H. Helman. Dordrecht: Kluwer Academic Publishers, 1988.

Salomon, Roger B. *Desperate Storytelling: Post-Romantic Elaboration of the Mock-Heroic Mode.* Athens: University of Georgia Press, 1987.

Sergeant, Elizabeth Shepley. "Good Greek Out of New England." In *Recognition of Robert Frost: Twenty-fifth Anniversary.* Edited by Richard Thornton. New York: Henry Holt and Co., 1937.

————. *Robert Frost: The Trial By Existence.* New York: Holt, Rinehart and Winston, 1960.

Sheehy, Donald G. "The Poet as Neurotic: The Official Biography of Robert Frost." *American Literature* 58 (1986): 393–410.

Siebenschuh, William R. *Fictional Techniques and Factual Works.* Athens: University of Georgia Press, 1983.

Smith, Barbara Herrnstein. *Poetic Closure: A Study of How Poems End.* Chicago: University of Chicago Press, 1968.

Spacks, Patricia Meyer. *Gossip.* New York: Alfred A. Knopf, 1985.

————. *Imagining a Self: Autobiography and Novel in Eighteenth Century England.* Cambridge: Harvard University Press, 1976.

Stevens, Wallace. *The Collected Poems of Wallace Stevens.* New York: Alfred A. Knopf, 1969.

Sutton, William A., ed. *Newdick's Season of Frost: An Interrupted Biography of Robert Frost.* Albany: State University of New York Press, 1976.

————. "Problems of Biography." In *Robert Frost: Studies of the Poetry,* edited by Kathryn Gibbs Harris. Boston: G. K. Hall, 1979.

Tharpe, Jac, ed. *Frost: Centennial Essays.* Jackson: University Press of Mississippi, 1974.

————, ed. *Frost: Centennial Essays II.* Jackson: University Press of Mississippi, 1976.

————, ed. *Frost: Centennial Essays III.* Jackson: University Press of Mississippi, 1978.

Thompson, Lawrance. "Cryptic" Lecture. Thompson-Frost Collection (# 10044-a). Clifton Waller Barrett Library, Manuscripts Division,

Special Collections Department, University of Virginia Library, Charlottesville.

———. "Frost Notes." Thompson-Frost Collection (# 10044-a). Clifton Waller Barrett Library, Manuscripts Division, Special Collections Department, University of Virginia Library, Charlottesville.

———. Notebooks. Thompson-Frost Collection (# 10044-a). Clifton Waller Barrett Library, Manuscripts Division, Special Collections Department, University of Virginia Library, Charlottesville.

———. "Notes on Robert Frost." TS, Thompson-Frost Collection (# 10044-a). Clifton Waller Barrett Library, Manuscripts Division, Special Collections Department, University of Virginia Library, Charlottesville.

———. "Revealing Notes." Thompson-Frost Collection (# 10044-a). Clifton Waller Barrett Library, Manuscripts Division, Special Collections Department, University of Virginia Library, Charlottesville.

———. Robert Frost: The Early Years, 1874–1915. New York: Holt, Rinehart and Winston, 1966.

———. Robert Frost: The Years of Triumph, 1915–1938. New York: Holt, Rinehart and Winston, 1970.

———. "Robert Frost and the Biographer as Critic." Thompson-Frost Collection (# 10044-a). Clifton Waller Barrett Library, Manuscripts Division, Special Collections Department, University of Virginia Library, Charlottesville.

———. "The Robert Frost Controversy, Jones Library, December 7, 1950 [1970]." Thompson-Frost Collection (# 10044-a). Clifton Waller Barrett Library, Manuscripts Division, Special Collections Department, University of Virginia Library, Charlottesville.

———. "Some Subtleties in Robert Frost's Art." Lecture, University of Miami, 3 April 1964. Thompson-Frost Collection (# 10044-a). Clifton Waller Barrett Library, Manuscripts Division, Special Collections Department, University of Virginia Library, Charlottesville.

———, and R. H. Winnick. Robert Frost: The Later Years, 1938–1963. New York: Holt, Rinehart and Winston, 1976.

Thoreau, Henry D. The Journal of Henry D. Thoreau. Edited by Bradford Torrey and Francis H. Allen. 14 vols. Boston: Houghton Mifflin Co., 1906.

———. The Selected Works of Thoreau. Edited by Walter Harding. Boston: Houghton Mifflin Co., 1975.

————. *Walden*. Edited by J. Lyndon Shanley. Princeton: Princeton University Press, 1971.

Thornton, Richard, ed. *Recognition of Robert Frost: Twenty-fifth Anniversary*. New York: Henry Holt and Co., 1937.

Tompkins, Jane, ed. *Reader-Response Criticism: From Formalism to Post-Structuralism*. Baltimore: Johns Hopkins University Press, 1980.

Turbayne, Colin. *The Myth of Metaphor*. Columbia: University of South Carolina Press, 1971.

Untermeyer, Louis. "Man and Poet." In *Recognition of Robert Frost: Twenty-fifth Anniversary*. Edited by Richard Thornton. New York: Henry Holt and Co., 1937.

Von Frank, Albert J. " 'Nothing That Is': A Study of Frost's 'Desert Places.' " In *Centennial Essays*. Edited by Jac Tharpe. Jackson: University Press of Mississippi, 1974.

Waggoner, Hyatt. *American Poets from the Puritans to the Present*. Boston: Houghton Mifflin Co., 1968.

Warren, Austin, and René Wellek. "Image, Metaphor, Symbol, Myth." In *Theory of Literature*. New York: Harcourt, Brace and World, 1949.

Warren, Robert Penn. "The Themes of Robert Frost." In *The Writer and His Craft: The Hopwood Lectures, 1932–1952*. Ann Arbor: University of Michigan Press, 1954.

Whicher, Steven. "Emerson's Tragic Sense." *American Scholar* 22 (1953): 285–92.

Wimmers, Inge Crosman. "Approaches to the Novel: Current Views on the Role of the Reader." Paper presented at the annual convention of the Modern Language Association, 28 December 1988.

————. *Poetics of Reading: Approaches to the Novel*. Princeton: Princeton University Press, 1988.

Winters, Yvor. "Robert Frost: Or the Spiritual Drifter as Poet." In *The Function of Criticism: Problems and Exercises*. Reprinted in *Robert Frost: A Collection of Critical Essays*. Edited by James M. Cox. Englewood Cliffs, N.J.: Prentice-Hall, 1962.

Youtz, Philip. "Robert Frost's Comments on His Poetry." TS, Robert Frost Collection. Amherst College Library, Amherst, Massachusetts.

Index

Accessibility: reader attracted by, 5

Adam and Eve: in "Never Again Would Birds' Song Be the Same," 246–52

Adam, Eve, and Eden, 224–54 passim

"Adonais" (Shelley), 61–62

Aging: in "An Old Man's Winter Night," 93–97; in "In Winter in the Woods Alone," 161; in "The Leaf Treader," 161–64; in "Gathering Leaves," 228–30; in "After Apple Picking," 236–39

Aging and time, 163–64

Alien entanglement: RF on braving, 1–2; other person as, 2; poem as, 2; risk of, 2; reading and writing as, 8; braving of, by reader, 31; reader as, 33; fear of, 78

Ambiguity, reader attracted by, xiv

Analogist, man as, in Emerson, 113

Analogy: nature used as, 10; distancing in, 12; in characteristics of poet and poems,
26–27; narrowness of, 46, 48; limitations of, 55; compared to metaphor, 55; as most comfortable relationship with nature, 142; with nature, 142–43; between mood and nature, 143

Appropriation of text, xiv

Aristotle: definition of metaphor, 71

Art and love, 252

Artist: doing by seeing, 165

Attraction of reader to RF, xiv, 5

Bagby, George: on RF's synecdochism, 55

Balance: in "Birches," 61–62; need for, in RF, 132

Barriers, need for, 91

Belief: in "Never Again Would Birds' Song Be the Same," 251; and poetry, RF on, 219–20; RF on, 310 (n. 34)

Biographers and RF, 20–21

Biographical method, Thompson's, 23–25

Black, Max, 293 (n. 44); interaction view of metaphor, 47;

Black, Max (*cont'd*)
on metaphor, 49, 267 (nn.
12, 13)
Blankness: identification with
and fear of, 157
Bondage, 186; in "The Silken
Tent," 186–92
Boundaries, 79, 153
Bounding and binding, 177
Brooks, Cleanth and Austin
Warren, 308 (n. 28)
Brower, Reuben, xiv, 30; on RF's
irony, xi; on RF and nature,
105; on RF's modernism,
106; on "The Most of It," 275
(n. 14)
Burnshaw, Stanley, 24; on
"saving" RF, 18

Ciardi, John, 31, 310 (n. 35); on
RF as teacher, 27; on "Mount
Frost," 108, 280 (n. 7); on
"Stopping by Woods," 151,
155, 288 (n. 20); on RF, 261
(n. 13)
Closure: opposed to openness,
3–4; impossibility of, 135, 254
Coale, Samuel, 287 (n. 18); on
emblem, 56
Communication, 209; in "Home
Burial," 193–97
Compression, in "Nothing Gold
can Stay," 225–26
Construction: by Thompson,
18–19; and fragmentation in
readings, 29
Control: fear of losing self, 103,
107; artistic, 270 (n. 41)

Correspondence: Swedenborg
doctrine, 52; RF compared to
Emerson, 107
Cowley, Malcolm, 205, 207
Cox, Hyde, 20
Craig, G. A., 295 (n. 11); on
wildness in RF, 102
Created Work: autonomy of,
in "Mowing" and "The Wood-
pile," 66–67
Creative powers, death of, 230
Creativity: of love, 210, 212; of
seeing, 214, 261 (n. 10), 261
(n. 11); and sexuality, 223

Dante, 256, 278 (n. 30); "The
Inferno," 62; terza rima, 97–
98; circular motion of charac-
ters, 98
Dark as metaphoric, 98
Darkness, 284 (n. 7); RF on
Emerson's, 134; in "Oft-
repeated Dream," 143–45
Dating poems: inaccuracy of,
xiv; RF on, 259 (n. 8)
Death: wish, in "Stopping by
Woods," 154–56; RF's fear of,
159; acceptance of, in "Home
Burial," 196–97; as "mother
of beauty" (Stevens), 222; in
"Gathering Leaves," 229
Devotion: test of, in "Into My
Own," 101
Dewey, John, 261 (nn. 10, 12);
on artist's approach to scene,
55; on reception theory, 260
(n. 8); on transformation in
perceiver, 262 (n. 19); on

nature and aesthetic emotion, 262 (n. 22); on reading poetically, 269 (n. 35); emotion pervading perceived object, 279 (n. 3); on aesthetic emotion and natural objects, 285–86 (n. 13)

Donne, John, 257, 298 (n. 22)

Dramatic monologues and dialogues: as fragmenting RF identity, 7

Echo, 89; in "For Once Then Something," 81; in "The Most of It," 86–87; as uniting, 98–99; Ragussis on, as ironic muse, 274 (n. 8); hollow (Nietzsche), 278 (n. 27)

Echo effect: in "Two Look at Two," 92; in "An Old Man's Winter Night," 96–97

Echoes: and solitude, 79; continuing, 79; mocking, 79

Eden: as myth to live by, 221, 253; and "After Apple Picking", 244–45. See also Adam, Eve, and Eden; Adam and Eve

Ellipse vs. self as single center, 77

Emblematic view of nature: Emerson and Swedenborg, 51

Emblemism, 267 (n. 16)

Emerson, Ralph Waldo, 13, 105–36, 142, 168, 274, 282 (n. 31), 287 (n. 16), 291 (n. 32); on the poet, 4, 109–11, 269 (n. 34); emblematic view of nature, 51; on poet and his readers, 106; calmness vs. RF's passion, 106, 120, 126; on reading world, 106–7, 111, 113; validating RF as poet, 108–9; RF on limitations of, 108, 273 (n. 5); on symbols and emblems, 109–10; on vision, lenses, 110, 114–15; on "reader" as central, 112–13; on man as analogist, 113; "Experience," 115, 118–26; as unafraid of nature, 117; failure in passion and grief, 117–126; real vs. ideal, 121–25; on Montaigne, 122, 125, 132; on value of experience, 123; on illusion, 125; on intellect vs. life, 125–26; compared with RF and Thoreau, 132–33; "dark sayings" RF admired, 134; influence on "Education by Poetry," 134; "Snow Storm," 283 (n. 1)

Engagement: lack of, in Emerson and Thoreau, 116–17; in love, 207–8. See also Entanglement

Entanglement: in texts, xiv; Iser on, 4; of reader, 26; readers' and writers' vulnerability to, 29; in object or other, 78; in love, 89; RF "making" out of, 103; barriers against, 145; in human dramas, 176; risks of, with others, 207. See also Alien entanglement, Engagement

Escape: and withdrawal in RF,

Escape (*cont'd*)
  101–2; danger and necessity
  of, in RF, 102–3

Fall of man, 224–33; in "After
  Apple Picking," 244. *See also*
  Adam, Eve, and Eden
Fish, Stanley, xii–xiii, 259 (n. 1)
Flower as image, 200, 209, 212
Forming, and Proteus, 14
Fragmentation: of self (James), 6;
  of RF identity, 7; sharing text
  as, 9; and loss of self, 14; in
  telling, 16; of vision, in "Range
  Finding," 38–41; as limiting
  vision, 40
Frost, Elinor, 184, 299 (n. 23),
  301–2 (n. 33), 309 (n. 32);
  and RF, 19, 21; effect of death
  on RF, 103; and courtship
  with RF, 276 (n. 21); and
  "Bereft," 283 (n. 5)
Frost, Irma, 301 (n. 32)
Frost, Jeannie, 285 (n. 9), 288
  (n. 21), 291 (n. 33), 295
  (n. 9), 301 (n. 32)
Frost, Lesley, 260 (n. 2), 284–
  85 (n. 8), 291–92 (nn. 37, 39),
  309 (n. 32)
Frost, Robert: modernism of,
  x–xii; postmodernism of, x;
  and alien entanglements,
  1–33 passim; attraction to
  accessibility of, 5; as reader
  of world, 9–17; as text, read
  as analogous to reading
  poems, 17; construction of, by
  Thompson, 18–19; as text in

"competition" with Thomp-
  son's, 18–19; and Thompson,
  18–25; and biographies, 20–
  21; characteristics analogous
  with poems, 26; as teacher,
  27, 34; fear of attracting,
  27; metaphors of metaphor,
  56–57; metonymic mode in,
  57–58; "On Emerson," 133–
  34; "Education by Poetry,"
  134–36, 299 (n. 23), 310
  (n. 34); on tears in writer,
  176; masks and characters,
  176; "A Constant Symbol,"
  184; as great poet of love
  and marriage, 205; "The
  Figure a Poem Makes," 222;
  on knowledge as construction,
  264 (n. 32); on gossip, 264
  (n. 35)
POEMS
—"Acceptance," 142
—"After Apple Picking," 236–45,
  268 (n. 32), 288 (n. 18)
—"Afterflakes," 144
—"The Aim Was Song," 233–36,
  271 (n. 42)
—"Bereft," 143–44
—"Birches," 59–63, 183, 270
  (n. 41)
—"A Boundless Moment,"
  167–68, 271 (n. 42)
—"Come In," 54, 140
—"The Cow in Apple Time,"
  308–9 (n. 31)
—"The Death of the Hired Man,"
  218–19, 262 (n. 17), 270
  (n. 42)

—"Desert Places," 11, 156–61, 217, 291 (n. 32)

—"Design," 53, 300 (n. 30)

—"Despair," 155, 301 (n. 31)

—"Directive," 3, 72, 132, 255–58

—"The Dream Pang," 145

—"The Drumlin Woodchuck," 142–43, 180

—"Dust of Snow," 128–29

—"Evening in a Sugar Orchard," 166

—"The Exposed Nest," 213

—"The Fear of God," 253

—"The Fear of Man," 32, 217

—"Fireflies in the Garden," 166, 271 (n. 42)

—"The Flood," 179

—"Flower Guidance," 200, 303 (n. 43)

—"For Once Then Something," 53, 79–83, 271 (n. 42)

—"The Freedom of the Moon," 165, 271 (n. 42)

—"Gathering Leaves," 228–30, 271 (n. 42)

—"The Gift Outright," 185–86

—"Going for Water," 213

—"The Grindstone," 232–33

—"A Hillside Thaw," 168–70, 271 (n. 42), 278 (n. 26), 306 (n. 13)

—"The Hill Wife," 262 (n. 17)

—"Home Burial," ix, 57, 124, 192–99, 214–16, 262 (n. 17), 124

—"Hyla Brook," 170–74

—"The Impulse," 296 (n. 15)

—"In the Home Stretch," 213, 291 (n. 35), 300 (n. 27), 310 (n. 33)

—"Into My Own," 99–101, 132

—"In Winter in the Woods Alone," 161

—"It is Almost the Year Two Thousand," 226, 305 (n. 10)

—"Kitty Hawk," 1, 218, 298 (n. 23)

—"The Leaf Treader," 161–64

—"Leaves Compared with Flowers," 144, 147–48

—"Love and a Question," 180

—"Maple," 44–49, 59, 271 (n. 42), 272 (n. 47)

—*The Masque of Reason,* 253

—"Mending Wall," 8, 56, 58, 79, 91, 177–79, 262 (n. 17), 270 (n. 37), 294 (nn. 5, 7), 309 (n. 31)

—"Misgiving," 146

—"A Missive Missile," 44, 272 (n. 48)

—"The Most of It," 79, 83–88, 90–91, 93, 98, 302 (n. 34)

—"Mowing," 31, 63–69, 270 (n. 42), 271 (n. 45)

—"The Need of Being Versed in Country Things," 54, 140

—"Neither Out Far Nor in Deep," 132

—"Never Again Would Birds' Song Be the Same," ix, 245–52, 302 (n. 34), 303 (n. 41), 309 (n. 32)

—"New Hampshire," 151–52

—"Nothing Gold Can Stay," 224–28, 248, 252–53

—"Now Close the Windows,"
165, 285 (n. 11)

—"The Oft-repeated Dream,"
143–45

—"An Old Man's Winter Night,"
88, 93–97, 275 (n. 17)

—"The Onset," 11, 135

—"Out, Out—," 56

—"The Oven Bird," 174, 230

—"Pan With Us," 236

—"The Pasture," 56

—"Paul's Wife," 32, 217–18, 271
(n. 42)

—"The Pauper Witch of Grafton," 205–6

—"Pertinax," 234

—"Putting in the Seed," 210,
222–23, 300 (n. 27)

—"A Question," 254

—"Range Finding," 38–41, 140

—"Revelation," 72, 101

—"The Rose Family," 69, 271
(n. 42)

—"A Servant to Servants,"
202–5, 216–17

—"The Silken Tent," 186–92,
246–47, 309 (n. 32)

—"Spring Pools," 127, 139–42,
159, 171, 212, 283 (n. 4)

—"Stopping by Woods on a
Snowy Evening," ix, 11, 56,
136, 148–56, 157–58, 161, 284
(n. 7), 290 (nn. 30, 31), 291
(n. 32)

—"Storm Fear," 11, 137–39, 143,
153–54

—"The Strong Are Saying Nothing," 206–7

—"The Subverted Flower," 199–
202, 209, 301 (n. 33), 302
(n. 34)

—"The Telephone," 98, 208–9,
213

—"They Were Welcome to Their
Belief," 164

—"Time Out," 49–50, 271
(n. 42)

—"To Earthward," 207, 209, 231

—"To Prayer I Go," 155

—"To the Thawing Wind," 170

—"Tree at My Window," 78,
145–46

—"Two Look at Two," 89–93,
98–99

—"Two Tramps in Mud Time,"
180–85

—"The Vantage Point," 35–38

—"West-running Brook," 226,
214, 218, 248, 256, 300
(n. 27)

—"Wild Grapes," 63

—"The Wind and the Rain,"
146, 162

—"The Woodpile," 67

Gaps: in RF poetry, 5; in RF, as
attracting reader, 7; readers
and poets drawn into, 135;
James on, 261 (n. 11)

Genesis, 220–54 passim

Gold, in "Nothing Gold Can
Stay," 224–27

Gombrich, E. H., 261 (nn. 10,
11), 263 (n. 24)

Gossip: RF on, 264 (n. 35);
Spacks on, 264 (n. 34)

Grail, 256

Hawthorne, Nathaniel, 111
Holding, in art and nature, 169–70
Holland, Norman N., 262 (n. 19); feedback loops, 25; on RF as synecdochist, 53; on people and psychology in theory, 116; on language as managing, 217; on RF's use of metaphor, 263 (nn. 25, 26); on importance of metaphor for RF, 291 (n. 36)
Hollander, John: on echoes, 80; echo and form, 97
Horney, Karen: theories of, as used by Thompson, 23–25, 260 (n. 2)
Human vs. animal vision, 40
Humor in "Never Again Would Birds' Song Be the Same," 250–52

Identification with leaves or trees, 143–47
Illusion, receptiveness to, 167–68
Imagination: and fact in "Birches," 60–61; and reality in RF, 83; affected by personal need, 83; role in seeing, 166–68; as flowing, 168; courting of, 168; in "Mending Wall," 178; shared, 213; and reality in "After Apple Picking," 240; and love, 251–52; "requisitioned," 292 (n. 39)

Imperfection: 184, 253; and creativity, 231; RF's need of, 231–32; delight in, 233; in "After Apple Picking," 242, 245
Incompletion in "After Apple Picking," 238
Insanity: fear of, in RF, 129; in "Servant to Servants," 180, 203–5, 216; as failure of language, 216–17
Interpretation: "sway" allowed reader, 34
Intertextuality of life, works, and reading, 28–30
Invasion: reading as, 6, 27; of RF by students, 27; of texts by readers, 29
Invitation, text as, 8
Irony: as defense against narcissism, 13; in "Home Burial," 195; in "The Aim Was Song," 235; in "Never Again Would Birds' Song Be the Same," 250–51
Iser, Wolfgang: xi, 261 (n. 10); on entanglement in constructing text, 4; on gaps and indeterminacy, 4; on text as invitation, 8; on participating in creating text, 9; on approach to RF, 15; on reading as shattering, 78; on "virtuality," 218; on reader-text interrelationship, 262 (n. 20)

Jakobson, Roman, 269 (n. 33); on metonymic mode, 57; on

Jakobson, Roman (*cont'd*)
    stress in "The Most of It," 276
    (n. 18)
James, Henry, Sr., on Adam and
    Fall, 232
James, William: 291 (n. 32); im-
    portance to RF, xi, 6; on con-
    cepts of self, 6; perception as
    shaping, 14; on subject-object
    relation, 14; influence on
    reception theory, 15; on sym-
    pathetic vs. unsympathetic,
    27–28; on breaches between
    men, 31–32; on Emerson, 122
Jarrell, Randall, 31; on "Home
    Burial," 199; on "The Pauper
    Witch of Grafton," 206; on
    "Gathering Leaves," 229

Keats, John, 15, 31, 269 (n. 37);
    "Ode to a Nightingale," 128
Knowledge: as construction, 264
    (n. 32); as loss of innocence,
    304 (n. 5)

Lacan, Jacques: mirror-stage, 77
Language: failure of, 214–16; as
    betrayal, 217–18; as creating
    reality, 217–18
Leaves: identification with, 162;
    as metaphor of metaphor, 164;
    as analogy for time, 226
Leaves and trees, identification
    with, 143–47
Lentricchia, Frank, 260 (n. 3),
    263 (n. 25); on RF's mod-
    ernism, xi; on linguistic
    self-creation, 32; on James,
    263 (n. 30), on sexuality in

"Oft-repeated Dream," 285
    (n. 9); on woods imagery, 286
    (n. 15)
Levin, Samuel, 58; theory of
    metaphoric world, 54
Linguistic analysis in "After
    Apple Picking," 308 (n. 27).
    See also Sound, analysis of;
    Stress; Syntax, analysis of;
    Tense and mode
Literary traditions: RF in tension
    with, xii
Lodge, David: on metonymic
    mode, 57
Loneliness: in "The Most of It,"
    84–88; in "An Old Man's
    Winter Night," 94–96
Losing self vs. being found, 101,
    103
Love: in "Two Tramps," 183–85;
    in "Birches," 183; as bound
    to earth, 191; as engagement,
    207; as creative, 210, 212;
    earth and reality in, 213; as
    figure of poem, 219; as tri-
    angle with death and creation,
    221; in "Never Again Would
    Birds' Song Be the Same,"
    246–52
Lynen, John: on RF pastoral,
    xii; on our physical nature,
    198; on "The Grindstone,"
    232–33; on nature as
    mechanical, 267 (n. 8)

McIntosh, James, 130, 132, 135;
    on man and nature, 108; on
    romanticism, 108

Manhood: stereotypic definition of, in "Home Burial," 193–94

Manliness: RF to Carol on, 299 (n. 24)

Mark, in "Directive," 3, 72, 260 (n. 7)

Marriage, 214; in "Home Burial," 192, 195–98; of language and object, 214–16; as figure, 219; "me" and "not me", 77

Material world: love of vs. use of, 34

Measure in "The Aim Was Song," 234

Memory: and reality in art, 171–74; and new creation, 230

Metaphor: and synecdoche, 12; functions of, 12, 44, 71, 222, 263 (n. 26); nature as, 44; "maple" on, 44–49; as causative, 45, 48; need for flexible reading of, 46; definitions of, 47, 49, 55, 56, 71; attempt to deny in "Mowing," 64; attempt to deny in "The Rose Family," 69–70; hiding of and behind, 70; metaphors of, 162, 268 (n. 32), 292 (n. 42); absence of, 172; and fact in "Hyla Brook," 172; and association, 172–73; as analogous to structure, 187; in "Silken Tent," 189, 191–92; understanding of, in "Home Burial," 195; fresh vs. stale, 272 (n. 47); importance of, to RF, 291 (n. 36)

Meter. *See* Prosody

Metonymy: in RF's realism, 57; and metaphor in "Mending Wall," 58

Milton, John, 31; and RF, 219; *Paradise Lost,* 247, 249, 252–54

Mimesis, 273 (n. 50); and mirror image, 103

Mirror imagery, 74–104 passim

Mirroring: in "For Once Then Something," 81–82; in "The Most of It," 86; in "Two Look at Two," 92

Modals. *See* Tense and mode

Modernism, x

Modes of seeing, creating by, 165–68

Montaigne, Michel de, 122–23; "On Experience" and pain, 281 (n. 19)

Morrison, Kathleen, 299 (n. 23), 309 (n. 32)

Myth: *Genesis,* to live by, 221, 253; definition of, 223

Naming, 216; in "West-running Brook," 214

Narcissism in reading, 13, 117

Narcissus, 79, 88, 117; and Echo, 74–79; "The Most of It," 87; RF in contrast with, 103

Nature: and man analogy, 10; emblematic view of, 10; limited vision in, 40; indifference of, 40–41, 141; human separateness from, 42–44; as book, 49, 78; as reflection of humans, 89; sexuality as, 89; excitement to RF, 105;

Nature (*cont'd*)
  insufficiency to RF, 106;
  RF's views of, compared to
  Wordsworth's, Emerson's,
  and Thoreau's, 106–9, 117;
  transforming power of, 106;
  human alienation from, 108;
  as text that invites reading/
  writing, 109; projection onto,
  116, 139–42, 143; danger of,
  136–42; as reflecting human
  feeling, 139–42; process in,
  140–42; transformation in,
  141, 170–74; analogies with,
  142–43; identification with,
  162; as partner in creation,
  164–68; as "arranged" by
  artist, 165–66; as model for
  artistic transformation, 165,
  168; projection onto, in "The
  Aim Was Song," 235; RF on
  cruelty of, 283 (n. 4)
Nature as text, 9–10, 106, 107,
  111; validated by Emerson and
  Thoreau, 136
Nature within us, 175, 198;
  harmony with, and love, 208,
  210; and aesthetic emotion,
  262 (n. 22), 286 (n. 13)
Negatives in "Into My Own," 100
Notable craftsman: RF on, 271
  (n. 43)

"Ode to the West Wind"
  (Shelley): form of, 278 (n. 30)
Other, as different from self, 77
Ovid, 74–76

Pathetic fallacy, 15, 42, 43,
  54–55, 140
Perception: as shaping, 15; in
  "Never Again Would Birds'
  Song Be the Same," 251
Percival, 256
Perkins, David, xii; on RF's
  romantic irony, 268 (n. 21)
Perspective and vision, 277
  (n. 23)
Play: seriousness of, in RF, 182
"The Poem That Took the Place
  of a Mountain" (Stevens), 50
Poet as reader, xii; of other
  poets, 31; Emerson's view, 110
Point of view in "Subverted
  Flower," 202
Poirier, Richard, xv, 219, 291
  (n. 32), 308 (nn. 24, 26); on
  "After Apple Picking," 268
  (n. 32); on reading/writing
  in RF poetry, 269 (n. 35); on
  "Spring Pools," 283 (n. 2);
  on woods, 287 (n. 15); on
  "Home Burial," 300 (n. 26);
  on married love in RF, 302
  (n. 34)
Possession in love, 185–86
Possessiveness of self in "Home
  Burial," 192
Postmodernism, RF's, x
Poulet, Georges: on text entering
  reader, 8–9, 13
"Pound-Eliot gang," x
Pritchard, William H.: value of
  biography, xiv
Process and making, 174
Prosody: in "Desert Places," 160;

in "Hyla Brook," 172; in "The Telephone," 209; in "Nothing Gold Can Stay," 225; in "Never Again Would Birds' Song Be the Same," 251
Proteus, 14, 229
Psychological projection onto nature, 142–46

Reader: fear of, xiv; fear of vs. need of, 3; roles of, 25, 35; as competition of RF, 25–26; relationship of, to natural text, 148; invitation to, in "Directive," 255–58; as affected by text constructing, 262 (n. 20)
Reader-response critics, 11; Emerson's closeness to, 114
Reader's rights: according to RF, 260 (n. 6)
Reader-text interaction, 4
Reading: as active process, xii; narcissism in, 13; role-playing in, 13; of RF as parallel with reading poems, 17; and writing as concentric circles, 28–30; and being read, 29; RF as teacher in poems, 34–35; influences upon, 35; as seeing, 35–38; of nature, 49, 106–7, 107–8, 163, 235; as synecdochic act, 59; risks of, 116; as closing gaps in nature/texts, 135; trancelike state in, 136; in "Two Tramps," 182; in "Subverted Flower," 201; of lovers, 209; in "Never Again

Would Birds' Song Be the Same," 251; Dewey on reading poetically, 269 (n. 35)
Realism in "Never Again Would Birds' Song Be the Same," 246
Reception theory: influence of James on, 15
Reflection, as thinking: 50, 80; with imagination, 82–83; nature of humans, 89
Renaissance poetry, 223
Repetend in "Stopping by Woods," 154
Response: RF on, 275 (n. 16)
Retreat, "strategic", 102
Rhyme. See Prosody
Romance of the Rose, 272 (n. 47)
Rosenblatt, Louise, 259 (n. 1), 261 (n. 10)
Rotella, Guy: on RF, indeterminacy and physics, 262 (n. 17); on RF and Emerson, 280 (n. 11)

Seeing, modes of, 36–38, 40
Seeing creatively: Emerson on, 112
Self: sharing vs. keeping of, 3, 5–6, 9; loss of, 12–14; as other, 75; love of, 76; as center of circle, 77; as individuated, 78; and not-self, 83; circle of, in "An Old Man's Winter Night," 96–97; going into, 99, 101; closed circle of and syntax, 101; analogy with trees, woods, 101–2; integrity of,

Self (*cont'd*)
179, 185; lack of, 180; giving
of, 185–86
Self-creation: linguistic, 32; with
objects (Dewey), 261 (nn. 12,
14)
Selfishness: RF on, as artist, 231,
295 (n. 8)
Sentence: analagous to metaphor,
187
Sentence sound: RF on, 271
(n. 43)
Sergeant, Elizabeth, 20, 155
Sestina, 98
Sexuality: buck as, 88, 92; and
nature, 89; absent in Thoreau's
writing, 120; fear of, in "Oft-
repeated Dream," 145; and
poetic creating, 170, 213, 223;
in "Two Tramps," 183–85; in
"Home Burial," 198–99; in
"Subverted Flower," 199–
202; distorted in "Subverted
Flower" and "Servant," 202;
in "The Pauper Witch of
Grafton," 205–6; implicit in
RF poems, 206–7, 209; in
"Never Again Would Birds'
Song Be the Same," 242; as
metaphor, 292 (n. 42); as
metaphor of matter and spirit,
299 (n. 23); and guilt in RF,
301 (n. 31); and RF's punning,
302 (n. 35)
Shakespeare, William, 31; Sonnet
116, 101; sonnets, 223; "My
Mistress' Eyes Are Nothing
Like the Sun," 249

Sharing vs. keeping: of self and
texts, 3, 5–6, 9; in RF, 25
Sheehy, Donald: on Thompson
biography, 23–25
"The Snow Man" (Stevens), 159
Socialist critics, and "Two
Tramps," 182–83, 295 (n. 9)
Solitude: RF on confronting self
in, 102; RF on need of, 279
(n. 35)
Song of Songs, 297 (n. 21)
Sonnet: turn in "Vantage Point,"
36; and terza rima, 98, 278
(n. 30); "Hyla Brook" as, 171;
"The Silken Tent," 187; and
dramatic monologue, 304
(n. 44)
Sound: analysis of, 141, 172; in
"Mowing," 65–66; in "Never
Again Would Birds' Song Be
the Same," 249
Sound of sense: RF on, 271
(n. 43); "Mowing" as example
of, 64
Spacks, Patricia M., 264 (n. 34);
on telling as control, 7; on
telling as self-creation, 7;
on gossip as telling, 16; on
Boswell and Johnson, 265
(n. 42)
Speech tones: in "Home Burial,"
196–97; RF on, 307–8 (n. 22)
Spending vs. keeping, 184–85
Stasis: compared to dynamism in
relationship, 77–78; compared
to motion, 161; compared to
process, 228, 245
"Stay," definitions of, 169, 227

Stevens, Wallace, 222
Stress, in "The Most of It"
    (Jakobson), 276 (n. 18)
Subject-object: James on relation,
    14; blurring of distinction, 78
Sutton, William A., on Thomp-
    son biography, 264–65
    (nn. 40, 41)
Swedenborg, Emanuel, 51, 232
Synecdoche: reading as, 59;
    Emerson's poet as, 269 (n. 34)
Synecdochism, 106
Synecdochist, RF as, 52, 53, 55
Syntax, analysis of: in "The Most
    of It," 85–87; in "Into My
    Own," 99–101; in "The Silken
    Tent," 187–90

Telling: importance of, to RF, 7;
    importance of, to identity, 7
Tense and mode: in "The Most of
    It," 86–87; in "Into My Own,"
    100–101; in "Never Again
    Would Birds' Song Be the
    Same," 247–48, 251. See also
    "The Most of It"
Terza rima, 98; and sonnet, 278
    (n. 30)
Text: RF on ways to read, 2;
    ownership of, 2, 3, 5–6, 9;
    person as, 6; risk in shared
    making, 9; RF as, 17–28;
    possessiveness of, 32
Thompson, Lawrance: value of
    biography, xiv; on RF masks,
    7; on RF biography, 18–25;
    The Story of a Biography, 19;
    on RF as synecdochist, 52;

on synecdochism, 106; on
    "Stopping by Woods," 151,
    155; on flower imagery, 200;
    on metaphors of metaphor,
    292 (n. 42); on "Home Burial,"
    299–300 (n. 25); on Elinor
    Frost, 300 (n. 29)
Thoreau, Henry David, 105–136
    passim; absence of humans
    or sexuality in writing of,
    120; passion in nature, 120;
    fear of bodies, 122, 132; as
    analogist, 127; on violence in
    nature, 127; on moral order
    in nature, 127–28; reality
    in, 127, 131; on wildness,
    128–32; universality of, 128;
    willingness to be lost, 132; on
    poet as "owner," 287 (n. 16)
Tragic sense: RF vs. Emerson and
    Thoreau, 120
Transformation: in nature and
    art, 170–74; in art, 234
Trees: fear of, 284–85 (n. 8); as
    time, 291 (n. 35)

Virgil, 256, 258
Vision, failure of: according to
    Emerson, 114

"The Wasteland" (Eliot), 5, 38
Whicher, Stephen: on Emerson
    and tragedy, 118–20
Wildness: 152–53; in self, 102–3;
    Thoreau vs. RF, 128–32; and
    woods, 286–87 (n. 15)
Wimmers, Inge Crosman, 136;

Wimmers, Inge Crosman (*cont'd*) on role-playing, 13; on empathy and identification, 13, 116–17; on narcissism in reading, 13, 274 (n. 6)

Withdrawal, RF and danger of, 102

Woods: and wildness, 148, 286–87 (n. 15); attraction of, 148

Wordsworth, William, 13, 54, 58, 131; on nature, 106

Work vs. play, 181–82

Writerly quality in RF poems, xi

Writer-reader interaction in "Mending Wall," 8